The Kingdom of God
Visualized

The Kingdom of God Visualized

by

RAY E. BAUGHMAN

Illustrated by

GERALD SCHMOYER

MOODY PRESS

CHICAGO

To my wife
Lucy

© 1972 by
THE MOODY BIBLE INSTITUTE
OF CHICAGO

Library of Congress Catalog Card Number: 70-181586

ISBN: 0-8024-4565-9

Printed in the United States of America

Contents

Illustrations

1

New Government to Be Established

NEWSPAPERS are constantly reporting new governments coming into power, whether established by elections, revolutions, military coups, coalitions, or by the death of one of the few remaining monarchs. As new leaders come into power, people wonder, What will the new government be like? How will it affect me? Higher taxes? Reform? War? Peace? Each new leader will have a platform or at least have made promises to his followers. Will he keep these promises?

Whom will he appoint to his cabinet and other important positions? Usually he will select those who have supported him in his campaign— those who worked hard, proved their ability, have unspotted records and, most of all, those who have shown unfaltering loyalty and faithfulness.

A new government will be established in the future that will be just as real as any existing now. Its territory will be definite, with certain people as its citizens, and with selected administrators to help in its rule. It will be the most important government in the world, the best that has ever existed, and it will last forever. It will be the kingdom of Jesus Christ. This is an important topic of study because the things that you are doing *now* and your *present* relationship with God will affect your future participation in, or relationship to, this promised kingdom. You can never see nor enter this kingdom unless you have been born again (Jn 3:3-5). Even as a Christian you can prove yourself unworthy of any inheritance or place of responsibility in His kingdom by your conduct (Gal 5:19-21; Eph 5:1-5). The study of this holy venture with God should be an incentive to all Christians to serve Him faithfully, and it should be a rebuke to all slothful Christians who will be happy if they "just get to heaven."

THE IMPORTANCE OF THE KINGDOM

Erich Sauer stresses the importance of the kingdom:

> All these mighty developments in the realm of the Divine, human, and Satanic belong to the history of the kingdom of God. The "Kingdom" is

7

the real basic theme of the Bible. It is the surrounding historical frame in which the whole course of revelation is being consummated. All ages and periods of the Divinely revealed ways; all groups and persons addressed, whether Israel, the nations, or the church; all temples, sanctuaries, and redeeming acts; all heavenly and demonic activities, whether in the foreground or background stand in some way, either positively or negatively, in connection with the history of the kingdom of God.[1]

The kingdom is important for the following reasons:

1. It is one of the great themes of prophecy in the Bible. The day of Jehovah, or the great tribulation, and the second coming of Christ introduce the kingdom. These references plus the many kingdom passages make up a large percentage of all prophecy. Redemption has its consummation as the curse is finally removed from creation in the kingdom (Ro 8:18-23).

2. It is a leading theme in the New Testament: of John the Baptist, Jesus, the twelve, and the seventy. Christ gave it top priority in His postresurrection ministry (Ac 1:3). Peter preached and wrote of it, and Paul, John, and the writer of the Hebrews all mentioned the kingdom in their epistles.

3. God, who does not lie, has promised in an unconditional covenant that He will establish His kingdom. When Jesus Christ returns, God the Son will establish His kingdom and fulfill this promise.

4. The past ages have all been building toward this climax in history. In the plan of God it was necessary for Christ to suffer first before His glory could be revealed (1 Pe 1:11).

5. The kingdom will demonstrate the wisdom of God as He works out His plan and overrules evil for good.

6. Christians are joint-heirs with Jesus Christ, but our rewards, place of responsibility, and honors in His kingdom will be won or lost according to our faithfulness in this life. We are to be good stewards (1 Co 4:2), "stedfast, unmoveable, always abounding in the work of the Lord" (1 Co 15:58).

METHOD OF INTERPRETATION

Because the kingdom is so common in Scripture, it has many varied and contradictory interpretations. It has been a popular subject for the cults. In the Dark Ages it was made synonymous with the church, and it is still popular among many people to spiritualize the promises concerning it. Misinterpretations and special problems concerning the kingdom are considered in more detail in the Appendix.

"You can make the Bible mean anything you want" is an expression that is often heard. This is true only when you ignore the basic rules of interpretation. One of the best formulas was given by Bible translator John Wycliffe who lived about six hundred years ago. He said, "It shall Greatly Helpe Ye to Understande Scripture, If Thou Mark Not only What is Spoken or Written, But of Whom, And to Whom, With what Words, At what Time, Where, To what Intent, With what Circumstances, Considering what Goeth Before and what Followeth."

This can be condensed into three main points:

1. interpret grammatically
2. interpret according to context
3. compare scripture with scripture

Believing in the verbal plenary inspiration of the Scriptures—that the very words of the Bible were inspired of God—it is necessary to interpret those very words. A word is a vehicle of thought, but words are not used by themselves. They are put together in phrases and sentences and have a definite relation one to another, so the context, or the passage as a whole, must be considered. Many portions of the Bible are self-explanatory, simple, clear-cut statements. Figures of speech are used in every language, but they can be recognized.* Jesus explained many of His own parables, so there is no question about their interpretation. The great commentary of the Scriptures is the Bible itself, letting scripture explain scripture. This brings into harmony the whole Word of God. Obscure or passages which appear to be contradictory cannot be used to support a doctrine that is opposed to the plain and general teaching of the Scripture.

Interpretation and application are different. Interpretation is trying to find *one* thing—what does the passage mean? In contrast it is possible to make *many* spiritual applications from a passage. These can be very profitable as long as it is clearly understood that they are applications.

Unfolding Revelation of the Kingdom

In the study of the Scriptures, the plan of redemption is of primary importance, but other important themes have often been neglected or misinterpreted.

The Scriptures cannot be rightly understood without a thorough knowledge of the kingdom, the key that unlocks many puzzles or seeming contradictions. It is interwoven with the great covenants of the Scriptures, the calling out of the church, the first and second comings of Christ, the resurrections, and the judgments.

The revelation of the kingdom of God can be compared to a jigsaw

---

*For an easy to understand presentation of figures of speech, see chap. 5 of the author's book, *Seeking Bible Treasures* (Oak Park, Ill.: Emmaus Bible School, 1965).

puzzle, for this truth is presented a piece at a time. As God gave His promises, covenants and prophecies, the picture of what the kingdom will be like became clearer. There is an unfolding revelation of His plan, but the kingdom itself has been planned from the foundation of the world (Mt 25:34; Rev 13:8).

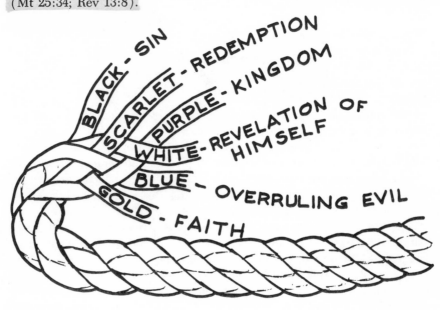

Fig. 1. Bible Themes

MAJOR BIBLE THEMES

The kingdom of Jesus Christ cannot be studied alone. Running through the Bible record are at least six major themes that must be considered. These can be compared to strands or threads in a rope (see Fig. 1) which do not appear in one continuous record, but keep reappearing.

BLACK THREAD

The black thread represents sin and its consequences: the rebellion in the Garden of Eden, sin down through the ages, the counterfeit kingdom of Satan, all the demonic activity, and the final revolt at the close of the millennium.

SCARLET THREAD

The scarlet thread symbolizes the promises of redemption from the Garden of Eden to the cross, and the offer of this redemption until the judgment before the great white throne.

PURPLE THREAD

The purple thread stands for the promise of a kingdom. This is the restoration of the rule of God over the earth. The scarlet thread and the purple thread are closely related. The promised redemption and the promised Kingdom are both to come through a promised seed.

BLUE THREAD

Representing God overruling evil for good as He works more or less "'behind the scenes" is the blue thread. While man has rebelled, God sets certain limits beyond which He does not let him go. He still sends judgment, such as the flood; raises up kings and puts down kings, such as Nebuchadnezzar; and promises a final accounting with all His creatures.

WHITE THREAD

The white thread is a symbol of God's revelation of Himself to man. Because of sin, man has lost fellowship with God and his knowledge of God has been greatly impaired. Throughout the Bible, God is in an educational process, teaching man what He is like: His love, power, holiness, justice, mercy, and other attributes. His greatest manifestation is in the person of Jesus Christ, for "he that hath seen me hath seen the Father" (Jn 14:9).

GOLD THREAD

The gold thread represents the faith exercised by man in the promises of God (1 Pe 1:6-7).

THE WORD "KINGDOM"

The word *kingdom* appears in the English Bible about four hundred times. The use of this word can be divided into three main categories: (1) the *realm* or territory that is ruled (Mt 4:8; 6:13; 24:7; Lk 4:5), (2) the *people* that are ruled or the people who accept God's rule in their lives (Mt 6:33; 21:31; Mk 10:15; Lk 16:16; Col 1:13; Ex 19:6); at other times the word is used when the kingdom is present in the person of the King (Mt 12:28; Lk 17:21), (3) the *reign* or rule itself. Sometimes the time factor—such as twenty years—is meant (Lk 19:12; 22:29; 1 Co 15:24-26).

Where the word *kingdom* is used, it must be decided by its context whether it is speaking about the realm, the people, or the reign. Many times when *kingdom* is used, it is speaking of the different earthly kingdoms. At other times it is speaking about the promised kingdom of God. There is one great kingdom in prophecy (Mt 25:34). The expressions "kingdom of God," "kingdom of heaven," "Christ's kingdom," and "kingdom of His dear Son" refer to one and the same thing. C. F. Hogg and W. E. Vine say:

> The expression "Kingdom of God" occurs four times in Matthew, "Kingdom of the Heavens" usually taking its place. The latter, cp. Daniel 4:26, does not occur elsewhere in the New Testament, but see II Timothy 4:18, "His heavenly Kingdom." The expressions cover the same ground, cp. Matthew 19:23 with verse 24, and again with Mark 10:23-24; Matthew 19:14 with Mark 10:14; Matthew 13:11 with Luke 8:10. This Kingdom is identical with the Kingdom of the Father, cp. Matthew 26:29 with Mark 14:25; and with the Kingdom of the Son, cp. Luke 22:30. Thus there is but one Kingdom, variously described: of the Son of Man, Matthew 13:41; of Jesus, Revelation 1:9; of Christ Jesus, II Timothy 4:1; "of Christ and God," Ephesians 5:5; "of our Lord, and of His Christ," Revelation 11:15; "of our God, and the authority of His Christ," Revelation 12:10; "of the Son of His love," Colossians 1:13.[2]

The Old Testament prophets described the kingdom as the restored kingdom of David with many glorious additions, which is how the Jews at Jesus' triumphal entry considered it: "Blessed be the kingdom of our father David, that cometh in the name of the Lord: Hosanna in the highest" (Mk 11:10).

The millennial kingdom is the first one thousand-year era of the kingdom. The kingdom itself is eternal.

In a general sense, all creation could be said to be the kingdom of God, for He sovereignly controls it, but it is doubtful that the expression "kingdom of God" is ever used this way in Scripture. This and other concepts of the kingdom are discussed in detail in later chapters and in the Appendix.

METHOD OF STUDY

What is the best method to approach this large and important subject of the kingdom? Alva J. McClain in *The Greatness of the Kingdom* says:

> The Kingdom of God in Scripture is a concept not easily handled by the conventional method of Systematic Theology. For one thing, it occupies a place in both Biblical history and eschatology. It is so vast in content, and so interminable in its reach both backward and forward, that it resists any attempt to shut it up in one department of theological treatment. Therefore, it is not enough to study a collation of texts on the subject; but the material must be examined in relation to the movement of history and the progress of divine revelation. This means that an adequate treatment must follow basically the method of Biblical Theology. Failure of students at this point has made no small contribution to the rise of the various one-sided notions about the Kingdom.[3]

Following McClain's suggestion, we will follow historically the unfolding revelation of the kingdom, noting many related subjects. It is difficult not to get on a tangent because of the central character of the kingdom in relation to biblical truth. Only as we get the overall view can we appreciate God's plan to bring this rebel planet back into a right relationship to Himself.

SUMMARY

1. Christ is going to establish His kingdom.

2. The things that you are doing now and your present relationship with Him will affect your future participation in this kingdom.

3. The doctrine of the kingdom is interwoven and related to all the other great doctrines of Scripture and it is one of the most important doctrines in the Bible.

4. Believing in the inspiration of the Scriptures, one should interpret grammatically, according to context, and compare scripture with scripture.

2

God's Plan of the Ages

SEVERAL QUESTIONS are common to all mankind: Who am I? What's going on in the world? Where do I fit in? Without the Word of God, all answers are guesswork—the wisdom or the imagination of men. But God has chosen to reveal at least the basic outline of His plan for the ages. Through the history and prophecy of the Bible we can understand God's program.

SURVEYING THE AGES

There are many possible ways of dividing this revelation into time periods. The Bible has already been divided into the Old and New Testaments. We could divide history up into two parts—everything that happened before the cross and everything that is to happen after the cross. There are important events in history which act as pivotal points, such as the flood, the exodus, the Babylonian captivity, the crucifixion, and the destruction of Jerusalem. Another method of division could be based on God's covenants with man: in the Garden of Eden, after the flood, with Abraham, with Moses, with David, and the new covenant. Bible students often divide time into seven dispensations. The author in his book *Bible History Visualized* has used sixteen key words, all beginning with the letter *C*, to visualize all of Bible history. We use these *C* titles to survey the kingdom emphasis:

1. *Creation.* Man was created and given dominion over the earth.

2. *Conscience.* Adam and Eve as they were tested, fell into sin, lost their dominion of the earth, and were expelled from the garden. The first promise was given of the seed who would redeem and rule the earth.

3. *Captain Noah.* The history of man, as he lived under the rule of his own conscience up to the flood, is covered in this period. He failed to govern himself properly.

4. *Confusion.* After Noah came out of the ark, God made a new covenant with him and established human government. When his descendants rebelled and built the Tower of Babel, God in judgment confused their

14

tongues and scattered the people across the face of the earth. Nations are formed from these language groups.

5. *Call of Abram.* God called out Abram and made with him an important new covenant covering a land, a seed, and a blessing for all the families of the earth. This period ended with the family of Jacob living down in Egypt with Joseph ruling under Pharaoh.

6. *Carrying burdens.* This was the period of the nation of Israel's slavery in Egypt, the ten plagues, and the crossing of the Red Sea.

7. *Camp.* After Israel arrived at Mount Sinai, God made a new conditional kingdom covenant, gave the instructions for building the tabernacle, and instituted the priesthood, the offerings, and the feasts. God was to be their King.

8. *Conquest.* After the nation of Israel wandered for forty years in the wilderness, Joshua led them into the promised land and conquered it.

9. *Crown.* The people desired a human king and God gave them Saul, and later, David and Solomon. After Solomon's death, the kingdom was divided. The people became very wicked and God sent judgment.

10. *Captivity.* The Northern Kingdom was carried into captivity by the Assyrians. The Southern Kingdom was taken into captivity by the Babylonians.

11. *Construction.* After the seventy years of captivity, the Jews were permitted to go back and rebuild the temple and the city. Only a few chose to do so. They were still under the dominion of Persia. In the intertestamental period they came under the successive rule of Greece, Egypt, Syria (with partial independence in the Maccabean period), and Rome.

12. *Cross.* The period of the cross started at the beginning of the New Testament. The King was presented and His kingdom announced as being at hand. But the King was rejected and crucified. The kingdom was postponed.

13. *Church.* On the day of Pentecost the church was founded. This is the age in which we are presently living. Christ is calling out Jews and Gentiles to reign with Him in His kingdom.

14. *Coming of Christ.* This period will cover the coming of Christ for His church and will be followed by the time on earth known as the great tribulation. At the end of this seven-year period Christ will come back to establish and rule His kingdom.

15. *Condemnation.* This period of one thousand years will begin and end with a judgment. The living nations of the world will be judged as to whom is to enter into Christ's kingdom. At the end of the one thousand years the wicked dead of all ages will be raised for their final judgment and cast into the lake of fire. These one thousand years are sometimes

called the millennium. This will be the first portion of Christ's kingdom. The kingdom will not end at this time but will continue on into the ages; it is to be forever.

16. *Consummation.* At the end of the one thousand years the lifting of the curse from the heavens and the earth will be completed and Christ's ministry of destroying the works of the devil (1 Jn 3:8) will be consummated. The kingdom of God will assume its eternal character. There are only faint glimpses given in the Word of God as to what this golden age is going to be like.

Where are we in God's program? The next great prophetic event in God's plan of the ages is Christ's return for His church. We do not know when it will be. There are no signs given to immediately warn us of His coming, although we are told of the general conditions of the times (2 Ti 3:1-13). We are told what His coming will be like (1 Th 4:13-18). The believers will then be judged for rewards (1 Co 3:9-15). This judgment is not for salvation. It is only of the saved, but it will determine what rewards the Christians will receive, and what places of responsibility and what ministries will be given to them when they return with Jesus Christ to rule upon the earth and in the eternal ages which follow. It is this important period of time covered by the kingdom and the events related to it to which we are going to direct our attention. Now let us study these periods in more detail.

PURPOSE OF LIFE

"Where did I come from?" the child asked his mother, and mankind continues to ask this question. The Bible reveals that man is a direct creation of God: "And God said, Let us make man in our image, after our likeness: and let them have dominion over the fish of the sea, and over the fowl of the air, and over the cattle, and over all the earth, and over every creeping thing that creepeth upon the earth. So God created man in his own image, in the image of God created he him; male and female created he them" (Gen 1:26-27). Man is the crown of God's creation. After creating all other things, His final act of creation was man (2:7).

The very first words of God concerning the purpose of man have to do with his having dominion: "And God blessed them, and God said unto them, Be fruitful, and multiply, and replenish the earth, and subdue it: and have dominion over the fish of the sea, and over the fowl of the air, and over every living thing that moveth upon the earth" (1:28). The human race was designed to be a generation of rulers over all the lower works of God (Gen 9:2; Ps 8:5-6).

Why was man created? Not just to rule, for he was created to have communion and fellowship with God. He was given abilities that no animal or plant had. God created man as a thinking, feeling, willing, living being who could appreciate, understand and know, at least in some measure, God's very character and being. Isaiah 43:7 says that man is to bring glory to God. He was created for this purpose, but man could do this only if he stayed in his proper relationship—subject to God. But something happened.

THE GARDEN REBELLION

Even though man was placed by God in a perfect environment, the Garden of Eden, this fellowship was interrupted by sin. When Adam became a sinner he lost his dominion, and nature came under the curse. The animals rebelled against man and only a few have been domesticated. This dominion will be restored in the promised kingdom.

Immediately the question comes to mind that has occupied the attention of Bible students through the ages: "Why did God permit sin?" When man was made as a thinking, feeling, living human being, he was given a will. A freedom of choice was presented so that he could exercise this will. Because God wanted man to respond in obedience to His love through his own choice, He did not make man as a machine. If it had not been possible to sin, man could not have been truly free. But God has overruled sin by providing a redemption from its curse and at the same time demonstrating His great love for us. "For God so loved the world, that he gave his only begotten Son, that whosoever believeth in him should not perish, but have everlasting life" (Jn 3:16). Through the ministry of Christ, all that man lost in the fall will be restored with additional blessings.

After Adam's fall, each succeeding generation was born in a state of sin (Ps 51:5). Sin always separates one from God (Is 59:1-2). Sin not only robs us of our fellowship but it also veils our vision of God. Our moral and spiritual condition reflects our limited knowledge of God. Mankind's loss of the knowledge of God is recorded in Romans 1:18-24. The present mess of world conditions can be directly attributed to man's lack of a proper relationship and understanding of God. Man's knowledge of God's character will determine his view concerning sin, duty, conduct, goals in life, and relation to the world around him. False ideals led to perverted conduct. A good example of this is the day of Noah: "And God saw that the wickedness of man was great in the earth, and that every imagination of the thoughts of his heart was only evil continually" (Gen 6:5).

This lack of fellowship with God leads to an emptiness of soul. Saved and unsaved man tries to fill this emptiness with houses, money, land, cars, boats, clothes, education, recreation, work, religious activities, drunkenness, or sex, but nothing satisfies. Nothing can take the place of God. The characteristic pattern of conduct of a man with this "emptiness of soul" is that he goes from one thing to another, trying in vain to fill his void with each in turn.

God, in planning that sin would be overruled for good, provided a way back into fellowship for all those who will by an act of the will receive it. His plan involved Christ's redemptive work on the cross, which is foundational because sin separates man from God, and sin deserves to be punished. Until the sin question is taken care of, nothing else can be considered. God also has plans for a golden age in the future. This present age has sometimes been called the *workshop for eternity*. It is important that all prepare now.

BEACON LIGHT OF HOPE

Immediately following the fall, God came seeking man and revealed to him some very important promises that can be compared to a beacon light shining in a dark and stormy night. In Genesis 3:14, God placed a curse upon the serpent. In Genesis 3:15 God prophesied about four important things:

1. He promised a seed of the woman.
2. He foretold that there would be enmity between the seed of the serpent and the seed of the woman. The word translated "bruise" (*shuph*) is literally "to lie in wait for" and has the idea of a prolonged conflict.
3. The serpent's seed would bruise the heel of the woman's seed. Many commentators have said that this is the first promise of the Redeemer in the Bible and that it points to the death of Christ upon the cross.
4. But the seed of the woman is also to bruise the head of the serpent. As Charles L. Feinberg says, this is the first Bible prophecy of a coming kingdom in which all evil will be put down and made subject to the promised seed.[1] In this verse are the *white thread*, the promised seed; the *black thread*, the enmity and warfare brought on by sin; the *scarlet thread*, the promised redemption in the bruising of the heel of the seed of the woman; and the *purple thread*, the final conquest and rule of the seed of the woman. The Bible later reveals that the "promiser" becomes the "promise." God the Son became the promised seed.

When Adam and Eve rebelled, they lost many blessings:

1. They lost their moral purity.
2. They became subject to disease and death.
3. They had to work for their livelihood.

4. They lost their personal fellowship with God.
5. They lost their dominion or rule over nature.
6. They were driven from the Garden of Eden.

In spite of the blackness of their sin and the terrible consequences that this had brought upon them, both Adam and Eve demonstrated their faith in the promises of God. Even though they were under the sentence of death, Adam named his wife Eve because he believed that she was to be the mother of all living (Gen 3:20). Eve demonstrated her faith when she bore her first son and said, "I have gotten a man from the LORD," or literally, "I have gotten a man, even Jehovah" (Gen 4:1). She evidently believed that this son was the promised seed. (This hope has been held by many Jewish women through the ages, who desired to bear the promised Messiah, until finally this privilege was given to the virgin Mary.) But sin reared its ugly head again and Cain, the firstborn, murdered his brother Abel.

God raised up another seed, Seth, but his descendants had no desire *? Gen 4:26* to subject themselves to the rule of God, and mankind became very wicked. "And God saw that the wickedness of man was great in the earth, and that every imagination of the thoughts of his heart was only evil continually" (Gen 6:5). God sent the flood to destroy the earth, but He had made promises to Adam and Eve, and He always keeps His promises, so Noah found grace in the eyes of the Lord. God preserved Noah and his family as a seed and destroyed the remaining people of the earth because of their wickedness.

HUMAN GOVERNMENT ESTABLISHED

After Noah and his family came out of the ark, God instituted something new—human government. Before the flood, man had lived under the rule of his own conscience. He had a knowledge of good and evil although he did not abstain from evil and do good.

Man is basically selfish and as a fallen, depraved, sinful being, he often harmed, stole from, or even killed his fellowman. It became absolutely necessary that these evil tendencies be restricted and controlled. The basic responsibility of human government is that of regulating the conduct of man with others of his society. God put government into the world to ← restrain sin (Ro 13:4). Murder had gone unpunished before the flood. Now God said, "Whoso sheddeth man's blood, by man shall his blood be shed: for in the image of God made he man" (Gen 9:6). The highest function of government is the judicial execution of murderers and other rebels. In subsequent revelation God reveals other sins that are worthy of death: rebellion of children (Ex 21:15, 17), witchcraft (22:18), idolatry

It is also true that God gave man a conscience to restrain sin.

(22:20), adultery and other sexual sins (Lev 20:10-16). It must be kept in mind that this is a governmental judgment and not personal vengeance. Upon his confession of faith the murderer can receive pardon from sin and eternal life, but God does deny him the right to continue to live on this earth.

Human government wasn't ordained of God only for Noah's day but for every age. "Let every soul be subject unto the higher powers. For there is no power but of God: the powers that be are ordained of God. Whosoever therefore resisteth the power, resisteth the ordinance of God: and they that resist shall receive to themselves damnation [judgment]" (Ro 13:1-2).

THE CONTINUING PROBLEM OF SIN

While creation was placed under a curse in the Garden of Eden, the continuing problem of sin caused further restrictions to be placed upon it later. After the flood God placed the fear of man in all animals and most became wild. The average life-span was shortened. God wanted man to be fruitful and multiply and replenish the earth, but the people rebelled and built the tower of Babel because they did not want to be scattered over the face of the earth (Gen 11:4). Because of this rebellion God confused their tongues so that they couldn't understand one another, which caused them to scatter and obey God's command. This language problem has continued throughout the ages and will go on into the future until the kingdom itself (Zep 3:9).

FIRST EARTHLY KINGDOM

From the descendants of Noah was born Nimrod, who "began to be a mighty one in the earth. He was a mighty hunter before the LORD: wherefore it is said, Even as Nimrod the mighty hunter before the LORD. And the beginning of his kingdom was Babel" (Gen 10:8-10).

The very meaning of Nimrod's name is "rebel." His kingdom was founded in the land of Babylon in Shinar and was called the seat and source of all idolatry (Zec 5:5-11; Rev 17:3-6; 18:24). This is the first use of the word "kingdom" in the Bible and it is a type of the great counterfeit kingdom under the Antichrist.

THE RESTORATION OF BLESSINGS

Through the devil, sin came into the world and sin wrought havoc. But through the promised seed, Jesus Christ, we have the remedy for the problems brought on by sin: "For this purpose the Son of God was manifested, that he might destroy [undo or put to naught] the works of the devil" (1 Jn 3:8). Everything lost by sin will eventually be restored with added blessings by Jesus Christ.

Summary

1. God does have a plan for the ages and He has revealed this plan in the Bible.

2. Man was created to have communion and fellowship with God.

3. Sin broke this fellowship with God and has left in man an emptiness of soul.

4. When Adam and Eve rebelled, they lost many blessings.

5. God has a plan to overrule evil for good and restore man to fellowship with Himself.

6. Human government was instituted by God.

7. The basic responsibility of human government is the restraint of sin, and the regulation of the conduct of man with others of his society.

8. Jesus came to destroy or undo the work of the devil.

3

God's Covenants

ONE KEY to understanding the Bible is to understand the importance of
the Abrahamic covenant, the basic covenant of Scripture whose promises
are expanded in later covenants. Four things must be stressed in the study
of this covenant:

1. The covenant is to be interpreted literally. When it speaks of land,
it means land and when it says forever, it means forever.

2. The covenant is eternal.

3. The covenant is made with Abraham and his seed.

4. When ratified, the covenant is unconditional on Abraham's part.
God is the one who ratified it. The only condition on the part of Abraham
was his original obedience to the call of God. There are no conditions to
keep the covenant in effect.

GOD'S CALL TO ABRAM

God's call to Abram had four conditions: "Get thee out (1) of thy
country, (2) and from thy kindred, (3) and from thy father's house, (4)
unto a land that I will shew thee" (Gen 12:1). God's future plan for
a kingdom required a *land* for them to live on, people to make up a
nation, and a *king* to rule the nation. It was God's plan to make them a
means of being a *blessing* to all the nations of the world.

THE ABRAHAMIC COVENANT

The Abrahamic covenant can be considered in three spheres: (1) personal promises to Abraham, (2) promises to his seed, (3) universal promises to all nations. See Figure 2.

PERSONAL PROMISES TO ABRAM

When God called Abram He made four personal promises to him
(Gen 12:2): (1) I'll make thee a great nation; (2) I'll bless thee; (3) I'll

Promises to -

Fig. 2. Abrahamic Covenant

make thy name great; (4) Thou shalt be a blessing. God did not actually ratify His covenant with Abram until he met the four conditions. These were conditions to enter into a covenant with God, and not conditions to keep or maintain the covenant. Genesis 11:31-32 says that Abram did leave his country, but he went with his father, Terah, and his nephew, Lot. He stopped short of the land that God was going to give him and stayed in Haran. After Terah died, Abram and Lot went down into the land of Caanan and God then promised the land unto Abraham's seed (12:7). This is the fifth personal promise to Abram. Not until Abram had separated from Lot, meeting the fourth condition—"from thy kindred"—did God promise to him and his seed the land forever (13:15). This is the sixth personal promise.

Abram worried because he had no seed, but God promised him that he would have an heir and that his seed would be as numerous as the dust of the earth (13:16). He compared them to the stars in the heavens (15:5). This is the seventh personal promise.

In Abram's reply the golden thread of faith is revealed: "And he believed in the LORD; and he counted it to him for righteousness" (15:6). Following this expression of faith, God made His covenant with Abram: "In the same day the LORD made a covenant with Abram, saying, Unto thy seed have I given this land, from the river of Egypt unto the great river, the river Euphrates" (15:18). Abram had previously met the four original conditions listed in Genesis 12:1. This is the first time God uses the word covenant with Abram. There is a progression in God's promise concerning the land. In 12:1 He told Abram to come to a land that He would "show" Him; in 12:7 and 13:15, He "promised" the land unto him and his seed; but in 15:18 He said, "I have 'given' the land"—a finished transaction. In 17:8 He promised that He had given them the land for an "everlasting possession." The eighth promise was that he would die in peace after a good old age (15:15). The ninth promise was that he would be the father of many nations (17:4-5), and God changed his name to Abraham, which means the "father of many nations." The tenth personal promise was that kings would descend from him (17:6).

PROMISES TO HIS SEED

The next sphere of blessing is to Abraham's seed. The word *seed* when referring to descendants in the Old Testament is always singular. When the seed is compared to the stars of the heaven and the dust of the earth, it is used as a collective noun. The argument in Galatians 3:16 is that the seed means Christ: "To Abraham and his seed were the promises made. He saith not, And to seeds, as of many; but as of one, And to thy seed, which is Christ."

There are several opinions as to what is meant by the seed of Abraham. Erich Sauer, in discussing the transferences of the Abrahamic covenant, says:

> In all, Abraham had three kinds of posterity:
> (a) purely *bodily:* Ishmael, children of Keturah (especially Midian, Genesis 25:1-4), and Esau (Edom);
> (b) *bodily* and *spiritual:* Isaac, Jacob, and Israel and
> (c) *purely spiritual:* the believers from all nations (Romans 4:11-12; Galatians 3:14).[1]

Walvoord has a similar classification that can be summarized as follows:[2]

1. natural lineage or natural seed
2. spiritual lineage within the natural
3. spiritual seed that are not natural

He limits the natural seed largely to the twelve tribes of Israel because he feels that the Gentiles "in Christ" make up the third class and only come under the universal promise of blessing given "to all the families of the earth."

These are helpful classifications. As Sauer has pointed out, a natural or bodily seed should include all the physical descendants of Abraham. There also is a national seed within the natural seed—the twelve tribes of Israel. The national seed can be divided into two classes: believing and non-believing Israelites. Within the natural, national, believing seed is the ruling seed, the line of the seed of the woman: Isaac, Jacob, Judah, David, Jesus. In the seed—Jesus Christ, there is a spiritual seed—the church made up of Jews and Gentiles from the present age.

The chart (Fig. 3) shows that the promised seed of Abraham is a continuation of the original promise made unto Eve in Genesis 3:15. Even though Lot was for a time a part of his household, he is not in the path of the seed. When Abraham had no children, he asked if Eliezer of Damascus could be his heir. But God told him no (15:2-4). Later Abraham tried to help God provide an heir by taking unto himself Sarah's handmaid, Hagar, who gave birth to Ishmael. But God told Abraham that this was not to be his heir (17:18-21). He is Abraham's first natural seed. But God said that Isaac was to be his son and heir (17:21). Later, He calls Isaac Abraham's "only son" (22:16). After Sarah died, Abraham married Keturah and had six sons by her and sons by concubines (25:1-6), but it was only to Isaac that God confirmed the covenant (26:2-5). "Neither, because they are of the seed of Abraham, are they all called children: but, In Isaac shall thy seed be called" (Ro 9:7).

Isaac had two sons, Jacob and Esau, and it was with Jacob that God confirmed the covenant (Gen 28:12-15). Jacob had twelve sons and all of these came under the covenant. This is the national seed. One of the sons was chosen for the line of the ruling seed. "The sceptre shall not depart from Judah, nor a lawgiver from between his feet, until Shiloh come; and unto him shall the gathering of the people be" (49:10). Later it was with David, who was of the tribe of Judah, that God expanded this covenant, "I will set up thy seed after thee, which shall proceed out of thy bowels, and I will establish his kingdom. . . . And thine house and thy kingdom shall be established for ever before thee: thy throne shall be established for ever" (2 Sa 7:12-16).

About a thousand years after David, the angel came to Mary who was of the tribe of Judah and said, "And, behold, thou shalt conceive in thy womb, and bring forth a son, and shall call his name JESUS. He shall be

[handwritten marginal note: Would Lot be a Gentile blessed by the Abrahamic Covenant?]

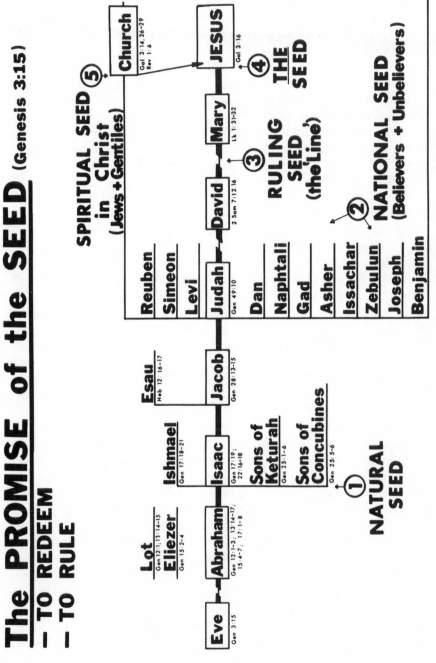

Fig. 3. The Seed

great, and shall be called the Son of the Highest: and the Lord God shall give unto him the throne of his father David: and he shall reign over the house of Jacob for ever; and of his kingdom there shall be no end" (Lk 1:31-33). Jesus is called the seed of Abraham (Gal 3:16). The lineage of the ruling seed is shown on the chart (Fig. 3) by the straight line from Eve to Christ.

All in this age who receive Jesus Christ as their personal Saviour are Abraham's seed by faith: "Know ye therefore that they which are of faith, the same are the children [sons] of Abraham" (3:7). "For ye are all the children [sons] of God by faith in Christ Jesus. For as many of you as have been baptized into Christ have put on Christ. There is neither Jew nor Greek, there is neither bond nor free, there is neither male nor female: for ye are all one in Christ Jesus. And if ye be Christ's, then are ye Abraham's seed, and heirs according to the promise" (3:26-29).

All believers today are brought into union with Jesus Christ and consequently become a part of the seed of Abraham that is promised to rule in the land. In this age all the families of the world can come under the promised blessings in Christ. As joint-heirs with Christ they will inherit with Him (Ro 8:17).

Seed compared to dust, stars, and sand. In promising that the seed could not be numbered, God used three illustrations: "The dust of the earth" (Gen 13:16), the stars in the heaven (15:5), and later "the sand which is upon the sea shore" (22:17). Commentators often explain that the stars in the heaven refer to the spiritual seed and the dust of the earth to the natural seed, but when God confirmed the covenants with Isaac He promised him that his seed would be as the "stars of heaven" (26:4) and when He confirmed his covenant with Jacob He promised that his seed would be as the "dust of the earth" (28:14). By no stretch of interpretation could Isaac's two sons, Jacob and Esau, be said to be spiritual, and Jacob's sons be only natural sons, for all of his twelve sons are picked to be under the covenant and one to be in the line of the ruling seed. Besides, the sons of Jacob are also the seed of Isaac.

It can be seen from the above discussion that when the word *seed* is used it must be interpreted according to its context, and this will show if it is referring to the following:

1. natural, physical seed
2. national seed, believing or unbelieving
3. the line of the "ruling seed"
4. Christ, "the seed"
5. spiritual seed "in Christ"

It is not always easy to know which promise is given to which seed. God does promise to make them a great nation (12:2; 13:16). He promised He would give them the land forever through His everlasting covenant (13:15; 17:7-8).

Abraham's seed has never occupied the land according to the covenant. George N. H. Peters says that since Galatians 3:16 refers to a single seed, "He meant that the land of Canaan should be inherited by a single person —preeminently the seed—descended from Abraham, even Jesus the Christ."[3] The land promises will be fulfilled when Jesus Christ rules and reigns. Many commentators believe that when Christ receives the seven-sealed book in Revelation it refers to the title deed of the land (5:9-12).

The promise that the Lord would give them kings is expanded in 2 Samuel 7:14-16 in the covenant made with David. This covenant has its great fulfillment in the birth of the Saviour (Mt 1:17).

Two covenants? Some believe that the covenant which God made with Abraham in Genesis 15 is different from the one made in Genesis 17.[4] In Genesis 17 the sign of circumcision was given. Both are called His covenants (15:18; 17:10). Ishmael and all those born in Abraham's house came under this covenant of circumcision by virtue of their belonging to the household (17:23-27). Yet Ishmael was not his promised seed or heir. This was an everlasting covenant and God was to be "their God." The individual relationship was forfeited if one failed to be circumcized (17:14). It is hard to be dogmatic, but there appears to be some basis for this two-covenant view.

UNIVERSAL PROMISES

The third sphere of blessing (see Fig. 3) includes all the families of the earth, the universal promises to all nations (12:3). Believers of all ages are saved through the finished work of Jesus Christ, for it is through Him that all the families of the earth are blessed. All Old Testament believers are not in the path of the seed, for example, Melchizedek, Job, and even Nebuchadnezzar.

In the present age of the church, all believers are placed into the body of Christ and through this union with Him become a part of the seed. People will be saved during the tribulation, but they will not be a part of the body of Christ. "After this I beheld, and, lo, a great multitude, which no man could number, of all nations, and kindreds, and people, and tongues, stood before the throne, and before the Lamb, clothed with white robes, and palms in their hands" (Rev 7:9). Verse 14 explains who these people are: "These are they which came out of great tribulation, and have washed their robes, and have made them white in the blood of the Lamb." They are saved by the work of Christ but are not "in Christ."

In the universal promises first given to Abraham, there were two blessings and a curse: "And I will bless them that bless thee, and curse him that curseth thee: and in thee shall all families of the earth be blessed" (Gen 12:3). This promise will be the basis of God's judgments on the living nations at the close of the great tribulation, after He has sent His 144,000 witnesses out proclaiming the gospel. Receiving the witnesses and their message is the same as receiving Christ (Jn 13:20; Lk 10:16; Mt 10:40; 25:31-46).

THE PURPOSE OF GOD'S CHOSEN PEOPLE

God has planned to establish His kingdom on the earth and restore His rule over it. He chose (elected) a man, Abraham, to start a new nation. Through this nation would come the promised seed, a seed that would provide redemption from sin and rule as King. The great requirement of God in Abraham's age, as well as in all the other ages, is faith. The Scripture says, "Abraham believed God, and it was counted unto him for righteousness" (Ro 4:3). Abraham showed his faith by odedience to God's command. About twenty-five years after Abraham came down into the land, God gave him his promised seed and Isaac was born. This was a supernatural birth because both Abraham and his wife Sarah were past the age of having children. His seed Jesus Christ also had a supernatural birth, being born of the virgin Mary.

After Abraham went to offer his son Isaac as an offering, God repeated His promise of universal blessing for the fifth time.

> And said, By myself have I sworn, saith the LORD, for because thou hast done this thing, and hast not withheld thy son, thine only son: that in blessing I will bless thee, and in multiplying I will multiply thy seed as the stars of the heaven, and as the sand which is upon the sea shore; and thy seed shall possess the gate of his enemies; and in thy seed shall all the nations of the earth be blessed; because thou hast obeyed my voice (Gen 22:16-18).

Notice that in this confirmation of the covenant, God again promised that the seed of Abraham would be victorious over his enemies. This is very similar to the garden promise in Genesis 3:15 when He promised to bruise the head of the seed of the serpent.

After Abraham's death, God unconditionally confirmed His covenant with Isaac (26:3-5). When Jacob was at Bethel and had his dream of the ladder extending from earth to heaven, God unconditionally confirmed the Abrahamic covenant with him (28:12-15).

God's people went into Egypt as a family and came out as a nation. God's chosen people are called His elect in Isaiah (42:1; 45:4; 65:9, 22), but the same word in other places is translated *chosen*. God chose them for a special purpose; this election was of grace and to a specific ministry and could be spurned. Just because they were born as Israelites does not mean that they automatically came under the covenant promises of Israel (Ro 9:6). Their election in Genesis 17:7 was not to eternal life but to a ministry in the plan of God. By faith they received eternal life, so to speak of them being *elected* to eternal life is a misuse of the word. Eternal life was not limited only to the chosen seed of Abraham. Melchizedek is an example of one who was not born of Abraham yet he was a priest of God. God could have chosen the seed of Ham or those of the Chinese nation or some other nation, but He chose Abraham and his seed.

THE ELECTION OF ISRAEL

The purpose and objectives of the election of Israel have been very clearly presented by Arthur W. Kac who gives six objectives which the election of Israel was expected to achieve:

1. To proclaim to the world the existence of God: "This people have I formed for myself, they shall set forth my praise" (Isaiah 43:21).

2. To proclaim to the world that Jehovah the God of Israel, is the one God of Revelation, the only one God who has revealed to Israel His purposes for the whole of mankind: "Hear, O Israel: Jehovah our God is one Jehovah" (Deut. 6:4). . . .

3. To demonstrate to the world the blessing to be derived from belonging to God: ". . . Happy is the people whose God is Jehovah" (Ps. 144:15).

4. To become the writers and preservers of the Word of God: "Behold, I have taught you statutes and ordinances, even as Jehovah my God commanded me, that you should do so in the midst of the land whither you go up to possess it. Keep therefore and do them; for this is your wisdom and your understanding in the sight of the peoples, that shall hear all these statutes, and say, Surely this great nation is a wise and understanding people" (Deut. 4:5-6). Notice what was to be Israel's most distinctive contribution in the world: "for this is your wisdom and your understanding in the sight of the peoples. . . ." The apostle Paul expresses the same truth in the Roman letter: "What advantage then hath the Jew? or what is the profit of circumcision? (i.e. of the Abrahamic Covenant). Much every way: first of all, that they were entrusted with the oracles of God" (Rom. 3:1-2). . . .

5. To become God's nation-priest to all the other nations of the world, a channel by which God's blessings would flow to all nations of the earth: "Now, therefore, if you will obey my voice indeed, and keep my covenant, then you shall be a peculiar treasure unto me from among all peoples: for all the earth is mine. And ye shall be unto me a kingdom of priests, and a holy nation . . ." (Ex. 19:5-6).

6. To bring into the world the world's Redeemer. . . .
   a. His human origin (Gen. 3:15).
   b. His national origin (Gen. 12:1-3).
   c. A descendant of the tribe of Judah (Gen. 49:10).
   d. A descendant of the royal house of David (Isa. 11:1-2).
   e. The place of the Redeemer's birth (Mic. 5:2).
   f. His divine nature (Isa. 9:6).

The fulfillment of the objectives of the election of Israel rests upon two premises: (1) Israel's possession of and her presence in the land of Israel and (2) the full realization of the objectives of the election of Israel will take place during the reign of the Messiah. Israel's uninterrupted possession of the land was dependent upon her faithfulness to God's covenant. Her ownership of the land, however, was never to be affected by her conduct for it was given by God through the unconditional Abrahamic Covenant.[5]

First Prophecy of a King for Israel

Before Jacob died, he gathered his sons together and prophesied about their descendants (Gen 49:1-28). Unto Judah he said, "The sceptre shall not depart from Judah, nor a lawgiver from between his feet, until Shiloh come; and unto him shall the gathering of the people be" (v. 10). This verse reveals that from the tribe of Judah the King was to come. By promise, the seed of the woman can now be traced to Seth, Shem, Abraham, Isaac, Jacob, and Judah. At this time it is not disclosed when the King will appear.

The Mosaic or Kingdom Covenant

When God called Abraham, He promised that He would make of him a great nation. When the book of Exodus opens, the chosen family has become a nation. God has kept His first promise. He also kept personal promises to Abraham—He gave him a seed and made his name great: he is respected to this day by Israelites, Arabs, and Christians.

After God brought them out of Egypt to Mount Sinai, He made a new covenant with the nation that had descended from Abraham—Bible students usually call it the Mosaic covenant. Sometimes called the law, this covenant is usually divided into three parts:

1. *The moral law* (Ex 20:1-26). The Ten Commandments are in this portion.

2. *The civil law* (Ex 21:1—24:18). This part of the law concerns their everyday activities, especially their social life or interpersonal relations, and it is quite detailed.

3. *The ceremonial law* (Ex 25:1—40:38). The final section regulates their religious life. (See Fig. 4).

The religious leaders of Jesus day concentrated on the outer ring and neglected the core.

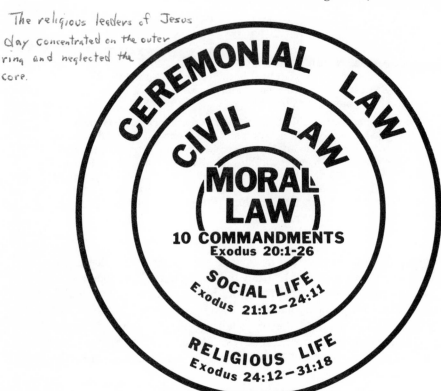

Fig. 4. Mosaic Covenant with Israel

THE PURPOSE OF THE MOSAIC COVENANT

The Mosaic covenant is a conditional covenant, but the purpose and promise given by God are often overlooked: "Now therefore, if ye will obey my voice indeed, and keep my covenant, then ye shall be a peculiar treasure unto me above all people: for all the earth is mine: and ye shall be unto me a kingdom of priests, and an holy nation" (Ex 19:5-6). In the promised land God wanted the nation to minister for Him as a nation of priests, and through this priestly nation would "all the families of the earth be blessed." A holy God demands a holy priesthood to minister and serve Him. In order to fulfill this high calling, they needed detailed instructions for their conduct and manner of service. They stayed at Mount Sinai about one year, during which time God gave instructions for building the tabernacle, the institution of the priesthood, the sacrificial offerings, and the feasts.

ISRAEL A THEOCRACY—GOD IS KING

Exodus 19, according to J. P. Lange, "records the establishment of the theocracy, or typical kingdom of God."[6] Josephus, the Jewish historian, is said to be the one who first used the term *theocracy*. A theocracy has been defined as a government of the state by the immediate direction of God. All legislative, executive and judicial power was held by God. He partially delegated executive and judicial authority to other people, but as Peters says, "All the people (Deut. 29:10-13) in their civil, religious, social, and family relations were to acknowledge, and be required at certain times in the year (Deut. 16:16, etc.) to visit the place of special manifestation, and renew their vows of allegiance."[7]

Moses said, "And he was king in Jeshurun, when the heads of the people and the tribes of Israel were gathered together" (Deu 33:5). McClain says, "That the pronoun 'he' must refer to Jehovah, not to Moses, is the opinion of the best commentators." (See Num 23:21; Ps 114:1-2; 1 Sa 8:7). (*The Greatness of the Kingdom*, p. 64).

The response of the people to God's offer of a covenant was good: "And all the people answered together, and said, All that the LORD hath spoken we will do. And Moses returned the words of the people unto the LORD" (Ex 19:8). They said this even before they knew the Lord's requirements and again affirmed it after they heard the words from Moses (24:3). One thing that the children of Israel had to learn was that even though they may have had the desire to live holy lives in obedience to what God required, by themselves they did not have the power.

One thing we all must learn

WHAT IS THE LAW?

The law or Mosaic covenant gives the requirements for those who would serve a holy God. It must be remembered that while the Bible often contrasts law and grace, yet there was grace in this covenant. The ceremonial law has many marvelous types and beautiful foreshadowings of the person and work of the Lord Jesus Christ.

PROPER USE OF THE LAW

Because of man's fallen condition he is unaware of his own sinfulness. It is through the law that guilty man gains his knowledge of sin and his utter helplessness in view of God's just requirements (Ro 3:19; 7:7; Gal 3:10; Ja 2:10). "Wherefore the law was our schoolmaster to bring us unto Christ, that we might be justified by faith" (Gal 3:24). Kenneth S. Wuest says:

> The word translated *schoolmaster* is the important word here. It is *paidagogos*. The word *schoolmaster* could better be the translation of

didaskalos which means "a teacher." It is true that our word *pedagogue* comes from the Greek *paidagogos*, and that it refers to a schoolmaster. But the Greek word did not have that meaning. The word designated a slave employed in Greek and Roman families who had general charge over a boy in the years from about 6-16. He watched over his outward behavior, and took charge over him whenever he went from home, as for instance, to school. This slave was entrusted with the moral supervision of the child. His duties were therefore quite distinct from those of a schoolmaster. Furthermore, the metaphor of a *paidagogos* seems to have grown out of the word *kept* (*phroureo*) of verse 23, which means "guard to." Thus the word refers to a guardian of a child in its minority rather than to a teacher or schoolmaster.

By describing the law as a *paidagogos*, Paul emphasizes both the inferiority of the law to grace, and its temporary character. The law was therefore the guardian of Israel, keeping watch over those committed to its care, accompanying them in a condition of dependence and restraint, and continually revealing to them sin as a positive transgression.[8]

The lawful use of the law will include these four uses:

1. It reveals a holy God's requirements for a people to serve Him as a nation of priests.

2. It reveals man's sinful condition.

3. It reveals man's utter helplessness to meet the standards which God requires.

4. It acts as God's guardian over His people until Christ came. Christ, in turn, supplied the means by which man could meet these holy requirements.

IMPROPER USE OF THE LAW

There are some definite things that the law cannot do: (1) justify man (Gal 2:16); (2) make perfect (Heb 7:19); (3) give the Holy Spirit (Gal 3:1-3); (4) give strength for holy living (Ro 8:3).

THE FUTURE OF THE LAW

The Scripture says that the law was our guardian until Christ should come (Gal 3:24).

The ability to live according to the holy standards of the law is promised in the new covenant given in Jeremiah. This is quoted in Hebrews 10:16: "This is the covenant that I will make with them after those days, saith the Lord, I will put my laws into their hearts, and in their minds will I write them." It is through an inward work of grace in the heart of believers and through the ministry of the Holy Spirit that it becomes possible. "This I say then, Walk in the Spirit, and we shall not fulfill the lust of the flesh" (Gal 5:16).

God's Basic Requirement

Under the Mosaic covenant, as in every age, God's basic requirement is faith. It is faith in God and His promised redemption that makes man right with God (Ro 3:21-24).

Summary

1. The Abrahamic covenant is the basic covenant of the Old Testament. It is an unconditional, eternal covenant and should be interpreted literally.

2. The Abrahamic covenant can be divided into three basic parts: (1) personal promises to Abraham, (2) promises to the seed, (3) universal promises to all nations.

3. The seed of Abraham can mean (1) natural physical seed; (2) national seed, believing or unbelieving; (3) the line of the "ruling seed"; (4) Christ "the seed"; (5) spiritual seed "in Christ."

4. God's plan is to establish His kingdom on the earth and establish His rule over it.

5. God chose Abraham to start a new nation through which He will establish His kingdom. It is through Israel that the promised Redeemer and King will come.

6. The Word of God came through Israel.

7. The ruling seed of the woman can now be traced from Eve to the tribe of Judah.

8. The Mosaic or kingdom covenant was given to the nation Israel.

9. The Mosaic covenant told how Israel could serve a holy God.

10. A theocracy is the government of the state by the immediate direction of God.

11. In a theocracy all the civil, religious, social, and family relations of the people are to be subject to God their King.

12. Trying to be justified by the works of the law is an improper use of the covenant.

13. The Mosaic covenant has been supplanted by the new covenant.

4

Israel's School in the Wilderness

GOD IS THE MASTER TEACHER. In preparing Israel as a "kingdom of priests" He used many teaching devices or visuals such as manna, water from the rock, the fiery pillar, the brazen serpent, and clothes that didn't wear out. He established and used institutions, for example, the tabernacle, the priesthood, the sacrificial system, the offerings, and the feasts. He also used their experiences: crossing the Red Sea and fighting Amalek.

We can learn many things today from the Old Testament. Paul, speaking of the experiences of Israel in the wilderness, said, "Now these things were our examples, to the intent we should not lust after evil things, as they also lusted. Now all these things happened unto them for ensamples: and they are written for our admonition, upon whom the ends of the world are come" (1 Co 10:6, 11; see also Lk 24:23-27; Ac 17:2-3; 1 Co 15:1-4). The law itself pointed toward things in the future: "For the law having a shadow of good things to come, and not the very image of the things, can never with those sacrifices which they offered year by year continually make the comers thereunto perfect. Then said he, Lo, I [Christ] come to do thy will, O God. He taketh away the first, that he may establish the second" (Heb 10:1, 9).

THE TABERNACLE WAS GIVEN TO A REDEEMED PEOPLE

Israel had been redeemed by the blood of the Passover lamb and brought out of Egypt by the very power of God. They belonged to Him; He had purchased them. They were to be His peculiar people, a nation of priests, and through them blessings were to flow out to all the families of the earth.

GOD TO DWELL WITH MAN

The reason God gives for the construction of the tabernacle is: "Let them make me a sanctuary; that I may dwell among them. And I will dwell among the children of Israel, and will be their God" (Ex 25:8; 29:45).

God revealed that it was His desire to again have fellowship with man and to dwell among them. The original relation in the Garden of Eden was to be restored with both God and man in their proper place, with man subject to God.

When Christ reigns, it will again be said of Jerusalem that "the LORD is there" (Eze 48:35). In the golden age that is to follow, "Behold, the tabernacle of God is with men, and he will dwell with them, and they shall be his people, and God himself shall be with them, and be their God" (Rev 21:3). We have a foretaste of this blessing today as God's dwelling place is said to be in the church (1 Co 3:16) and in the individual believer (6:19-20).

TEACHING MINISTRY OF THE TABERNACLE

The design of the tabernacle was given by God Himself, who told Moses, "And look that thou make them after their pattern, which was shewed thee in the mount" (Ex 25:40). The tabernacle is called a pattern and a figure and evidently represents God's heavenly throne (see Heb 8:2, 5; 9:8-9, 23-24; see Fig. 5).

About four hundred years later David gives to Solomon the pattern of the temple. He had received this from the Lord (1 Ch 28:11-12, 19). It was an expanded and glorified copy of the tabernacle. The ministry and service in the temple were more elaborate than the service for the tabernacle, but they were then in the land that God had promised Abraham.

Ezekiel 40–43 describes a temple that will be built and used during Christ's millennial reign. It will be larger than Solomon's, and at that time the nation will assume its ministry as a nation of priests ministering to the world.

In the New Jerusalem, God will tabernacle or dwell with men (Rev 21:3). There will be no temple, for as John says, "And I saw no temple therein: for the Lord God Almighty and the Lamb are the temple of it" (21:22).

The tabernacle as it was first given in the wilderness was God's kindergarten school of service which He used to teach His people to serve Him. It emphasized three important things:

1. the holiness of God
2. their own sinfulness
3. the only way to approach a holy God, through the high priest and the shedding of blood

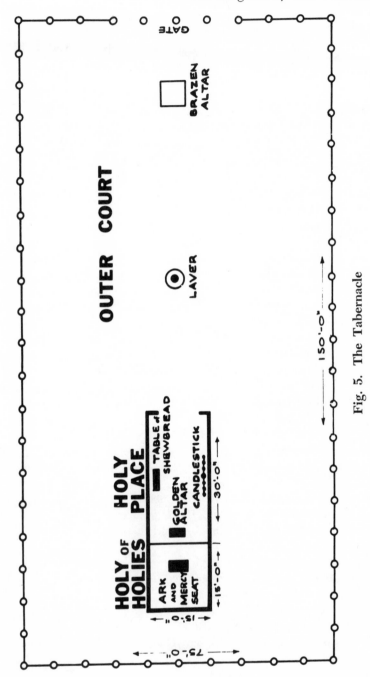

Fig. 5. The Tabernacle

PRIESTHOOD

The basic ministry of the priesthood is the representation of men before God. Out of the tribe of Levi, God chose one family, the family of Aaron, to minister at His altar, and Aaron himself was the first high priest (Ex 28:1). Walter C. Wright points out three things about the Old Testament priesthood:

(a) That God wanted them to draw near; else why should He have appointed the ritual?

(b) That they could not come into His immediate presence, else why would they be represented by one man who went to and fro on their behalf?

(c) That every approach must satisfy the requirements of holiness.[1]

The functions of the Levites and the priests were not limited to worship in the tabernacle nor to attendance upon the altar. They were also to be teachers of the law and advisors of the judges (Deu 17:8-11; Eze 44:24; Mal 2:7). So God chose one family and tribe to minister to the nation which, in turn, was to minister to the world.

The book of Hebrews says that the Aaronic priesthood was replaced by another priesthood "after the order of Melchizedek" of which Christ is the High Priest (chaps. 5–7). This is the order of an unending priesthood.

Christians are called to a priestly ministry: "But ye are a chosen generation, a royal priesthood, an holy nation, a peculiar people; that ye should shew forth the praises of him who hath called you out of darkness into his marvellous light" (1 Pe 2:9).

QUALIFICATIONS FOR PRIESTLY MINISTRY

Being the son of Aaron did not automatically qualify one to minister as a priest. There were three basic requirements:

1. The priest had to be ceremonially pure and holy (Lev 21:10-11). He was not to rend his clothes (as the high priest did at the trial of Jesus) or defile himself.

2. The priest's life had to be above reproach. His wife had to be a virgin. He could not marry a widow, a divorced person, or a harlot, and the virgin had to be of his own people (vv. 13-15).

3. The high priest had to be physically perfect. Any physical defect, infirmity or deformity disqualified him from officiating as priest (vv. 17-21). God provided for his needs and his food was supplied, but he could not minister (vv. 22-23). These qualifications pointed toward the high priesthood of Jesus Christ and His holy character, conduct and ministry.

If it was true of Israel that they could be disqualified from the priest-hood, what a warning this should be to believers! They too can be dis-qualified through sin. Our priestly calling is given in 1 Peter 2:9. Com-pare the standards in Galatians 5:19-21 and Ephesians 5:5.

THE OFFERINGS

The first five chapters of Leviticus explain the five basic offerings of the sacrificial system: (1) the burnt offering, (2) the meat (meal) offering, (3) the peace offering, (4) the sin offering, and (5) the trespass offering. All point to the redemptive work of Jesus Christ. When the offerer came bringing a sacrifice, he laid his hands upon it and identified himself with it, and confessed his sins. He said in effect, "Here is my substitute that I have brought in obedience to your commands to atone for my sins." This was done millions of times.

Erich Sauer figures that according to Numbers 28–29 there were 1,273 official annual offerings.[2] Therefore, from Moses to Christ almost two million sacrifices were made, plus all the private offerings designated in Leviticus 1–5, which must total in the millions.

God was teaching the people that an innocent one would have to die for the guilty, and many years later John the Baptist pointed to Jesus and said, "Behold the Lamb of God, which taketh away the sin of the world" (Jn 1:29).

FEASTS AND SET TIMES

The most important set time for Israel was the Sabbath. First men-tioned in the Bible in Genesis 2:2-3 in connection with the creation of the world, the basic idea of the word *Sabbath* is *rest* or *ceasing from labor*. God did not rest on the seventh day because He was tired but because His work was finished. The Sabbath is mentioned in the times of Noah (Gen 7:4, 10) and Laban (29:27), where it was used as a means of mark-ing or counting time, but it was not necessarily kept as a rest. It is also used in connection with the giving of manna in Exodus 16:23. With the giving of the Mosaic covenant, it became the sign of the covenant (Ex 20:8-11; 31:13-17). It set Israel apart from the nations of the world.

THE TEN SABBATHS

The word *Sabbath* is used for other than the weekly Sabbath. In Leviticus 19:3, God said, "Keep my sabbaths." There are ten ways that it is used in the Bible:

1. The weekly Sabbath (Ex 20:8)
2. The first day of the feast of Passover (unleavened bread) (Lev 23:7-8)

3. The seventh day of unleavened bread
4. The feast of Pentecost (vv. 15-16, 21)
5. The first day of the seventh month of the feast of trumpets (v. 24)
6. The Day of Atonement (tenth day of the seventh month) (v. 32)
7. The first day of the Feast of Tabernacles (v. 39)
8. The eighth day of the Feast of Tabernacles
9. The sabbatical year—every seven years (25:4)
10. The year of jubilee—the year following seven sabbatical years, or every fiftieth year (25:10-11)

The first Sabbath came at the completion of creation when God expressed His satisfaction with what He had done: "It was very good." This blessedness, however, was lost through the fall, but through the mercy of God He will restore it through the redemption of Christ.

Keeping the Sabbath was commanded to compensate to some degree for the losses which came to man through the curse of sin. He had to earn his livelihood by the sweat of his brow, and he was also under the oppression and slavery of sin (Jn 8:34). Perhaps the Sabbath was to remind them of the promised rest of God which will be realized in the kingdom. Colossians 2:16-17 says that the Sabbaths and holy days are a "shadow of things to come."

THE CHURCH AND THE SABBATH

Neither by commandment nor by tradition has the church been taught to keep the Sabbath. It was a covenant sign for Israel.

Jesus, "the Lord of the Sabbath," met with His disciples on the first day of the week after His resurrection. Pentecost, the birthday of the church, was the day after the weekly Sabbath which commemorated the deliverance of Israel from Egypt: "And remember that thou wast a servant in the land of Egypt, and that the Lord thy God brought thee out thence through a mighty hand and by a stretched out arm: therefore the Lord thy God commanded thee to keep the sabbath day" (Deu 5:15). Christ's resurrection on the first day of the week commemorates a greater deliverance.

THE SABBATICAL YEAR

Every seventh year God provided a vacation for His people. In the sixth year He would provide a surplus so that during the seventh year only that which grew by itself without being cultivated was to be taken from the fields. This was a gracious provision for the poor, the slaves, and even the animals, for there was no planting or harvesting in the normal manner. Everyone, whether they owned land or not, was permitted to gather from the fields, but only enough to meet their daily needs (Lev 25:4-7). This was the year in which debts were suspended (Deu 15:1-3).

THE YEAR OF JUBILEE

The year of jubilee was called the year of "liberty." At the beginning of this year, every slave was freed, all debts were canceled, and the land was returned to the descendants of the original owners. The year of jubilee gave the original four freedoms:

1. freedom from slavery
2. freedom from debt
3. freedom from hunger
4. freedom from toil

The forty-ninth year, the sabbatical year, was followed by the year of jubilee, which was also a Sabbath. So for two years in a row there was no laboring in the fields, but this required a dependence or trust in the Lord to supply food and the necessities of life. The sabbatical year and the year of jubilee both seem to point toward the coming kingdom of Jesus Christ when creation will have the curse lifted and there will be the restoration of all things.

THE THREE MAIN FEASTS

Exodus 23:14-17 lists the three important feasts of Jehovah: the feasts of Passover, Pentecost, and Tabernacles. Each year all male Jews who were physically able were to go to Jerusalem to appear before the Lord and to celebrate these feasts which were to begin when they entered the land.

In Leviticus 23 additional feasts of the Lord are given. These six feasts prophetically foreshadow great events in the future: The feast of the Passover—the redeeming work of Christ; the feast of unleavened bread which immediately followed Passover—a holy walk of believers; followed by the feast of firstfruits—Christ's resurrection from the dead (1 Co 15:23); the feast of Pentecost—the birthday of the church; the feast of trumpets—the regathering of Israel; the feast of Tabernacles—the kingdom of Christ. There is also an important set time—it was not a feast but a fast—the great Day of Atonement which again points to the finished work of Christ.

LESSONS IN FAITH

Little by little God taught His people, using feasts, rituals, sacrifices and experiences. He taught them about His power as He humbled the Egyptians with the ten plagues and led His people safely through the

Red Sea. He used physical signs to demonstrate His holiness while they were at Mount Sinai: fire, lightning, thunder, trumpets and clouds. Through the tabernacle, the priesthood, the offerings, and the feasts, God taught them the conduct that He required and the manner in which they were to serve Him. He provided manna and quail to feed them and brought water from the rock to quench their thirst. After one year at Mount Sinai He led them out toward the promised land.

If the period at Mount Sinai can be compared to a kindergarten, the next period can be compared to a grade school. There was one thing above all else that He wanted of His priestly nation—faith or absolute trust in Him. He led them out by the pillar of cloud, so there was no question about where and when He wanted them to go. When they arrived at Kadesh-Barnea, they sent twelve spies into the land. All the spies agreed that the land was a wonderful land just as God had promised, but ten of them said that there were giants in the land and walled cities and "we be not able to go up against the people; for they are stronger than we" (Num 13:31). They flunked the test of faith.

This should be a warning to Christians. Disobedience or lack of faith can cause missed blessings now and in the kingdom of Christ. How could one minister as a priest, teaching men or representing men before God, if he is disobedient or if he doesn't believe Him? Who would want a government of this kind?

PROPHECIES OF BALAAM

As the new generation moved toward the land of Moab, Balak the Moabite king and his people became very worried. So Balak called for a very unusual person, Balaam, a Gentile prophet, to come and curse the Israelites. Although God would not permit Balaam to do this, the prophet did give several unusual prophecies about the king and the kingdom of the Israelites (see Num 23:19-21; 24:7, 17-25).

PREPARATION AND ENTRANCE INTO THE LAND

Deuteronomy records the history of the final preparations of the new generation to enter the land. Everyone over the age of twenty who came out of Egypt, with the exception of Joshua and Caleb, had died in the wilderness, and Moses' final ministry before he died was to prepare this new generation for entering the land. Moses reminded them that God "brought us out from thence, that he might bring us in, to give us the land which he sware unto our fathers" (Deu 6:23).

They were to be given an opportunity to be a "kingdom of priests, and an holy nation" (Ex 19:6). At Sinai when God gave the conditional kingdom covenant there were blessings as well as penalties attached to it. The extreme national penalty for breaking the covenant, given in both Leviticus and Deuteronomy, is a dispersion of Israel and the desolation of the promised land (Lev 26:32-33; Deu 28:63-68).

PALESTINIAN COVENANT

"These are the words of the covenant, which the LORD commanded Moses to make with the children of Israel in the land of Moab, beside the covenant which he made with them in Horeb" (Deu 29:1). The covenant made at Mount Sinai (Mount Horeb) was a conditional covenant. The first generation did not keep it so God is now giving this new generation an opportunity to keep it. Sometimes it is called the "Palestinian covenant" by Bible students. Dr. C. I. Scofield lists seven parts to the Palestinian covenant,[3] but Sidlow Baxter says that there is nothing given in this passage that has not already been included in such passages as Leviticus 26, and that it is a new covenant only in the sense that it is now being given to a new generation.[4] Upon close examination this seems to be the case.

RELATION OF MOSAIC AND ABRAHAMIC COVENANTS

Israel did not keep the Mosaic covenant but this does not annul the unconditional covenant that God made with Abraham. "And this I say, that the covenant, that was confirmed before of God in Christ, the law, which was four hundred and thirty years after, cannot disannul, that it should make the promise of none effect. For if the inheritance be of the law, it is no more of promise: but God gave it to Abraham by promise" (Gal 3:17-18).

OWNERSHIP—POSSESSION

Eternal ownership of the land is given unto Israel in Genesis 17:8, "And I will give unto thee, and to thy seed after thee, the land wherein thou art a stranger, all the land of Canaan, for an everlasting possession; and I will be their God." God has a purpose for the land as well as a purpose for the people. Abraham, Isaac and Jacob all lived in the land promised to them, and this new generation and their descendants will also live in the land for a total of about eight hundred years. It is important to see that neither Abraham nor the nation has ever yet taken possession of the land under the unconditional Abrahamic covenant. Even under the reigns of David and Solomon, all the land promised was never occupied.

NATIONAL OWNERSHIP VERSUS PERSONAL POSSESSION

It can also be pointed out that Israel's ownership of the land is unconditional as a nation, but possession or enjoyment of that land is based upon the obedience of each generation. Leviticus 26:28 lists a series of seven different chastisements for disobedience, and the final one was a desolation of the land and a scattering of the people among the nations. Israel was being taught a new lesson—that obedience to the Lord's commands can only come about through conversion (Deu 30:6). This promise of conversion was explained and expanded in the new covenant.

SUMMARY

1. The Old Testament contains many promises, prophecies, and types concerning Christ and His ministry (Lk 24:23-27).

2. God had Israel build a tabernacle so that He might dwell among them.

3. The tabernacle emphasizes the holiness of God, the sinfulness of Israel, and the way to approach God through the high priest and the sacrifice.

4. Priests were picked to represent men before God.

5. Priests can disqualify themselves from the ministry of the priesthood.

6. The sacrifices pointed toward the work of Christ upon the cross.

7. The act of sacrifice taught the important truth of substitution—an innocent one must die for the guilty.

8. The Sabbath foreshadows the rest in Christ's millennial kingdom.

9. The feasts of Israel foreshadow important events in God's program.

10. In the school in the wilderness God tried to teach His people to trust Him. Most of them flunked the test.

11. The generation that came out of Egypt forfeited by unbelief their right to enter the land.

12. There are blessings and penalties connected with the Mosaic covenant, for it is a conditional covenant.

13. Failure to keep the conditional Mosaic covenant does not annul the unconditional Abrahamic covenant.

5

Establishment of the Historical Kingdom

Upon Israel's entrance into the promised land, the historical kingdom was established, and while God was the King, He ruled through Joshua, the judges, and the kings whom He appointed. But because of Israel's failure to live up to the requirements of the conditional kingdom covenant, the historical kingdom never became the promised kingdom in which the seed of the woman was to rule.

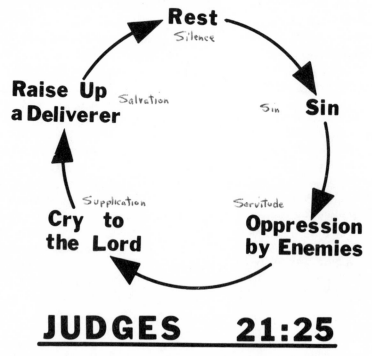

Fig. 6. Cycle of Sin in Judges

46

FAILURE OF THE JUDGES

Israel in the land utterly failed to keep the covenant which God made with them at Mount Sinai. "In those days there was no king in Israel: every man did that which was right in his own eyes" (Judg 21:25). The children of Israel went through a cycle of sin six times: They did evil again in the sight of the Lord, and the Lord brought in their enemies to oppress them; they cried out in prayer and supplication unto the Lord; He, in turn, raised up a judge to deliver them, and the land had rest. But they never seemed to learn from their discipline (see Fig. 6).

Samuel, the last judge of Israel, illegally made his sons judges over Israel, but they did not serve honestly. Finally the elders of Israel came together "and said unto him, Behold, thou art old, and thy sons walk not in thy ways: now make us a king to judge us like all the nations" (1 Sa 8:5).

A KING FOR ISRAEL

God had planned for Israel to have a king because He had told Abraham that "kings shall come out of thee" (Gen 17:6). Jacob had prophesied about the scepter not departing from Judah (49:10), and Balaam had prophesied about a scepter rising out of Israel (Num 24:17). God had given detailed instructions concerning a king in Deuteronomy 17:14-20, but there were some restrictions and requirements:

1. The choice of king was to be God's alone.
2. There were certain things he could not do: multiply horses, wives, or wealth.
3. He was to write a personal copy of the law, which he was to read, study, and keep all the days of his life, thus subjecting himself to God's will. If he kept these regulations, he was promised that it would "prolong his days in his kingdom, he, and his children, in the midst of Israel" (v. 20).

The people were wrong in demanding, "Make us a king . . . *like all the nations.*" They probably thought that a king would forge them into a strong nation and this, in turn, would free them from the oppression of their enemies. But they failed to recognize that this oppression was direct discipline from the Lord because of their sinful ways. Their request for a human king was really an insult to God, for how could a human king give greater blessings and promises than God had given them? They wanted all the blessings without the obedience God required.

REJECTION OF GOD AS KING

Samuel felt the people's request was a rejection of himself, but God explained to him that they actually were rejecting Him: "But they have rejected me, that I should not reign over them. According to all the works which they have done since the day that I brought them up out of Egypt even unto this day, wherewith they have forsaken me, and served other gods, so do they also unto thee" (1 Sa 8:7-8).

THE REJECTION OF KING SAUL

Saul was rejected because he committed three major sins:

1. He spurned God's order and presumptuously intruded into the priesthood by offering sacrifices (1 Sa 13:13-14).

2. He rebelled against the command of God and did not destroy the Amalekites (15:22-23).

3. He turned from God to demonism when he consulted the witch at Endor (28:7-19).

THE KINGDOM TO BE A THEOCRACY

The kingdom in its final form will be a theocracy, and God Himself in the person of Jesus Christ, the Son of David, will rule over the kingdom as its earthly Ruler. Peters says, "The theocracy must, in the very nature of the case, include a *manifested reign* of God as earthly ruler and the exhibition of an intimate and abiding union of the civil and religious."[1]

GOD'S CHOICE OF A KING

After God rejected King Saul, He chose David to be king. At Saul's coronation Samuel had referred to him as the king whom the people had chosen (12:13). When God sent Samuel to the house of Jesse, He said, "I have provided me a king among his sons" (16:1); and when David was brought before Samuel, the Lord said, "Arise, anoint him: for this is he" (16:12).

The Lord blessed David and the nation and gave them victory over their enemies. David made Jerusalem the capital city and brought the ark to Jerusalem, "and it came to pass, when the king sat in his house, and the LORD had given him rest round about from all his enemies; that the king said unto Nathan the prophet, See now, I dwell in an house of cedar, but the ark of God dwelleth within curtains" (2 Sa 7:1-2). David had a desire to build a house for the ark of God, but God had a better plan for David than to build a beautiful building. He revealed to Nathan that David's posterity was to be his "house." Through his descendants, or "house," his throne and his kingdom were to continue forever. This same terminology is used of Christ: "But Christ as a son over his own house; whose house are we, if we hold fast the confidence and the rejoicing of the hope firm unto the end" (Heb 3:6). The covenant with David is one of the important covenants of Scripture.

THE DAVIDIC COVENANT

Now therefore so shalt thou say unto my servant David, thus saith the LORD of hosts, I took thee from the sheepcote, from following the sheep, to be ruler over my people, over Israel: and I was with thee whithersoever thou wentest, and have cut off all thine enemies out of thy sight, and have made thee a great name, like unto the name of the great men that are in the earth. Moreover I will appoint a place for my people Israel, and will plant them, that they may dwell in a place of their own, and move no more; neither shall the children of wickedness afflict them any more, as beforetime, and as since the time that I commanded judges to be over my people Israel, and have caused thee to rest from all thine enemies. Also the LORD telleth thee that he will make thee an house. And when thy days be fulfilled, and thou shalt sleep with thy fathers, I will set up thy seed after thee, which shall proceed out of thy bowels, and I will establish his kingdom. He shall build an house for my name, and I will stablish the throne of his kngdom for ever. I will be his father, and he shall be my son. If he commit iniquity, I will chasten him with the rod of men, and with the stripes of the children of men: but my mercy shall not depart away from him, as I took it from Saul, whom I put away before thee. And thine house and thy kingdom shall be established for ever before thee: thy throne shall be established for ever (2 Sa 7:8-16).

This covenant contains personal promises to David, promises to his yet unborn son (Solomon), and promises to the nation of Israel (see Fig. 7). David is promised four things:

1. A house or posterity or family or dynasty.

2. He is to have a son yet to be born who shall succeed him and establish his kingdom and "thy seed after thee."

3. He was promised a throne or royal authority.

4. He was promised a kingdom or sphere of rule. The house, throne and kingdom were to be forever.

God promised Solomon:

1. that he would build the temple instead of David;

2. that he would be chastised for disobedience;

3. that the throne would not be taken from him, even though his sins would justify it.

Solomon's throne, but not his seed, was promised to be established forever. Notice that the promise was not that the throne would be occupied forever. It was only necessary that the lineage never be lost. Solomon's line was cut off because of sin (Jer 22:30; 36:30). Joseph was Christ's legal father from the line of Solomon (Mt 1:7), but Mary, Jesus' mother, was from the line of Nathan, another son of David (Lk 3:31).

First Chronicles 17:14 is either talking about David or is looking forward to David's greater Son, Jesus Christ: "But I will settle him in mine house and in my kingdom for ever: and his throne shall be established

Promises to –

NATION

SOLOMON

DAVID

1. House
2. Seed
3. Throne
4. Kingdom

1. Build Temple
2. Chasten with Mercy
3. Throne

1. Permanent Place
2. Rest from Enemies

2 Samuel 7:8-16

Fig. 7. Davidic Covenant

for evermore." Notice the emphasis on "mine house" and "my kingdom."
This is an unconditional covenant that God, in grace, made to David.

The Northern Kingdom had nineteen kings from nine different families
before it was carried into captivity, but the kings of the Southern Kingdom were all from the family of David.

God promised the nation:

1. that He would plant them, that they would dwell in a place of their
own, and that He would move them no more;

2. that they would not be afflicted by their enemies.

This covenant is built upon the promises to Abraham and will be fulfilled when Jesus reigns in His kingdom.

David subdued the enemies on every side of Israel: the Philistines on the west, the Syrians and Hadadezer on the north, the Ammonites and Moabites east of the Jordan, and the Edomites and Amalekites to the south (2 Sa 8:12-14).

CONTRASTS OF SAUL AND DAVID'S KINGDOMS

Hottel makes an interesting contrast between Saul and David's kingdoms:

> The kingdom of Saul and the kingdoms of David and Solomon stand in marked and sharp contrast in the record of the Books of Samuel; the former being man's kingdom, demanded by Israel and ruled over by a king whose very spirit and principle reflected Israel's spirit and principle of independence of God, as well as of unbelief and self-will; the latter being the expression of the Kingdom of God, inaugurated by the will of God and ruled over by one whose heart was with Him. The kingdom of Saul is therefore a clear foreshadowing of the kingdom of Satan, ruled over by the coming Antichrist, the willful king and the lawless one (Dan. 11:36-39; II Thess. 2). It was clearly a counterfeit kingdom as the kingdom of Antichrist will also be, while the kingdom of David, supplemented by that of Solomon, is the foreshadowing and expression of the Kingdom of God in the Person of His Son, the Lord Jesus Christ.[2]

David could not build the temple because he was a man of war, so it was built by Solomon; but David established the kingdom over which Solomon reigned. Together they foreshadowed the coming reign of Christ who will conquer all His foes and establish His kingdom, as David did, and He will rule as the Prince of Peace, even as Solomon's reign was peaceful.

THE TEMPLE

The temple was designed by God and resembled the basic pattern of the tabernacle given to Israel about four hundred years previously. Built in Jerusalem on Mount Moriah, it is thought to have been on the same mountain to which Abraham took his son Isaac: "Take now thy son, thine only son Isaac, whom thou lovest, and get thee into the land of Moriah; and offer him there for a burnt-offering upon one of the mountains which I will tell thee of" (Gen 22:2). In David's time the site was a threshing floor that he purchased from Ornan. David had also gathered many of the materials for the construction of the temple.

Compared to some heathen temples, the temple was not large. Its beauty was in its workmanship, coverings and ornaments, but its main glory was the Shekinah glory or the divine presence of God manifested by a visible cloud resting over the mercy seat. When the temple was completed, God showed His acceptance of it by sending down fire from

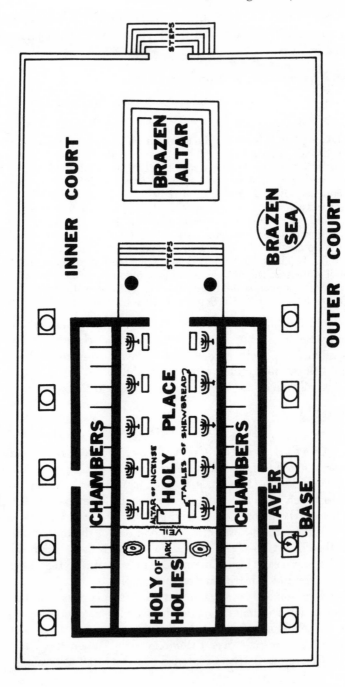

Fig. 8. Solomon's Temple

heaven to consume the offerings upon the altar, and filling the temple with His Shekinah glory. "And the priests could not enter into the house of the LORD, because the glory of the LORD had filled the LORD's house. And when all the children of Israel saw how the fire came down, and the glory of the LORD upon the house, they bowed themselves with their faces to the ground upon the pavement, and worshipped, and praised the LORD, saying, For he is good; for his mercy endureth for ever" (2 Ch 7:2-3; see Fig. 8; the dimensions of the outer court are not given.)

The tabernacle was built in the wilderness, and from the outside its beauty was largely hid. It can be compared to the Saviour's earthly ministry. He was meek and lowly as He took on the form of a man; His glory was veiled by human flesh. The temple can be compared to the exalted Lord of glory as He will be when He reigns in His kingdom.

Arthur E. Smith says:

> The reason why the New Testament throws so much light on the Tabernacle, rather than on the Temple, is because the Tabernacle is a type of wilderness journey, the Church in the wilderness—condition during this age of grace. The world has become a wilderness to the saints because of their identification with the rejected Christ.
>
> On the other hand, the Temple in the land is a picture of a risen Christ with His ransomed people as stones in a spiritual house.[3]

In the plan of God, a temple should have an important place in the ministry of a nation of priests, but Israel failed to keep its covenant with God and eventually this temple was destroyed.

SUMMARY

1. Israel's oppression by their enemies during the time of the judges was a discipline of God for their sins, but they failed to learn the lessons.

2. When Israel requested a king like the nations they rejected God as King.

3. God planned for Israel to have a king, but there were certain restrictions concerning His choice and conduct.

4. God rejected Saul as king because of his sins.

5. The theocracy of Israel was an introductory form of the kingdom.

6. The Davidic covenant is an important unconditional covenant of the King.

7. The Davidic covenant will be fulfilled when Jesus rules in His kingdom.

8. While Saul's kingdom foreshadows the coming kingdom of the Antichrist, David and Solomon's kingdoms foreshadow the coming kingdom of Christ.

9. The temple will be rebuilt in the millennial kingdom.

6

The Disruption of the Historical Kingdom

SIN BRINGS TROUBLE (Ro 6:23). The apostasy of Israel brought forth a harvest of judgment. In grace God attempted to turn Israel back to her covenant responsibilities and to Himself by giving her a new order of servants—the prophets—who were His spokesmen with His message to man. Four prophets were sent to Israel and seven to Judah, but the people failed to heed the message and consequently were carried into captivity.

After Solomon's death the kingdom was divided, with the ten northern tribes choosing Jeroboam as their king, while Judah and Benjamin were ruled by Solomon's son Rehoboam.

THE NORTHERN KINGDOM

Because Jeroboam did not want his people to go down to Jerusalem to worship and to attend the feasts, he established two new centers of worship, one in Dan in the northern section of his kingdom, and the other at Bethel in the southern part. Ordering two golden calves to be made and placed at these locations, he then claimed that they were Israel's gods which had led them out of the land of Egypt. Evidently these idols were to represent Jehovah. Jeroboam also built high places for the new worship, selecting a new group of people to be priests, ordaining a new feast to replace the Feast of Tabernacles, and instituting a sacrificial system. It was a totally counterfeit religion through which Jeroboam "made Israel to sin," a foreshadow of the counterfeit religion of the false prophet in the end time. Despite the prophetic ministries of Elijah, Elisha, Hosea and Amos, the ten tribes continued on their downhill track away from God.

THE KINGDOM IN HOSEA

Hosea compared Israel to an adulterous wife who would be chastened but eventually restored because of the love of the Lord for Israel: "For

54

the children of Israel shall abide many days without a king, and without a prince, and without a sacrifice, and without an image, and without an ephod, and without teraphim: afterward shall the children of Israel return, and seek the Lord their God, and David their king; and shall fear the Lord and his goodness in the latter days" (3:4-5). Hosea saw a chastened Israel repenting and turning back to the Lord in the end time.

THE KINGDOM IN AMOS

Amos prophesied against the wickedness of Israel and Judah, telling them that their worship was an abomination unto God, and that some of them had been worshiping idols. Because of their sin, God would send an invader to carry them away captive: "Therefore will I cause you to go into captivity beyond Damascus, saith the Lord, whose name is The God of hosts" (5:27). He also prophesied about a coming day of judgment called the day of the Lord (5:16-20), the great tribulation in the New Testament. Amos closed with a prophecy about the future kingdom, promising a restoration to the land and that the land would become fruitful: "And I will plant them upon their land, and they shall no more be pulled up out of their land which I have given them, saith the Lord thy God" (9:15).

In fulfillment of the prophecy of the captivity, the Assyrians conquered the land in 722 B.C. and carried the Israelites off captive.

THE SOUTHERN KINGDOM

The Southern Kingdom continued about 140 years longer than the Northern Kingdom, but its spiritual trend was also downward. In the Bible the northern kings are compared to Jeroboam, who made Israel to sin. In the Southern Kingdom the kings are compared to David and said to be good when they are like their father David. None of the nineteen kings in the Northern Kingdom was called good. They were from nine different families, while the kings from the Southern Kingdom were all from the family of David. Five of Judah's kings were called good. God gave these seven prophets to Judah before they were carried into captivity: Joel, Isaiah, Micah, Zephaniah, Hakakkuk, Obadiah and Jeremiah.

THE KINGDOM IN JOEL

Joel had much to say about the future of Israel. He phophesied about the following:

1. A plague of insects which would destroy the land, used as a type to describe an enemy army in the coming day of the Lord (1:15)

2. A promised pouring out of the Spirit of God (2:28-29)

3. The signs before the day of the Lord (2:30-32)
4. The return from captivity (3:1)
5. The judgment of nations (3:2-8)
6. A final cleansing of Israel and restoration to the land (3:17-21)

THE KINGDOM IN ISAIAH

The book of Isaiah is filled with prophecies concerning the kingdom. Beginning his ministry about forty years before the Northern Kingdom went into captivity and about 175 years before the Babylonian captivity of the Southern Kingdom, the prophet Isaiah repeatedly warned Israel of punishments that would come upon them for their terrible sins. A great deterioration of the nation had occurred from the times of David and Solomon; but even as God warned of judgments and punishments coming upon the nation, He also promised wonderful things in the latter days: "And it shall come to pass in the last days, that the mountain of the LORD's house shall be established in the top of the mountains, and shall be exalted above the hills; and all nations shall flow unto it" (Is 2:2; cf. 1:25-28; 2:1-5; 4:1-6).

SIN OF JUDAH

The book of Isaiah is a good example of the interrelationships of the great themes of the Bible. In the first thirty-nine chapters the *black thread* of sin is very prominent. In the opening chapter God says that they have rebelled against Him (1:4-6).

SOVEREIGNTY OF GOD

The *blue thread*, which represents God the sovereign Ruler of the universe overruling evil for good, is also very prominent in Isaiah's prophecy. Behind the scenes God overruled sin, using man's own wickedness to accomplish His ends. The day of the Lord, God's final great judgment for sin, is mentioned again and again in the first thirty-nine chapters.

The prophecy about God's judgment for sin takes the shape of a spiral (see Fig. 9). Imagine the spiral superimposed over a map of the land. The temple was at Jerusalem, the capital city of God's chosen people. The prophecies of judgment begin with Judah and extend out. Chapters 1–6 foretell the day of the Lord and Judah in the south; chapters 7–12 tell of the day of the Lord and Israel in the north; chapters 13–23 prophesy about ten "burdens" or judgments on the nations surrounding Israel. Chapters 24–27 have to do with the day of the Lord and the whole world. Then the prophecy turns back to Jerusalem itself, and chapters 28–33 include the six woes upon Jerusalem (compare this to the three woes

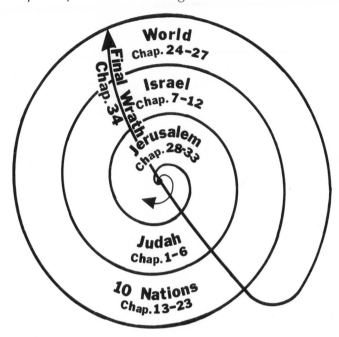

Fig. 9. Spiral of Judgment in Isaiah

given in Rev 9:12). Finally, chapter 49 has the final wrath—the description of the Battle of Armageddon: "And I feed them that oppress thee with their own flesh; and they shall be drunken with their own blood, as with sweet wine: and all flesh shall know that I the LORD am thy Saviour and thy Redeemer, the mighty One of Jacob" (v. 26).

VISION OF GOD

The *white thread* which represents God's revelation of Himself appears many times in Isaiah. One outstanding passage is Isaiah's vision of God sitting upon the throne of His heavenly temple (6:1-8). In chapters 40–48 God revealed many additional things about Himself: His omnipotence, omniscience, omnipresence, holiness, wisdom and righteousness.

Because the Saviour and the King are to be the same Person, many of the prophecies concerning the Redeemer and the King overlap.

PROPHECIES ABOUT THE KING

The *purple thread* of royalty is a prominent theme in the book of Isaiah, who gave unto the unbelieving King Ahaz the prophecy of the virgin birth: "Therefore the Lord himself shall give you a sign; Behold, a virgin shall conceive, and bear a son, and shall call his name Immanuel" (7:14). His name "Immanuel" means God with us (Mt 1:23). Israel's only hope would be in this promised King, of whom Isaiah gives a further prophecy: "For unto us a child is born, unto us a son is given: and the government shall be upon his shoulder: and his name shall be called Wonderful, Counsellor, The mighty God, The everlasting Father, The Prince of Peace. Of the increase of his government and peace there shall be no end, upon the throne of David, and upon his kingdom, to order it, and to establish it with judgment and with justice from henceforth even for ever. The zeal of the LORD of hosts will perform this" (9:6-7).

The revelation concerning the coming King takes a giant stride in these prophecies. Starting with the first prophecy of the seed of the woman (Gen 3:15), through the seed of Abraham (17:6), through the tribe of Judah (49:10), through the family of David (2 Sa 7:16), it is clear that the King is going to have a supernatural birth but He will not just be a man; He will be God ruling forever (Is 9:6-7).

THE KINGDOM PROMISED

Chapters 11 and 12 foretell the establishment of the kingdom following the great tribulation and give details about the King:

> And there shall come forth a rod out of the stem of Jesse, and a Branch shall grow out of his roots: And in that day there shall be a root of Jesse, which shall stand for an ensign of the people; to it shall the Gentiles seek: and his rest shall be glorious. And it shall come to pass in that day, that the Lord shall set his hand again the second time to recover the remnant of his people, which shall be left, from Assyria, and from Egypt, and from Pathros, and from Cush, and from Elam, and from Shinar, and from Hamath, and from the islands of the sea (11:1, 10-11).

Note the following:

1. His ancestry (11:1)
2. His anointing by the Spirit of God (11:2)
3. The character of His righteous reign (11:3-5)
4. Nature during the kingdom (11:6-9)
5. The gathering of His people from the four corners of the earth (11:10-16)
6. His kingdom—a "rest" (11:10)
7. Worship in His kingdom (chap. 12)

RESURRECTED BELIEVERS IN THE KINGDOM

Isaiah also foretells about the resurrection: "And they shall be gathered together, as prisoners are gathered in the pit, and shall be shut up in the prison, and after many days shall they be visited. Then the moon shall be confounded, and the sun ashamed, when the LORD of hosts shall reign in mount Zion, and in Jerusalem, and before his ancients gloriously" (24:22-23).

Isaiah is one of the three writers (along with Peter and John) who prophesied about the new heavens and new earth: "For, behold, I create new heavens and a new earth: and the former shall not be remembered, nor come into mind" (65:17). He also prophesied about the second coming of Christ (61:1-2).

THE SAVIOUR

The *scarlet thread* in Isaiah is the most graphic picture of the crucifixion in all of the Old Testament. This was given over seven hundred years before it took place. Isaiah 52:14 foretold that in His appearance He would be so marred by the crucifixion brutalities that His appearance would no longer be like that of a man; He would look inhuman. Isaiah 53 is a graphic description of the work of the Saviour.

THE KINGDOM IN MICAH

Micah prophesied of a coming judgment for Judah (chaps. 1–3), but he also told about the promised kingdom and regathering of the people back to the land (chaps. 4–5). He gave a remarkable prophecy about the birthplace of the promised King: "But thou, Bethlehem Ephratah, though thou be little among the thousands of Judah, yet out of thee shall he come forth unto me that is to be ruler in Israel; whose goings forth have been from of old, from everlasting" (5:2). King Herod's scribes and chief priests quoted this prophecy to the wise men.

THE KINGDOM IN ZEPHANIAH

There is a seventy to one hundred-year interval between Micah and Zephaniah. Used of God to prophesy to Judah about the coming captivity, Zephaniah also told of God's judgments on the surrounding nations; but he closed his book with a prophecy about the coming kingdom: "The LORD hath taken away thy judgments, he hath cast out thine enemy: the king of Israel, even the LORD, is in the midst of thee: thou shalt not see evil any more. The LORD thy God in the midst of thee is mighty; he will save, he will rejoice over thee with joy; he will rest in his love; he will joy over thee with singing" (3:15, 17). These two verses emphasize that their King will be in their midst, and He is the Lord who will save them and bring happiness to them.

THE KINGDOM IN HABAKKUK

Habakkuk could not understand why God permitted sin to go unpunished, but God revealed to him that He was going to use the Chaldeans to punish His people for their wickedness. "But the just shall live by his faith" (2:4). Of the promised kingdom, Habakkuk said, "For the earth shall be filled with the knowledge of the glory of the LORD, as the waters cover the sea" (2:14).

THE KINGDOM IN OBADIAH

This short book concerns the land of Edom which was located south of Judah and was originally given to Esau's descendants. A judgment will come upon them during the great tribulation, but Edom will be included in the kingdom (1:17-21).

THE KINGDOM IN JEREMIAH

Jeremiah the prophet ministered in the Southern Kingdom to the last generation before the Babylonian captivity. The conduct and attitude of the priests, rulers, prophets and people can be seen in these verses: "The priests said not, Where is the LORD? And they that handle the law knew me not: the pastors also transgressed against me, and the prophets prophesied by Baal, and walked after things that do not profit" (2:8). "The prophets prophesy falsely, and the priests bear rule by their means; and my people love to have it so: and what will ye do in the end thereof?" (5:31). The king himself showed his utter scorn for God by burning God's message (36:27).

Jeremiah preached against the sin of Judah and foretold that the Babylonians would carry them off into captivity. His message was not well received, and he was physically mistreated.

FAITH UNDER TRIAL

Jeremiah's life demonstrates the life of faith despite opposition, slander and persecution. He suffered *with* his people as the land was invaded by Nebuchadnezzar's armies, and *under* his people as he was carried against his will by the Jews down into Egypt. Yet, Jeremiah faithfully declared the whole counsel of God to this unrepentant people, and for this God will reward him.

This illustrates a very important lesson: God does not count the value of service for Himself merely in terms of success. He had a message He wanted delivered, even though the people failed to respond to it. The same is true of the message of salvation today. We are to evangelize, or give the message of the grace of God, to all. We cannot force people to believe, for that is not our job. Neither are we to judge people and witness only to those who we think will respond. We must learn to be faithful, even where we cannot be successful.

THE BRANCH

Jeremiah also prophesied about the coming King of Israel: "Behold, the days come, saith the LORD, that I will raise unto David a righteous Branch, and a King shall reign and prosper, and shall execute judgment and justice in the earth. In his days Judah shall be saved, and Israel shall dwell safely: and this is his name whereby he shall be called, THE LORD OUR RIGHTEOUSNESS" (23:5-6).

Jeremiah foretold the restoration of the nation (23:1-24; 33:1-26), and said that the length of their captivity would be seventy years (25:1-14).

In foreseeing the resurrection, he said David would have a place in the coming kingdom: "But they shall serve the LORD their God, and David their king, whom I will raise up unto them" (30:9).

THE NEW COVENANT

Because of Israel's inability to keep the Mosaic covenant and enter into the promised blessings, God promised a new covenant:

> Behold, the days come, saith the LORD, that I will make a new covenant with the house of Israel, and with the house of Judah: not according to the covenant that I made with their fathers in the day that I took them by the hand to bring them out of the land of Egypt; which my covenant they brake, although I was an husband unto them, saith the LORD: but this shall be the covenant that I will make with the house of Israel; After those days, saith the LORD, I will put my law in their inward parts, and write it in their hearts; and will be their God, and they shall be my people. And they shall teach no more every man his neighbour, and every man his brother, saying, Know the LORD: for they shall all know me, from the least of them unto the greatest of them, saith the LORD: for I will forgive their iniquity, and I will remember their sin no more (31:31-34).

Several features of the new covenant should be emphasized:

1. It is an everlasting covenant.

2. With the new covenant comes a promise of a renewed mind and heart which is called the new birth or regeneration.

3. The new covenant provides for a restoration to the favor and blessings of God: their God, His people.

4. The new covenant provides for the forgiveness of sin.

5. The teaching ministry of the Holy Spirit will be manifested as He indwells their hearts (Eze 36:27).

Jeremiah 31:31 plainly teaches that this new covenant is to be made with the nation of Israel, but these promises will extend on to "all the families of the earth" in this age, as later revealed in the New Testament. This is an expansion of the third sphere of the Abrahamic covenant, the universal promises (Gen 12:3; see Fig. 27).

THREE VIEWS OF THE NEW COVENANT

Who is under the new covenant? There are three general views: (1) the covenant is exclusively with Israel, (2) there are two covenants—one with Israel and one with the church, and (3) there is one covenant with a twofold application—first promised to the Jews for the kingdom age, and presently enjoyed by the church. The latter view seems best.

Lewis S. Chafer points out that seven important features are in the covenants (except the Mosaic covenant) which God made with Israel. They are all related to the kingdom:

1. A nation forever
2. A land forever
3. A king forever
4. A throne forever
5. A kingdom forever
6. A New Covenant
7. Abiding blessings[1]

UNHEEDED WARNINGS

After 140 years the Southern Kingdom followed the Northern Kingdom into captivity. With the exception of a few short periods, the nation has demonstrated about eight hundred years of unfaithfulness since they entered into the kingdom covenant with God at Mount Sinai. But before He punished them, God promised the new covenant which they will be able to keep.

SUMMARY

1. Sin brought about the disruption of the kingdom.

2. Hosea and Amos, the prophets to the Northern Kingdom, both prophesied of the coming captivity, a restoration, and a future kingdom.

3. Joel prophesied about the day of the Lord, the pouring out of the Spirit of God, the return from captivity, the judgment of nations, and restoration to the land.

4. Isaiah prophesied about the coming captivity, a judgment upon the nations, the birth and death of the Messiah-King, the resurrection, the establishment of the kingdom, and the new heaven and earth.

5. Micah prophesied about a coming judgment for Judah, a restoration back to the land, and the birthplace of the Messiah.

6. Zephaniah prophesied about a coming captivity and a restoration to the land when the Lord would be their King.

7. Habakkuk prophesied that God would punish the wicked, but in the coming kingdom the earth would be filled with the knowledge of the glory of the Lord.

8. Obadiah sees a judgment coming upon Edom but prophesied that she would be included in the kingdom.

9. Jeremiah prophesied of the Babylonian captivity and that the coming King will be a righteous branch of David. He prophesied that God would make a new covenant with Israel because they had been unable to keep His old one, the Mosaic covenant.

7

The Overthrow of the Historical Kingdom

EVEN THOUGH God punished His people, He did not leave them without a witness. Ezekiel and Daniel had much to say about Israel's restoration and the coming kingdom. After the captivity a faithful remnant was allowed to return to the land, but the restoration of the kingdom is yet future (Ac 1:6).

THE KINGDOM IN EZEKIEL

Ezekiel, who ministered during the Babylonian captivity, was taken captive in the second wave of the conquerors in 598 B.C. A key to understanding the book of Ezekiel is in the phrase, "They shall know that I am the LORD," which occurs some seventy times with slight variations.

VISION OF CORRUPT JERUSALEM

Ezekiel's vision in chapter 8 came just five years before the fall of Jerusalem. In this vision he was transported from the captivity in Babylonia to Jerusalem where God revealed to him the terribleness of the people's sin:

1. An idol had been set up in the very temple of the Lord (v. 5). God's commandment was "Thou shalt not make unto thee any graven image, or any likeness of any thing that is in heaven above, or that is in the earth beneath, or that is in the water under the earth" (Ex 20:4).

2. The elders of Israel were secretly worshiping and burning incense before animal or beast gods (Eze 8:7-12).

3. The women were involved in the sex-corrupted worship of a Greek god (vv. 13-15).

4. Twenty-five men, evidently the high priest and the twenty-four chief priests of the temple had turned their backs upon the holy place and were worshiping the sun (v. 16).

5. The spiritual breakdown had caused a moral breakdown, and the land was filled with violence (v. 17). Because of the condition of the

people, God said that He was going to judge the people and judge them severely (v. 18).

God promised to spare the remnant and restore them to their land (11:14-21). Ezekiel also speaks of a new covenant called an everlasting covenant under which God would bring His people at a future time (16:60, 62; 20:37). Chapters 36—39 are important descriptions of the end-time activities, with Israel's restoration to the land and with the wars in the great tribulation period. Through Ezekiel the prophet, King David is again promised a place in the kingdom as a prince forever (37:24-25).

Chapters 40—48 describe the kingdom age and tell of the temple that is to be built, with a description of its size, offerings and worship. God promised that His throne would be in the midst of Israel forever (43:7). These themes are studied in detail in a later chapter.

THE KINGDOM IN DANIEL

What about the promises of the kingdom that God said He would establish in the land? The nation had been taken into captivity, and Jerusalem and the temple destroyed. Did God change His mind? Through Ezekiel, God said that these judgments had come upon them so that "they shall know that I am the LORD." In the book of Daniel, He states an additional purpose three times: "that the living may know that the most High ruleth in the kingdom of men, and giveth it to whomsoever he will" (4:17, 25, 32). Daniel shows that five world empires will arise.

God gave Daniel the interpretation of Nebuchadnezzar's dream of the great image which represented four great world empires: Babylon, Medo-Persia, Greece and Rome. But the fifth empire is the important one:

> And in the days of these kings shall the God of heaven set up a kingdom, which shall never be destroyed: and the kingdom shall not be left to other people, but it shall break in pieces and consume all these kingdoms, and it shall stand for ever. Forasmuch as thou sawest that the stone was cut out of the mountain without hands, and that it brake in pieces the iron, the brass, the clay, the silver, and the gold; the great God hath made known to the king what shall come to pass hereafter: and the dream is certain, and the interpretation thereof sure (2:44-45).

The kingdom has its origin in heaven and is heaven's kingdom. It was known by the Jews and referred to many times in the book of Matthew as the kingdom of heaven.

Nebuchadnezzar had to learn his lesson. He was personally humbled; he became insane and for seven years ate grass as an ox until he knew "that the most High ruleth in the kingdom of men, and giveth it to whomsoever he will" (4:32). Daniel lived to see the Babylonian kingdom fall to the Medo-Persians.

VISION OF SEVENTY SEVENS

The angel Gabriel told Daniel that "seventy weeks [sevens] are determined upon thy people and upon thy holy city" (9:24). Note that the word "weeks" can also be translated "sevens." In Hebrew there is no separate word for week. Daniel said that these seventy weeks were being given to accomplish certain things: (1) to finish the transgression, (2) to make an end of sins, (3) to make reconciliation (atonement) for iniquity, (4) to bring in everlasting righteousness, (5) to seal up the vision and prophecy, and (6) to anoint the Most Holy.

The seventy weeks (or sevens) are to be divided into three parts. From the going forth of the commandment to restore and rebuild Jerusalem there will be seven sevens, or forty-nine years. After sixty-two more weeks, or 430 years, the Messiah shall be cut off (9:25-26). Daniel then prophesied about a coming prince, evidently the Antichrist who will destroy the city and the temple in the period of the great tribulation. This prince will make a covenant with the nation for one week, or seven years, but in the middle of the week he will cause their sacrifice to cease and set himself up as God to be worshiped (Dan 9:26-27; 11:31; 2 Th 2:3-4; Mt 24:15).

The prophecy of seventy sevens was interrupted at the close of the sixty-ninth week at the rejection of the Messiah. The unspecified interval between the sixty-ninth and the seventieth week has lasted over nineteen hundred years. The fulfillment of this prophecy will begin again when the Jews make a covenant with this wicked prince. This is evidently the covenant mentioned in Isaiah 28:15-18, where it is called a covenant with death and an agreement with hell. The seventieth week of Daniel is the subject of much of the Lord's Olivet discourse in Matthew 24 and 25 (see Figs. 16 and 19).

THE FALSE MESSIAH

A. C. Gaebelein says,

> During the last seven years, the final prophetic week, when the prince of the Roman power makes a covenant with the Jews, they will build a temple in Jerusalem. In the middle of this week this willful king will come and take his seat in that temple and claim divine worship. Then Satan will be working in great power, signs, and lying wonders. This willful king deceives them that dwell on the earth (Rev. 13:14) by the means of those miracles. Apostate Jews and Gentiles will believe the lie, and thus hasten

on to the judgment which is prepared for them when God's true king appears out of the open heavens.[1]

THE KINGDOM IN THE PSALMS

The Psalms give abundant testimony to the fact that Israel was to be a theocracy—a nation ruled by God (5:2; 44:4; 68:24; 74:12; 84:3; 89:18; 95:3; 98:6). Other prophecies point toward a coming eternal kingdom (24:7-8; 145:1, 11-13; cf. 10:16; 22:28; 29:10; 45:6; 91:1; 93:-1-2; 97:1; 146:8-10).

Psalm 2:6-7 reveals that the King will be God's Son: "Yet have I set my king upon my holy hill of Zion. I will declare the decree: the LORD hath said unto me, Thou art my Son; this day have I begotten thee."

Psalm 89:3-4, 20-37 especially stresses the relationship of God's covenant with David and the kingdom, while several other psalms seem to prophesy about Christ's reign as King of kings and Lord of lords when the nations of the world will bow down to Him or bring tribute (72:1, 10-11, 17; 68:29; 82:8).

THE KINGDOM IN EZRA AND NEHEMIAH

In the book of Ezra God permits a remnant to go back and rebuild the temple under the leadership of Zerubbabel. The wall was rebuilt around Jerusalem under the leadership of Nehemiah. Notice the progression of the work: from the altar to the temple to the wall. This temple, later remodeled by Herod the Great, is the temple that stood during the ministry of Christ.

The seed of David has never occupied the throne of David since the time it was sent into the Babylonian captivity. God did permit the temple to be rebuilt, and that rebuilt temple should have reminded them of several things:

1. The way was not yet opened into the presence of God. The altar was still blocking the path until that time when Jesus would provide a new and living way (Heb 10:19-20).

2. The temple was a symbol of the former unity of the nation which had split some five hundred years before.

3. The temple was a reminder of the nation's high calling—a nation of priests.

4. The temple was a challenge to the elect nation to a renewed consecration.

THE KINGDOM IN HAGGAI

Haggai is a prophet of the postexile period whose ministry of exhortation was directed toward the rebuilding of the temple, but the last three

verses refer to the establishment of the kingdom and the promised place
in it for Zerubbabel:

> Speak to Zerubbabel, governor of Judah, saying, I will shake the
> heavens and the earth; and I will overthrow the throne of the kingdoms,
> and I will destroy the strength of the kingdoms of the heathen; and I will
> overthrow the chariots, and those that ride in them; and the horses and
> their riders shall come down, every one by the sword of his brother. In
> that day, saith the LORD of hosts, will I take thee, O Zerubbabel, my
> servant, the son of Shealtiel, saith the LORD, and will make thee as a
> signet: for I have chosen thee, saith the LORD of hosts (2:21-23).

THE KINGDOM IN ZECHARIAH

Zechariah was a contemporary of Haggai who also ministered during
the rebuilding of the temple in the postexile period. He had much to say
about the Messiah, His kingdom, and the end-time activities:

1. the Messiah, the Branch and my Servant (3:8)
2. the Messiah entering into Jerusalem on a colt (9:9)
3. the Messiah, the good Shepherd (9:16; 11:11)
4. the Messiah, the smitten Shepherd (13:7)
5. the Messiah betrayed for thirty pieces of silver (11:12-13)
6. the Messiah's hands pierced (12:10)
7. the Messiah wounded in the house of His friends (13:6)
8. the Messiah coming on the Mount of Olives (14:3-8; Ac 1:11)
9. the Messiah's coming and coronation (chap. 14)
10. The extent of the Messiah's kingdom (14:9)
11. the "pierced" Messiah recognized (12:10)
12. the Spirit poured out on the Messiah's people (12:10)
13. the Messiah's kingdom set up on earth (chap. 14)
14. the Messiah's people regathered (10:9-12)

MALACHI AND THE DAY OF THE LORD

Malachi does not have anything directly to prophesy about the kingdom, but he does prophesy about the coming day of the Lord (4:5).

INTERTESTAMENTAL CHANGES

With the writing of the book of Malachi the Old Testament closed,
and for four hundred years there was a silent interval in the written Word
of God. During this intertestamental period many changes took place.
The Old Testament closed with Persia ruling over Palestine, and this rule
continued until 333 B.C. when Alexander the Great led the armies of
Greece and set up his world empire. Alexander died ten years later and
his empire was split into four parts. Egypt ruled over Palestine from

323 to 204 B.C., when Syria conquered the country and held control until the Maccabbean rebellion which began in 167 B.C. Various parts of Palestine were practically independent under the Maccabbees until 63 B.C. when Rome took control of the land: Rome continued to rule over Palestine through the New Testament period. After a rebellion by the Jews, Rome destroyed the city of Jerusalem in A.D. 70 and took many captives.

The four great world empires prophesied in Daniel have been established: Babylon, Medo-Persia, Greece and Rome. The fifth kingdom—the kingdom that has its origin in heaven—Christ's kingdom, is yet future.

FIVE NEW PARTIES

When the New Testament opened there were five new parties in existence that were not seen in the Old Testament. Three were religious: the Pharisees, Sadducees, and Essenes. Two were political: the Herodians and Zealots.

FIVE NEW INSTITUTIONS

The New Testament opened with five prominent new institutions: the Sanhedrin, the synagogue, the oral law, the scribes, and the publicans.

SUMMARY

1. Ezekiel said God's judgment came upon Jerusalem because of her sins, especially because of her perverted worship.

2. God promised to restore a remnant to the land.

3. God promised a new and everlasting covenant with Israel.

4. The book of Daniel tells of five great world empires.

5. The fifth great world empire will be heaven's kingdom.

6. Daniel tells of a great prophetic schedule of seventy sevens for the nation of Israel.

7. The seventieth seven applies to the future and will begin when Israel makes its covenant with the Antichrist.

8. The Psalms reveal many things about the kingdom, including the fact that the King will be God the Son.

9. Ezra and Nehemiah record the return of a remnant to the land. They rebuild the temple but the throne is still empty and they are under the rule of Persia.

10. Haggai prophesied that Zerubbabel will have an important place in the kingdom.

11. Zechariah prophesied fourteen important things about the Messiah and His kingdom.

12. Malachi does not mention the kingdom, but his last words are a warning about the coming day of the Lord.

13. Israel's restoration is necessary and important in the plan of God.

14. In the intertestamental period, Palestine comes under the successive rule of Greece, Egypt, Syria, the Maccabbees, and Rome.

15. Five new parties are formed in the intertestamental period: Pharisees, Sadducees, Essenes, Herodians and Zealots.

16. Five new institutions arise during the intertestamental period: the synagogue, the Sanhedrin, the publicans, the oral law, and the scribes.

8

The Place of the Kingdom in Old Testament Prophecy

HAVING TRACED the development of the theme of the kingdom through the Old Testament, we need to stop and evaluate what this meant in the thinking of the Jew in New Testament times. If we try to "stand in his shoes," we can better understand his response and thinking when John the Baptist appeared on the scene proclaiming that the kingdom of heaven was at hand.

Charles L. Feinberg, after briefly surveying the kingdom theme in the Old Testament, said,

> It has been our purpose in this chapter to show by a consistent and connected study of the Old Testament Scriptures that the kingdom finds, not accident or incident, but purposely and intentionally, a place in God's revelation preparatory to the New Testament age. Writer after writer and prophet after prophet added a line here and a line there to complete the Old Testament picture of a kingdom under the King of the Davidic line. With such a prophetic testimony to guide them and shape their thinking, what kind of a kingdom, think you, the Jews of those days and we who study the Word in this day, should expect? Were the Jews at fault in expecting God to fulfill His oft-reiterated word and guarantee that on the throne of David in Jerusalem over regathered and cleansed Israel, there would one day reign in unexcelled glory and righteousness a King of the house of David? If they were, then how shall we with any fair show of reason or wisdom explain away all the various and painstakingly minute prophetic utterances that we have taken time to persue?[1]

ONE KINGDOM PROPHESIED

Peters shows that the prophets described but one kingdom as he says,

> 1. There is *one* Kingdom under the Messiah, David's Son, and Lord, in some way linked with the election of the Jewish nationality which is *the great burden* of prophecy.
> 2. This Kingdom, too, according to the grammatical sense, is one here *on the earth*, not somewhere else, as e.g. in the third heaven or the Uni-

verse. Take the most vivid descriptions, such as are contained in Isa. 60 and Dan. 7, etc., and they refer this Kingdom *exclusively to this earth*, which, of course, follows naturally *from the relation* that this Kingdom sustains to the Jewish nation and Davidic throne. Any other portraiture of it would be incongruous, and hostile to covenant and fact.[2]

THE MESSIANIC HOPE

What was the Messianic hope at the time of Christ's birth? From our brief survey of the Old Testament we have found that God revealed many things about His Messiah, His salvation, and His kingdom. W. B. Hill, in describing this yearned-for age, says:

> The Messianic Age, in the widest sense of the term, is the glorious time when, through the favor of Jehovah, all the desires of His people, Israel, shall be satisfied. Because the Jews were usually a subject nation and without a strong leader, their most persistent desire was for a king who would crush their foes and achieve an independent kingdom. Such a king must be the chosen agent of God; accordingly he is called the Messiah (the Christ) which means the Anointed (Ps. 2:2), i.e. the one whom God has placed on the throne; or, because in him is fulfilled Jehovah's promise to David concerning some descendant, "I will be his father, and he shall be my son" (II Sam. 7:14), he is called . . . the Son of God.[3]

It is interesting to notice how the yearnings of the Jewish people parallel in many cases the prophetic promises about the coming kingdom:

> The Messianic hope was usually for the coming of a personal Messiah and the establishment of his kingdom—the kingdom of God. But there were periods when the Jews had independence, or enough of liberty to satisfy them; then they ceased to yearn for a future kingdom: and there were periods when they were content with their present leaders; then they ceased to desire a Messiah. Still the present was never so ideal as to destroy all longing for a better future. Sickness and suffering made them yearn for a day when physical ills would disappear; the barrenness of Judea's hills set them to dreaming of a time when the ground would bring forth abundantly with little or no labor; the contempt of other nations created an emphasis on a glorious day when all nations would stream as humble learners to the temple at Jerusalem. Whenever national events aroused a feeling of sin and impurity, the hope was for purification and spiritual blessings; but when religion grew dead, such higher aspirations were exchanged for more sensuous and selfish desires. . . .[4]

Alfred Edersheim, writing on the same theme, says:

> The most important point here is to keep in mind the organic unity of the Old Testament. Its predictions are not isolated, but features of one grand prophetic picture; its ritual and institutions parts of one great system; its history, not loosely connected events, but an organic development tending towards a definite end. Viewed in its innermost substance, the history of the Old Testament is not different from its typical institu-

tions, not yet these two from its predictions. The idea, underlying all, is God's gracious manifestation in the world—the Kingdom of God; the meaning of all—the establishment of this Kingdom upon earth. That gracious purpose was, so to speak, individualised, and the Kingdom actually established in the Messiah.[5]

Edersheim points out that generally speaking there was not felt among the people a need for the deliverance from sin. Because of this there was no place in their thinking for the priestly office of the Messiah, and even His claims to be "the Prophet" that Moses said would come, are almost entirely overshadowed in their desire to have a King and a Deliverer.[6]

O. C. S. Wallace describes the hopes of the rabbis:

> The rabbis were Pharisees in doctrine and pedants in scholarship. Fierce bigotry and nonsensical puerilities characterized their religious and ecclesiastical opinions. They were looking eagerly for a Messiah who would establish at once, by force of arms, a splendid Jewish kingdom. When he appeared, extraordinary prosperity would dawn. That the Jews might be rich and at ease, marvels would be accomplished. At the touch of God's words the white flour would drop from the ripened ears of wheat. From a single grape, wine would be drawn as from a cask. Jerusalem would be enlarged immensely, and as some believed, filled with houses three miles high. There would be no sickness or pain, and nothing would occur to mar the glory and happiness of the new kingdom.[7]

Scriptures Considered Messianic by the Rabbis

From ancient rabbinic writings, Edersheim has compiled a list of 456 scriptural references that are attributed to the Messiah or His time.[8] He has given 558 separate quotations from the Targumim, the two Talmuds, and the most ancient Midrashim. He does not consider that his list is complete but only that it gives examples of the most prominent verses. This is important because it shows what the Jewish teachers thought and taught about the Messiah.

The first reference that they refer to is Genesis 1:2, where the expression "Spirit of God" is explained as the Spirit of the King-Messiah with a cross-reference to Isaiah 11:2.

Genesis 3:15 is paraphrased with the express reference to the promised seed being the Messiah.

It is interesting to note that they say that when the fall took place, Adam lost six things: (1) his glorious sheen (Job 14:20); (2) life (Gen 3:19); (3) his stature (Gen 3:8); (4) the fruit of the ground; (5) the fruit of the trees (Gen 3:17); and (6) the heavenly light. These six things are to be restored by the "son of Pharez" or the Messiah (Ruth 4:18).

In Genesis 4:25 the language of Eve at the birth of Seth, "another seed," is explained as meaning seed coming from another place and referred to the Messiah.

Exodus 16:25 is applied to the Messiah. It is said that if Israel kept only one Sabbath according to the commandment that Messiah would immediately come.

In Numbers 23:21 the term "king" is expressly referred to the Messiah, with the same thing being said of Balaam's prediction of the star and scepter in Numbers 24:17.

Psalm 2 is treated as being full of Messianic references.

In Isaiah 53:11, the Targum renders "my servant" by the words "my servant, the Messiah."

Ezekiel 29:21 is among the many passages applied to the time when the Messiah should come.

Daniel 2:22, 35, 44 are all applied to the coming Messiah.

Micah 4:8 has the unusual commentary, "And thou Messiah of Israel, who shall be hidden on account of the sins of Zion, to thee shall the kingdom come." The well-known prophecy of Micah 5:2 about the birthplace of the Messiah is readily admitted to be Messianic.

The rabbis applied Zechariah 11:12 to the Messiah, but they interpreted that the thirty pieces of silver represented thirty precepts which the Messiah was to give to Israel. From this brief sampling of Jewish Messianic scripture verses, it can be seen that many were cited in the New Testament as referring to Jesus Christ.

SUMMARY

From the various responses given by different individuals in the gospel accounts, there must have been all kinds of ideas about the kingdom. But the teaching concerning the Messianic kingdom in the Old Testament can be summarized as follows:

1. *It is based upon the covenants of God.* The formal covenants and the informal covenants or promises are given in Genesis 3:15, 12:1-3; 2 Samuel 7:11-16; Jeremiah 31:31-40; etc.

2. *God will be King.* His name will be "Immanuel . . . God with us" (Is 9:6; cf. Mt 1:23), yet He will be of the family of David (2 Sa 7:16), born of a virgin (Is 7:14), in the city of Bethlehem (Mic 5:2).

3. *He will rule over regathered and converted Israel.* It will be the restored Davidic kingdom (Deu 30:3-6; Is 11:11-12; Jer 33:7-9).

4. *Jerusalem will be His capital* (Is 2:1-3).

5. *He will be King of kings and Lord of lords.* He will be King of Israel, and Israel will be exalted over the other nations of the earth (Ps 72:11; Is 55:5; Dan 7:13-14; Zec 8:22; cf. Rev 19:16).

6. *His kingdom will be characterized by righteousness and holiness.* It will bring (1) forgiveness of sins, (2) a new heart, (3) a knowledge of God, (4) the outpouring of the Spirit of God upon all flesh, (5) inward harmony to the laws of God in contrast to outward conformity, (6) the restoration of joy to the human race (Is 35:10; Jer 31:28-34; Eze 36:24-34).

7. *Peace will come.* War and all its associated evils will be alleviated (Ps 72:1-14; Is 65:21-22; Zec 9:10).

8. *He will bring changes of nature.* The curse upon nature will be at least partially lifted. People will live longer, disease will be abolished, and there will be a great productivity of the soil (Is 11:6-9; 32:14-16; 35:5-6; 65:20, 22; Eze 36:34-36).

9. *Satan will be defeated.* The angelic rebellion led by Satan is defeated and punished (Is 14 and Eze 28, cf. Rev 20:2).

10. *The Old Testament saints will be resurrected.* The Old Testament saints to whom God promised the kingdom will be resurrected and will have a part in the kingdom. For instance, Abraham in the flesh never realized all of the promises given to him (Jer 30:9; Eze 37:24-25; Dan 12:2-3; Lk 13:28).

9

The Advent and Preparation of
the King

GOD'S PLAN is to make it possible for man to be restored to fellowship with Himself, and for the earth to be placed back under man's dominion. The key figure in His plan is Jesus Christ, the God-Man, who provides redemption and reigns as King. All enemies will be put down; the curse will be lifted from creation; all blessings will be restored; and additional blessings will be given.

Israel was one of the instruments God chose to bring about His plan. As Samuel Andrews says,

> The Lord came to a nation in covenant with God—His elect people. He had chosen for them a land in which they might dwell apart from the nations, and in a wonderful manner had given them possession of it. He had given them laws and institutions, which, rightly used, should secure their highest national well-being. He had established His temple in their chief city, in which He revealed Himself in the Visible Glory, and which was appointed to be "a house of prayer for all nations." How highly they had been honored and blessed of God is seen from his words (Exod. xix. 5-6) "If ye will obey my voice indeed, and keep my Covenant, then ye shall be to me a peculiar treasure above all people, and ye shall be unto me a kingdom of priests and a holy nation." And from among them should the great Deliverer, the Seed of the woman, come. The Messiah should reign at Jerusalem, and from thence establish justice and judgment throughout the earth.[1]

HOW COULD THEY KNOW THAT JESUS WAS THE MESSIAH?

The author in his book *The Life of Christ Visualized* has shown that enough Old Testament prophecies were given so that a birth certificate could have almost been filled out in advance.[2]

THE BIRTH OF THE KING

The prophecies and testimonies given before and at the time of Jesus' birth clearly point to Him as the Messiah, the Saviour-King. The angel

Gabriel told Mary that the child that she would bear would be (1) called the Son of the Most High, (2) given the throne of His father David, (3) reign over the house of Jacob forever, (4) that of His kingdom there would be no end and so fulfill the promises made by God in the Davidic covenant (Lk 1:31-33).

The angel appeared unto Joseph in a dream and told him that the child that Mary would bear was conceived by the Holy Ghost (of the seed of the woman, Gen 3:15) and that He would save His people from their sins (Mt 1:20-21).

Angels announced the Prince of Peace to the shepherds and said, "For unto you is born this day in the city of David a Saviour, which is Christ the Lord. . . . Glory to God in the highest, and on the earth peace, good will toward men" (Lk 2:11-14). One of the great characteristics of the kingdom is peace.

"Where is he that is born King of the Jews?" (Mt 2:2) the wise men asked Herod. Herod, the chief priests and the scribes, and all Jerusalem were troubled by the arrival of the wise men. They told them that He was to be born in Bethlehem (Mic 5:2), where the wise men later found Him. The giving of gifts to Him by the wise men foreshadowed the worship of the nations of the world in the kingdom as they will come to pay tribute to Christ (Ps 86:9; Is 66:23; Zec 14:16-19).

The amazing thing about the birth of Christ is the utter lack of response on the part of "religious" Israel. There is no evidence that the religious leaders journeyed the five miles to Bethlehem to see if the Messiah had been born. With the exception of King Herod's brief attempt to kill anyone who would be a threat to his throne and the brief Passover appearance when Jesus was twelve years old, the next thirty years slipped by with Israel unaware that their Messiah had come.

Repent, the Kingdom of Heaven Is at Hand

In the summer of A.D. 26 God raised up a voice in the wilderness, John the Baptist. Clothed in camel's hair with a leather girdle, John was an unusual person who ate locusts and wild honey while he lived in the wilderness and preached in Judea along the Jordan River. His message was "Repent ye: for the kingdom of heaven is at hand. . . . Prepare ye the way of the Lord, make his paths straight" (Mt 3:2-3). He is identified as fulfilling the prophecy of Isaiah 40:3-5: "As it is written in the book of the words of Esaias the prophet, saying, The voice of one crying in the wilderness, Prepare ye the way of the Lord, make his paths straight" (Lk 3:4). The people knew something unusual was happening because he promised, "And all flesh shall see the salvation of God" (Lk 3:6).

It is easy to understand why John called the nation to repentance. The Messiah's kingdom was to be a kingdom of holiness and righteousness, and Israel had been promised a special place and ministry in this kingdom. They were to be a nation of priests (Ex 19:6; Lev 11:44). But under the Mosaic covenant it was clearly shown that priests who were defiled could not minister. The nation was defiled by sin and wickedness, and so John called for it to repent of its sins.

Many people thought John was actually the Christ, but he said he was not and that one was coming after him who was greater than he. To emphasize this contrast, he said, "I indeed baptize you with water unto repentance: but he that cometh after me is mightier than I, whose shoes I am not worthy to bear: he shall baptize you with the Holy Ghost, and with fire" (Mt 3:11).

John's Baptism

There has been much controversy through the centuries about baptism, the rite which appears upon the scene in the New Testament without explanation. While baptism was something new, it was not foreign to the Jewish system of thought, for it was related to purifying, as shown by John 3:25-26: "Then these arose a question between some of John's disciples and the Jews about purifying. And they came unto John, and said unto him, Rabbi, he that was with thee beyond Jordan, to whom thou barest witness, behold the same baptizeth, and all men come to him."

Spiritual Purity Symbolized by Washing

In the scriptural and traditional background of the Jews at least six different washings were used to symbolize cleansing or purity:
1. cleansing of lepers
2. purification from the defilement of death by ashes of the red heifer
3. hand-washing traditions
4. becoming a proselyte
5. entering into a covenant
6. preparation for the priestly ministry

LEPROSY

In the Old Testament, leprosy is a type of sin and death. Lepers were to be excluded from society, wear mourning costumes, rend their clothes, leave the hair of their head uncovered, and keep a covering over their upper lip and cry, "Unclean, unclean" (Lev 13:45). Leprosy is a vivid symbol of how sin will contaminate the whole person and bring death.

A specific ceremony prescribed for the purification of persons cured of leprosy was given in Leviticus 14, and one part of this ceremony included the cleansing with water: "And he that is to be cleansed shall wash his clothes, and shave off all his hair, and wash himself in water, that he may be clean: and after that he shall come into the camp, and shall tarry abroad out of his tent seven days" (v. 8).

THE RED HEIFER

After preparing the ashes of a red heifer, which were used to cleanse from the defilement of death, the priest washed his flesh and his clothes. Defilement from the dead lasted seven days. The ashes were placed in a vessel, where living (running) water was poured upon them; then a branch of hyssop was dipped into the mixture and sprinkled upon the one defiled on both the third and seventh day, after which he had to wash his clothes and bathe his flesh. Death, of course, was the greatest of all defilements (see Num 19).

HAND-WASHING TRADITIONS

In the time of Christ, ceremonial hand-washing was very important to the Pharisees. One rabbi is said to have starved in prison during the late Maccabean period because his captors wouldn't give him enough water to ceremonially wash his hands. Another is quoted as saying, "He who eats bread without hand-washing is as if he went in to a harlot." Jesus was criticized because His disciples did not practice this tradition (Mt 15:1-20).

Cunningham Geikie gives a good description of what this traditional hand-washing was like:

> It was laid down that first the hands were to be washed clean. The tips of the ten fingers were then joined and lifted up so that the water ran down to the elbows, then turned down so that it might run off to the ground. Fresh water was poured on them as they were lifted up, and twice again as they hung down. The washing itself was to be done by rubbing the fist of one hand in the hollow of the other. When the hands were washed before eating they must be held upwards; then after it, downwards, but so that the water should not run beyond the knuckles. The vessel used must be held first in the right, then in the left hand; the water was to be poured first on the right, then on the left hand, and at every third time the words repeated "Blessed art thou who hast given us the command to wash the hands." It was keenly disputed whether the cup of blessing or the hand-washing should come first; whether the towel used should be laid on the table or on the couch; and whether the table was to be cleansed before the final washing or after it.[3]

LEVITICAL DEFILEMENTS, PROSELYTES, AND ENTERING A COVENANT

Alfred Edersheim has an interesting comment about the use of water and washings:

> What John preached, that he also symbolised by a rite which, though not new itself, yet in its application, was wholly new. Hitherto the Law had it, that those who had contracted Levitical defilement were to immerse before offering sacrifice.
>
> Again, it was prescribed that such Gentiles as became "proselytes of righteousness," or "proselytes of the Covenant," were to be admitted to full participation in the privileges of Israel by the threefold rites of circumcision, baptism and sacrifice—the immersion being, as it were, the acknowledgement and symbolic removal of moral defilement, corresponding to that of Levitical uncleanness. But never before had it been proposed that Israel should undergo a "baptism of repentence," although there are indications of a deeper insight into the meaning of Levitical baptisms.
>
> Was it intended, that the hearers of John should give this as evidence of their repentence, that, like persons defiled, they sought purification, and, like strangers, they sought admission among the people who took on themselves the rule of God? These two ideas would, indeed have made it truly a "baptism of repentence." But it seems difficult to suppose, that the people would have been prepared for such admissions; or, at least, that there should have been no record of the mode in which a change so deeply spiritual was brought about.
>
> May it not rather have been that as, when the first Covenant was made, Moses was directed to prepare Israel by symbolic baptism of their persons (Gen. 35:2) and their garments (Ex. 19:10, 14), so the initiation of the new Covenant, by which the people were to enter into the Kingdom of God, was preceded by another general symbolic baptism of those who would be the true Israel and receive, or take on themselves, the Law from God? In that case the rite would have acquired not only a new significance, but be deeply and truly the answer to John's call. In such case also, no special explanation would have been needed on the part of the Baptist, nor yet such spiritual insight on that of the people as we can scarcely suppose them to have possessed at that stage. Lastly, in that case nothing could have been more suitable, nor more solemn, than Israel in waiting for the Messiah and the Rule of God, preparing as their fathers had done at the foot of Mount Sinai.[4]

PREPARATION FOR A PRIESTLY MINISTRY

The priests had to wash themselves each time at the laver of brass before they went into the tabernacle to minister. Even more significance can be seen in the high priest's ministry on the Day of Atonement. Before he ministered he was told, "He shall put on the holy linen coat, and he shall have the linen breeches upon his flesh, and shall be girded with a linen girdle, and with the linen mitre shall he be attired: these are holy garments; therefore shall he wash his flesh in water, and so put them on" (Lev 16:4).

As a nation of priests they needed a spiritual cleansing before they could minister for Messiah. The spiritual cleansing that John called for is accomplished by the "washing of regeneration" (Titus 3:5) or new birth promised under the new covenant. It was only symbolized by water baptism, but the symbolism would have been something that the Jews understood.

JESUS' BAPTISM BY JOHN

When Jesus came to John and asked to be baptized, John didn't want to do it, for he thought he should be baptized by Jesus. Various explanations have been given for Jesus' baptism. It can be definitely stated that Jesus was *not* baptized for the forgiveness of sin and He was *not* repenting of sin, because the Scriptures say that He was without sin (Heb 4:15). Some have suggested that He was identifying Himself with the nation of Israel, but the answer that Jesus gave was that He wanted to "fulfil all righteousness" (Mt 3:15). Immediately after His baptism in water, He was anointed by the Spirit of God (Mt 3:16). These two things—His sinlessness and anointing—make His baptism different from all others.

ANOINTING FOR MINISTRY

Priests were anointed for ministry: "And thou shalt anoint Aaron and his sons, and consecrate them, that they may minister unto me in the priest's office" (Ex 30:30). Kings were also anointed: "Then Samuel took the horn of oil, and anointed him in the midst of his brethren: and the Spirit of the Lord came upon David from that day forward" (1 Sa 16:13). God had some prophets anointed, although the Scripture does not record a formal anointing with oil for most of them. "And Jehu the son of Nimshi shalt thou anoint to be king over Israel: and Elisha the son of Shaphat of Abelmeholah shalt thou anoint to be prophet in thy room" (1 Ki 19:16).

MESSIAH'S MINISTRIES

One of the ministries of the Messiah was as a priest. The book of Hebrews speaks of Jesus as being of a new order of priesthood after the order of Melchizedek. But since Jesus was a Prophet, a Priest, and a King, and of a newer and greater order than of any of the Old Testament, God would not have to exactly follow any Old Testament patterns. After all, they only pointed toward His ministry.

It would appear that as Jesus began His ministries, He was symbolically

washed in baptism, anointed by the Holy Spirit, and accepted by the
Father. The Father gave His approval by saying, "This is my beloved
Son, in whom I am well pleased" (Mt 3:17). He was also identifying Him
as "His Son," the promised King of Psalm 2:6-12. Christ assumed His
ministries not by virtue of any ritual or human ordination but by God's
appointment and approval. It seems reasonable to understand that God
was presenting Jesus to the nation of Israel in this way and in a manner
reflecting these Old Testament teachings.

Jesus did not begin all three ministries at the same time. He performed
a prophetic ministry at His first coming, He entered into His high-priestly
ministry at His ascension, and His kingly ministry will begin at His second
coming.

WATER, ANOINTING, AND BLOOD

One element is missing in the symbolism of the Old Testament—the
blood. "Moreover he sprinkled with blood both the tabernacle, and all
the vessels of the ministry. And almost all things are by the law purged
with blood; and without shedding of blood is no remission" (Heb 9:21-22;
cf. Lev 8:12, 23). On the Day of Atonement the high priest first offered
a sacrifice for himself and then for the nation; but because Jesus was
sinless, no personal sacrifice was necessary.

No animal sacrifice would do for Christ because He was going to minister by virtue of "his own blood" (Heb 9:12). After His temptation when
He had been proved holy, John the Baptist pointed Him out as the "Lamb
of God" (Jn 1:29). We are redeemed by "the precious blood of Christ,
as of a lamb without blemish and without spot" (1 Pe 1:19).

BAPTISMAL DISTINCTIONS

John's baptism was of repentance and directed toward the nation:
"Repent ye: for the kingdom of heaven [or kingdom of God] is at hand"
(Mt 3:2). The promised King had arrived and was ready to set up His
kingdom. Jesus' disciples practiced this same baptism of repentance (Jn
4:1-2). As we have shown, Jesus' baptism by John was different. And
Christian baptism practiced after Pentecost and after Christ's death and
resurrection is also different. It has a different formula: "in the name of
the Father, and of the Son, and of the Holy Ghost" (Mt 28:19). There is
also a new and deeper meaning as we symbolically are identified with His
death, burial and resurrection (Ro 6:3-6). But this identification is not
just with His past; we are also identified with His glorious future. We are
called as kings and priests unto God (1 Pe 2:9; Rev 1:6). As Christ's new
body, the church, we continue His prophetic ministry by proclaiming the

gospel to the world— speaking for God to men. We have a present and future ministry as priests—speaking for men to God. When Christ returns and establishes His kingdom we will rule with Him—ruling men for God. Baptism symbolizes what faith in Christ's death has accomplished for us: we have been cleansed, anointed, and called to share in the ministry of Jesus as prophets, priests and kings.

MESSIAH IDENTIFIED BY JOHN

After Jesus returned from His forty days of temptation, John the Baptist pointed Him out as "the Lamb of God, which taketh away the sin of the world" (Jn 1:29). Some of John's disciples became acquainted with Jesus and later became His disciples. Andrew went and told his brother Simon that he had found the Messiah (1:41). Philip told Nathaniel, "We have found him, of whom Moses in the law, and the prophets, did write" (1:45). After Nathaniel had met Jesus, he said, "Rabbi, thou art the Son of God; thou art the King of Israel" (1:49).

SUMMARY

1. The King, the seed of the woman, was born according to promise.

2. He came of the seed of Abraham, the tribe of Judah, and the house of David.

3. He was conceived by the Holy Spirit of the virgin Mary.

4. John the Baptist called for the nation to repent so they could fulfill their ministry as a "nation of priests."

5. In the Jewish background at least six different washings were used to symbolize cleansing or purity: of lepers, for defilement of death, handwashing tradition, of proselytes, entering a covenant, and for priestly ministry.

6. Jesus' baptism, anointing by the Holy Spirit, and approval of the Father seem to initiate Him into His threefold ministry as Prophet, Priest and King.

7. Christian baptism of the believer symbolizes our identification with Christ's work on the cross and our entering into His ministry as prophets, priests and kings.

8. John the Baptist points out Jesus as the Lamb of God, the promised Messiah.

10

The Offer and Rejection of the King and His Kingdom

THE KING AND THE KINGDOM are inseparably joined in Scripture. Many would have gladly received the kingdom and its blessing, but they refused Jesus as King. They resented the call to repentance, assuming they were entitled to the kingdom because they were "sons of Abraham."

JESUS AND HIS KINGDOM MESSAGE

The first recorded conversation of Christ about the kingdom is with Nicodemus: "Verily, verily, I say unto thee, Except a man be born again, he cannot see the kingdom of God. . . . Except a man be born of water and of the Spirit, he cannot enter into the kingdom of God" (Jn 3:3-5). Nicodemus didn't understand what this meant, so Jesus explained, "That which is born of the flesh is flesh; and that which is born of the Spirit is spirit" (3:6). A new birth is the foundational requirement for all who would have a part in Christ's kingdom for it brings together the Messiah's work as Saviour and King, and solves the sin problem which must be taken care of first. The benefits of Christ's work are received by believing or trusting in Him: "For God so loved the world that he gave his only begotten Son, that whosoever believeth in him should not perish, but have everlasting life" (3:16).

Israel had tried to keep the law and enter into the promises made in the Mosaic covenant, but had found themselves totally incapable. To meet this need, God promised, in the new covenant, forgiveness of sins and that the Spirit of God would work in the hearts and indwell believers. This is what Jesus spoke of as being born again. It is not only necessary for a person to be born again to see or enter Christ's kingdom but also to receive eternal life. It is obtained by faith.

In the first summer of Jesus' ministry following His discourse with Nicodemus, Jesus and John the Baptist carried on parallel ministries in the land of Judea, where they preached that "the kingdom of God is at

84

hand." When John publicly reproved Herod Antipas for living with his brother's wife, Herod put John into prison. Jesus returned to Galilee and taught in the synagogues, saying, "The time is fulfilled, and the kingdom of God is at hand: repent ye, and believe the gospel" (Mk 1:15; cf. Mt 4:17; Lk 4:15). It is important to see that Jesus presented Himself as the King and offered the kingdom unto Israel. This can be traced through every period of His ministry.

THE SERMON ON THE MOUNT

In the Sermon on the Mount Jesus gave His standard of righteousness for the kingdom: "Except your righteousness shall exceed the righteousness of the scribes and Pharisees, ye shall in no case enter into the kingdom of heaven" (Mt 5:20). The scribes and Pharisees thought they were all right and that they alone would be accepted by God because of their knowledge of the law and their many traditions. But Jesus was actually saying, "This is not enough. You must be born again. You must have the righteousness that I alone can give." In Matthew 5 Jesus taught that outward conformity to the law and traditions was not enough. God requires an inward conformity to the law as promised in the new covenant in order to enter His kingdom. In chapter 6 He said that religious observances are not enough, and in addition, they are often done in a hypocritical manner. This teaching brought Him into sharp conflict with the scribes and Pharisees.

SIGNS OF THE KINGDOM

Jesus' ministry was validated by sign-miracles which can be divided into four main classes:

1. miracles over nature
2. miracles of physical healing
3. miracles over demons
4. miracles over death

Starting in the spring of A.D. 27, when Jesus changed water into wine, He performed miracles in every period of His ministry.[1] These miracles had at least a threefold purpose: (1) they showed that He was God, (2) they brought kingdom conditions wherever He ministered, and (3) they fulfilled Old Testament prophecies.

KINGDOM CONDITIONS FORESHADOWED

It is interesting to compare the results of these miracles with the prophesied conditions of the kingdom. For instance, turning water into wine and feeding the four thousand and the five thousand point to times of plenty. The land will be very productive and there will not be famine or lack of food in the kingdom age.

The many physical healings remind us of the prophecy that life will be greatly extended and the curse of disease lifted. The casting out of demons foreshadows the time in the kingdom when Satan will be bound and the forces of evil greatly restricted. The miracles over death remind us that the believers who have died will be raised to have their part in the kingdom, and eventually death itself will be abolished.

FULFILLING OLD TESTAMENT PROPHECIES

After John the Baptist had been in jail about a year, he began to wonder if Jesus was really the Messiah, so he sent some of his disciples to ask. Jesus performed a special series of miracles that day to answer their question and told them to go back and tell John "how that the blind see, the lame walk, the lepers are cleansed, the deaf hear, the dead are raised, to the poor the gospel is preached" (Lk 7:22). These were the Old Testament prophecies of the Messiah—His credentials (Is 29:18-19; 35:5-6; 61:1).

A few weeks before this Jesus had healed a leper and sent him down to Jerusalem to show himself to the priest. The leper was to be a special testimony to them, but the Jewish leaders did not receive this testimony (Mk 1:40-44). Two years later, just before He was crucified, Jesus healed ten more lepers and told them to do the same thing. One was a Samaritan, so it is doubtful that he would go to Jerusalem, but this would still be a ninefold sign-miracle to prove His Messiahship (Lk 17:11-19).

TWO ISSUES IN CONFLICT

Early in Jesus' ministry a conflict arose between Him and religious Israel concerning His person and His teaching. One day in Capernaum, the friends of a sick man opened the roof and let him down into the midst of the crowd of people so Jesus could heal him. Jesus said, "Thy sins are forgiven thee. And the scribes and Pharisees began to reason, saying, who is this which speaketh blasphemies? Who can forgive sins, but God alone?" (Lk 5:20-21). This was the issue: "Is Jesus God?" Jesus knew their hearts and knew what they were thinking, so He asked, "Whether is easier, to say, Thy sins be forgiven thee; or to say, Rise up and walk?" (v. 23). Then He commanded the man to take up his bed and to go to his house, and he did.

In John 5:19-30 Jesus gave additional proofs of His deity: (1) He and the Father are equal in works—He can do what the Father can, (2) He and the Father both have power of life, (3) the Father has the power to judge, but He has committed all judgment to the Son, (4) He and the Father are equal in honor so you cannot honor the Father and reject the Son, and (5) He and the Father have the power of resurrection. Jesus then pointed out four witnesses that testified to His deity (Jn 5:30-47): (1) John the Baptist, (2) Jesus' own works, (3) the Father—at His baptism, and (4) the Scriptures.

Jesus taught that in order for a person to come into a right relationship with God, he must be born again (Jn 3:3, 6). The Pharisees believed that if they kept the law and all the traditions handed down by the fathers, that they would be accepted by God. The most important thing in their system was the keeping of the Sabbath, the fourth commandment, which was also the sign of the Mosaic covenant. The Pharisees had compiled many regulations for what one could do and not do on the Sabbath, so when Jesus healed on the Sabbath or in some other way broke with their traditions, they became very angry. As far as they were concerned, if a person didn't keep the Sabbath according to their traditions, he couldn't possibly be from God.

THE CRUCIAL DECISION

When Jesus healed a demon-possessed blind and dumb man, the scribes and Pharisees couldn't deny that the man was healed, but they didn't want to attribute this power to Jesus as God or even as a servant of God. Instead they said that He cast out demons by the power of Beelzebub, the prince of demons. Jesus met their accusations with a threefold argument:

1. If what they said was true, was Satan casting out Satan? If so, he was divided against himself.

2. Some of the scribes also cast out demons at various times, so He asked, "By whom do your sons cast them out?"

3. If He cast out demons by the Spirit of God, however, then the kingdom of God had come unto them. This was proof of His person and ministry. It was a sign—even as Satan will be cast out of His kingdom into the abyss.

Christ's rejection by the religious leaders of Israel, a pivotal point in His ministry, took place about two years before the crucifixion. For almost two years Jesus and His disciples had been preaching that the kingdom of heaven was at hand. Because the religious rulers attributed His miracles to evil powers and rejected Him as the Messiah, the character of His ministry changed. He then revealed some new facts about the kingdom in a series of parables.

KINGDOM OF HEAVEN PARABLES

The word *mystery* is used several times in the New Testament, but it does not necessarily mean something that is mysterious or hard to understand. Charles Ryrie says, "To most people, a mystery is something unintelligible—unless you know the secret of it! In Greek the word 'mystery' was used of the sacred rites of the Greek mystery religions—secrets shared only by those who had been initiated into the religion."[2]

Mystery refers to unrevealed truth that can be known only by revelation. Jesus gave His explanation in Matthew 13:35: "I will open my mouth in parables; I will utter things which have been kept secret from the foundation of the world." (Cf. Ro 16:25-26).

Many different interpretations and applications have been made of the kingdom of heaven parables. They can be and often are used to illustrate scriptural truth, but in order to understand their primary meaning they must be considered in their context as they relate to the overall revelation of the kingdom and the historical situation in which they were given. To try to interpret them as relating to the church will only bring confusion. The church was unknown in the Old Testament. A different mystery that was revealed later, it was mentioned for the first time by Christ about one year *after* these parables were given. Because of Old Testament usage and the parallel accounts in the other gospels, the kingdom of heaven and the kingdom of God as given in these parables are considered to be one and the same. Other interpretation of these parables and usages of these terms are considered in the Appendix. Briefly, in these parables Jesus revealed for the first time that because of His rejection by Israel there would be a delay between the time that the kingdom was first offered and the time it will be literally set up on the earth.

The disciples had just returned with Jesus from the third Galilean tour where they had seen the response He received from the common people and had witnessed His rejection by religious Israel, so it is no wonder that they were puzzled. Would he start an insurrection like the Maccabees, or call down fire from heaven? To answer these unspoken questions, Jesus gave the parables on the kingdom of heaven.

MYSTERIES OF THE KINGDOM

The kingdom itself was not a mystery, for it was spoken of in the Old Testament in great detail. What wasn't known or clearly revealed was that (1) the kingdom would be rejected when offered, (2) there would be a delay between the offer and the final setting up of the kingdom, and (3) the day of the Lord would usher in the kingdom. When the Lord was speaking about the mysteries of the kingdom, He was not speaking about a "mystery form" of the kingdom (Lk 8:10). Ryrie says, "The kingdom of heaven (literally *of* the heavens, not *in* the heavens) which Christ faithfully offered on earth was the very same earthly, Messianic, Davidic kingdom which the Jews expected from the Old Testament prophecies. But it is a matter of history that such a Kingdom was not ushered in at the first advent of Christ."[3]

NO "MYSTERY FORM" OF THE KINGDOM

McClain says:

> The fiction of a present "kingdom of heaven" established on earth in the Church, has been lent some support by an incautious terminology sometimes used in defining the "mysteries of the kingdom of heaven" (Matt. 13:11). The parables of this chapter, it is said carelessly by some, describe the kingdom of heaven as now existing in "mystery form" during the Church age. Now it is true that these parables present certain *conditions* related to the Kingdom which are contemporaneous with the present age. But nowhere in Matthew 13 is the establishment of the Kingdom placed within this age. On the contrary, in two of these parables the setting up of the Kingdom is definitely placed at the end of the "age" (vss. 39 and 49 ASV, with 41-43). And it is to be noted that in each of these references, our Lord is speaking as the infallible interpreter of His own parable.[4]

PARABLE OF THE SOWER (Mt 13:3-23)

Jesus Himself interpreted the parable of the sower. Saying that the word that was sown was "the word of the kingdom" (Mt 13:19), He told about the different responses that it received. Satan prevented some from responding, while others let the cares of the world, the deceitfulness of riches, the pleasures of this life, or the lusts of other things choke the word so it became unfruitful. But the word was fruitful in a small minority.

PARABLE OF THE SEED (Mk 4:26-29)

Only Mark records the short parable of the seed which demonstrated how the word of the kingdom of God would be received. Like a seed, it was planted by John the Baptist, Jesus and the disciples; but it did not bring forth an immediate response or the literal kingdom. When a seed is planted in the garden, it may appear to be dead for it is hid from sight, but after a period of time, when conditions are right, it will germinate and break through the soil, gradually developing until it ripens. The simple teaching of the parable is that after the word of the kingdom is proclaimed there will be a period of time before there is any visible response but it will grow to maturity as prophesied.

PARABLE OF THE TARES (Mt 13:24-30; 36-43)

Charles Ryrie points out that, except for the first, each of the seven kingdom of heaven parables begins with the phrase, "The kingdom of heaven is like." He says, "Literally, The kingdom of the heavens has become like unto. . . ."[5] The status of the kingdom had changed. Jesus, the Messiah-King, had offered the kingdom to Israel. John the Baptist, Jesus, and Jesus' disciples had been preaching that the kingdom of heaven was at hand, and now, because of rejection, its present status is illustrated in these parables.

Jesus, identifying Himself as the one who sows the good seed, says that the field is the world, the devil sows the bad seed, the harvest is the end of the age, and the angels will be executors of this judgment. Jesus will be the Judge directing the execution of the judgment. The good seed is the sons of the kingdom, the ones who will inherit it. The wicked will be removed and judged; their judgment is explained in more detail in other parables and in the Olivet discourse.

PARABLES OF THE MUSTARD SEED AND THE LEAVEN (Mk 4:30-32; Mt 13:31-35; Lk 13:18-21)

These parables teach that the kingdom began in a very small way with the announcement of one man, John the Baptist (Lk 16:16), but it will eventually grow into the mighty kingdom of Christ. It continues the teaching of the little parable of the seed, which is directly related to the dream of Nebuchadnezzar in Daniel 2 as it talks about a stone cut out of the mountain without hands: "And the stone that smote the image became a great mountain, and filled the whole earth" (vv. 35, 44). Because leaven is sometimes used in the Bible in an evil sense, some say it cannot be used in a good sense here. It is present in the loaves used at the feast of Pentecost. If there is a constant symbolical meaning of leaven, it would be the silent steady way it works until "all is leavened." Figures are often used symbolically in more ways than one in the Bible, for example, both Christ and Satan are referred to as lions. The woman in the parable does not have to represent a false religious system, because often in the Bible a woman represents good (cf. Rev 12:1-5; 17:1-6).

This parable does not teach that the world will be converted by the gospel, but it does teach that the world will eventually be ruled by Christ. Even as it takes a tiny seed time to grow, it takes time for leaven to spread through the dough, and it will take time from the announcement of the kingdom until it is set up.

THE PARABLES OF THE HIDDEN TREASURE AND THE PEARL OF GREAT PRICE
(Mt 13:44-46)

The parables of the hidden treasure and the valuable pearl seem to illustrate the good response of two kinds of individuals. In the former, a man unexpectedly heard the word of the kingdom and realized it was a great treasure. Nathaniel is an example of this kind of hearer (Jn 1:44-50). In the latter, a man was seeking for something, and when he heard the word of the kingdom, he recognized it as valuable. Cornelius illustrates this kind of hearer (Ac 10:1–11:18); he was unsaved until Peter brought the message (11:14). In both parables the hearers joyfully sold all because they realized the value of the treasure (which represents the kingdom).

PARABLE OF THE NET (Mt 13:47-50)

The primary teaching of the parable of the net is that at the end of the age there will be a judgment, the same one spoken of in the parable of the tares, at which time the wicked who will be living at the time of Christ's second coming will be judged. In the Olivet discourse Jesus gives more details (Mt 25:31-46).

The kingdom will come after the execution of judgment on the world, and the wicked will be cast into a furnace of fire. Matthew 25:46 says this is an "everlasting punishment." Revelation 19:20 calls it "a lake of fire burning with brimstone."

PARABLE OF THE HOUSEHOLDER (Mt 13:51-52)

Jesus taught that a scribe who is a disciple of the kingdom and a student of the Scriptures will take the prophecies concerning the kingdom from the Old Testament and add to them the new things revealed in these parables, and the new things will supplement the Old Testament prophecy.

In these parables Jesus revealed for the first time that there would be a delay between the time the kingdom was first offered and the time it will be set up. This delay is caused by the rejection of the King.

McClain summarizes the teachings of the parables in relation to the present age:

> What is certain in the teaching of these difficult parables is that the present age, viewed from the standpoint of the Kingdom, is a time of *preparation*. During this period the Son of man is sowing seed (vs. 37), generating and developing a spiritual nucleus for the future Kingdom, a group called "sons of the kingdom" (vs. 38, ASV). At the same time He is permitting a parallel development of evil in the world under the

leadership of Satan (vss. 38-39). It is the purpose of God to bring both
to a "harvest," when the good and bad will be separated, and then to
establish the Kingdom in power and righteousness (vss. 41-43, 49). . . .
The absence in Matthew 13 of any mention of the *ekklesia*, or of its
pretribulation Rapture, is not strange; for such mention at this point
would be completely unhistorical in the progress of divine revelation.[6]

FOURTH GALILEAN TOUR

The response from the fourth Galilean tour is another pivotal point in
the revelation of the kingdom. Jesus had sent His disciples out two by
two, giving them the power to perform the same type of sign-miracles of
the kingdom that He had performed, including the power to raise the
dead. But He limited their ministry to the lost sheep of the house of
Israel (Mt 10:6) because the covenants were made with Israel and it was
to Israel that the kingdom was promised (Lk 9:1-6; Mt 10:1-7). This
tour seems to foreshadow also the ministry of the 144,000 mentioned in
the book of Revelation. During this tour they were able to see for themselves the response to the message of the kingdom foretold in the kingdom
of heaven parables. The twelve were sent out to offer the kingdom, and
a few months later the seventy were sent out to declare the King.

After they had returned, Jesus asked them, "Whom do men say that
I the Son of man am? And they said, Some say that thou art John the
Baptist: some, Elias; and others, Jeremias, or one of the prophets" (Mt
16:13-14). This was a report of rejection. The people liked His miracles,
they wanted to be fed and healed, but the majority did not believe that
He was the promised Messiah.

"He saith unto them, But whom say ye that I am? And Simon Peter
answered and said, Thou art the Christ, the Son of the living God" (16:15-
16). At this pivotal point these four doctrines are introduced or expanded: (1) the rejection of the Messiah, (2) the future building of the
church, (3) His coming death and resurrection, and (4) His second
coming.

SOMETHING NEW—THE CHURCH

"He came unto his own [Israel], and his own received him not. But as
many as received him, to them gave he power to become the sons of God,
even to them that believe on his name" (Jn 1:11-12). This truth is explained in more detail in Ephesians 2. The blessings promised to come
through Abraham would be extended to all the families of the earth.

After Peter's response, Jesus, using the future tense in Greek, revealed
that He was going to build something new: "I will build my church." His
church is to be built upon Christ the Rock or, as others interpret this

verse, upon the confession of faith that He is the Christ. He didn't explain what He meant by the church. The word itself, *ekklesia*, just means "called-out assembly." It is unreasonable to believe that the disciples at this time had any concept of what the church would be like. Perhaps they remembered the unbelieving generation that had come out of Egypt, and how God had allowed only the two faithful spies, Joshua and Caleb, and a new generation to enter the promised land. The church was still a mystery or unrevealed truth (Eph 3:3-6; 5:25-32).

THE KEYS OF THE KINGDOM

Jesus promised that He would give the keys to the kingdom of heaven. The key that provides entrance into the kingdom (as well as eternal life) is personal faith in Jesus as the Christ, the Son of the living God. By this faith man is born again. He later told the scribes that they had taken away the keys of the kingdom from the people, that they weren't entering and they were preventing others from entering. They considered themselves to be the interpreters of the law and thought that the common people were cursed because they didn't know the law.

The expression "binding and loosing" meant giving permission or forbidding certain things. A false idea is prevalent today that Peter is a gatekeeper for the gates of heaven, but heaven and the kingdom of heaven are not synonymous.

A literal translation of Matthew 16:19 would be: "Whatsoever thou shalt bind [forbid] on earth shall already have been bound [forbidden] in heaven: and whatsoever thou shalt loose [permit] on earth shall already have been loosed [permitted] in heaven." The words *bound* and *loosed* are in the perfect tense in Greek.

JESUS FORETOLD HIS DEATH AND RESURRECTION

When His rejection became apparent, Jesus began to teach in detail about His death and resurrection. His death would be in Jerusalem and be brought about by the elders, chief priests, and scribes (Mt 16:21).

SECOND COMING PREVIEWED

Teaching about the second coming, Jesus gave three of His disciples a preview in miniature of what it would be like. They saw Him transfigured on a mountain top, revealed in the glory He will have at His second coming (2 Pe 1:18).

Jesus never stopped preaching about the kingdom, but He did stop preaching that the kingdom of God was at hand. Just a short time before He went up to Jerusalem to be crucified, He gave the parable of the pounds "because they thought that the kingdom of God should immediately appear" (Lk 19:11). There is a new emphasis in this parable about the second coming, for He uses such phrases as "and to return," "occupy till I come," and "when he returned."

In the parable of the pounds a nobleman goes to a far country where he receives the title deeds to his kingdom. When he returns to establish it, his first step is to call his servants and deal with them and reward them. According to their faithfulness, they are given places of responsibility in his kingdom. Those who have been unfaithful are denied the privilege of reigning with him. The second step is to deal with his enemies, whom he judges, commanding that they be put to death: "But those mine enemies, which would not that I should reign over them, bring hither, and slay them before me" (Lk 19:27). This is the same judgment spoken of in the parable of the tares, the dragnet, and the sheep and the goats—the judgment of the living nations at the close of the great tribulation period.

Triumphal Entry of the Messiah

In fulfillment of Zechariah 9:9, Jesus came riding into Jerusalem on a "colt the foal of an ass." The people shouted "Hosanna," which in the Hebrew means "save, we pray." "And they that went before, and they that followed, cried, saying, Hosanna; Blessed is he that cometh in the name of the Lord: Hosanna in the highest." (Mk 11:9-10). The common people were happy, for Jesus went into the temple where the blind and lame came to him and He healed them. But all this made the religious rulers very indignant.

THE PARABLES OF REJECTION

In the final week Jesus taught from many parables, warning the religious rulers by the three parables of rejection: the two sons (Mt 21:28-32), the wicked husbandmen (21:33-41), and the marriage of the king's son (22:1-14). He taught the following:

1. Many will reject the King: the self-righteous (scribes, Pharisees, religious rulers, and the proud).

2. Some will receive Him: those who realize that they are sinners (publicans, harlots, common people, and some rulers).

3. The King, the Son of God, will be killed.

4. The rejecting generation will be judged.

5. The kingdom will be given to another generation that will receive the King. The Bible does not teach that God will break His promise to Israel by giving the kingdom to another (a Gentile nation), and it does *not*

teach that the kingdom has been given to the church. It will be given to another generation that receives Jesus at His second coming.

OLIVET DISCOURSE

On the Mount of Olives Jesus' disciples asked Him three questions:
1. When will Jerusalem be destroyed?
2. What will be the sign of His coming?
3. What would be the sign of the end of the world (age)?

Jerusalem was destroyed in A.D. 70, but the Olivet discourse seems to speak of another destruction in the end time. The sign for this destruction is the "abomination of desolation" spoken of by Daniel the prophet (Mt 24:15; Dan 9:27; 11:31; 12:11). In the Olivet discourse Jesus tells many things about the period of the great tribulation which will immediately precede the setting up of His kingdom.

PARABLES OF READINESS

The proper attitude of a disciple is to be ready for Jesus' second coming. Jesus emphasized this by telling the parables of the porter (Mk 13:33-37), the master of the house (Mt 24:43-45), the faithful and evil servant (24:46-51), and the ten virgins (25:1-13).

PARABLES OF JUDGMENT

Jesus gave the parable of the talents (25:14-30) in which He taught His disciples to be faithful because they were accountable. The parable of the sheep and goats (25:31-46) describes the judgment of living nations at the return of Christ before He sets up His kingdom.

THE INSTITUTION OF THE NEW COVENANT

The night before the Lord was crucified, He observed the Passover with His disciples. At the conclusion of this meal, He instituted the new covenant promised in Jeremiah 31:31. The word translated *testament* in the King James Version is the same word that is also translated *covenant*. "For this is my blood of the new testament [covenant], which is shed for many for the remission of sins" (Mt 26:28). In John 14:16-18 He promised the indwelling of the Holy Spirit, who does the internal work in the heart of the believer (14:16; 16:13). Through the Word of God and the ministry of the Spirit of God, man is born again and receives a new heart and a new mind (Jer 31:33; Eze 36:26-27; 1 Pe 1:23; Jn 3:3, 6).

God placed the rainbow in the sky to remind man that He would keep the promise He made with Noah to never again destroy every living thing. Jesus gave the Lord's Supper as a memorial of the new covenant to remind believers of His death until He comes (see Mt 26:26-29; Mk 14:22-25; Lk 22:17-20; 1 Co 11:23-26). While the church enjoys the blessings of the new covenant now, Israel as a nation will come under the new covenant at Jesus' second coming (Eze 34:25-31; Ro 11; see Fig. 27).

Jesus instituted the Lord's Supper as a memorial observance for believers who gather together in His name. The Lord's Supper itself has no magical power. The bread is to be a reminder that His body was broken for them, while the cup symbolizes His blood shed on Calvary for the remission of sins. All the animals sacrificed at the institution of previous covenants point toward this great sacrifice as Jesus gave Himself.

KINGDOM YET FUTURE

At the Lord's Supper Jesus said that He would not drink of the fruit of the vine again "until the kingdom of God shall come" (Lk 22:18). The parallel account in Matthew 26:29 shows that the Father's kingdom and the kingdom of God are one and the same thing. Jesus offered Israel the kingdom, and it was rejected. It is not a "spiritual kingdom" nor a "mystery form" of the kingdom, but the kingdom promised from the Old Testament that will be set up when Christ returns the second time.

The Lord's Supper was given for a specific length of time: "For as often as ye eat this bread, and drink this cup, ye do shew the Lord's death till he come" (1 Co 11:26). When He comes it will cease to be observed.

THE BETRAYAL, ARREST, AND TRIAL

Jesus was betrayed for thirty pieces of silver according to prophecy (Zec 11:12; Mt 26:15; Lk 22:3-6). He was arrested and brought before the deposed high priest, Annas. This was the first of three religious trials. In the second trial He was taken before Caiaphas, the high priest, and the chief priests, elders, and scribes who were also assembled there. They tried to get false witnesses to testify against Him but the witnesses couldn't agree. Jesus was asked under oath whether He was Christ, the Son of God, and He said "yes" (very emphatic in the original language). The high priest said this was blasphemy. Christ repeated that He was the Christ in His third trial before the Sanhedrin, but they also said that He was guilty of blasphemy. They didn't prove that He was not the Christ, the Son of God, or even attempt to.

THE CIVIL TRIALS

When they brought Him before Pilate, they changed the indictment. Instead of blasphemy, they charged Jesus with three things: (1) perverting the nation, (2) forbidding to give tribute to Caesar, and (3) saying that He Himself was Christ their King (Lk 23:2). Since the Romans did not permit the Jews at this time to execute their criminals, the Jews tried to make Pilate believe that Jesus was leading a rebellion against Rome so he would execute Him for them. When asked about this, Jesus literally said, "My kingdom does not have its origin in this world system" (Jn 18:36). Jesus did come as a King, but the people He came to and offered the kingdom—the Jewish people—rejected Him. Pilate's verdict was "not guilty" (Lk 23:4).

Because Jesus was from Galilee, Pilate sent Him to Herod, who was in Jerusalem for the feast of Passover. Herod wanted to see Jesus perform a miracle but Jesus didn't utter a word. After mistreating Him, he returned Him to Pilate. The Jewish religious leaders, determined to have Jesus put to death, told Pilate that if he let Jesus go, he was not a friend of Caesar. Finally Pilate asked them, "Shall I crucify your King?" The chief priests answered, "We have no king but Caesar" (Jn 19:14-15). He then gave the order for Jesus to be crucified and put this inscription over His head: "JESUS OF NAZARETH THE KING OF THE JEWS" (19:19).

THE CRUCIFIXION OF THE KING

With the piercing cry from the cross, "It is finished," the work of redemption was finished. This is also the classic example of God over-ruling evil for good. His enemies tried to destroy Him by crucifixion. "But we speak the wisdom of God in a mystery, even the hidden wisdom, which God ordained before the world unto our glory: which none of the princes of this world knew: for had they known it, they would not have crucified the Lord of glory" (1 Co 2:7-8). But not only the wisdom of God is shown at the cross; here also is revealed God's love: "For God so loved the world, that he gave his only begotten Son, that whosoever believeth in him should not perish, but have everlasting life" (Jn 3:16). Because of the cross a holy God can also be righteous and just and yet have something to do with guilty sinners: "To declare, I say, at this time his righteousness: that he might be just, and the justifier of him which believeth in Jesus" (Ro 3:26). And these blessings all come upon those who exercise faith in Him: "Therefore we conclude that a man is justified by faith without the deeds of the law" (3:28).

What was the basic cause of the rejection of Christ? It was because of their misconceptions about the Messiah and His ministry. Explaining this, Samuel Andrews says:

> It is apparent that, thus mistaking the character and work of the Messiah, the very intensity of their desire for His coming would but the more certainly insure His rejection. They had formed the conceptions

of Him which Jesus could not realize. Their ideal Christ was not the
Christ of the prophets. To be at once received by them. Jesus must act
in a manner corresponding to their preconceived opinions, and thus fulfill their expectations. But this He could not do, since these expectations
were based upon misconceptions of their own moral needs, and of God's
purpose.[7]

ALL IS NOT LOST

Lewis S. Chafer draws a good comparison between Israel in the wilderness and the crucifixion of Christ:

> This first offer of the kingdom had been typified by the events at
> Kadesh-Barnea. There this same nation, which had already tasted the
> discomforts of the desert, were given an opportunity to immediately enter
> their promised land. Thus left to choose, they failed to enter, and
> returned to forty years more of wilderness wandering and added judg-
> ments. They might have entered the land in blessing. God knew they
> would not; still it was through their own choice that the blessing was
> postponed. Later they were brought again to the land after their judg-
> ments and afflictions in the wilderness. This time, however, it was with-
> out reference to their own choice. With the high hand of Jehovah God
> they were placed in their own land. So Israel, already five hundred years
> out of the land, and without a king, rejected the King and the kingdom
> as offered in Christ, and still continues the wilderness afflictions among
> all the nations of the earth whither the Lord God hath driven them. But
> He will yet regather them, else the oath of Jehovah will fail, and that
> regathering will be without reference to their own choosing, or merit.
> Under an unconditional covenant He has pledged to place them in king-
> dom blessings, under the glorious reign of their Immanuel King and in
> their own land (Deut. 30:3-5; Isa. 11:10-13; Jer. 23:3-8; Ezek. 37:21-
> 25). This, too, shall be done by no human processes, but by the mighty
> power of God.[8]

POSTRESURRECTION MINISTRY OF CHRIST

Before His death, Jesus had promised His twelve apostles that they
would reign with Him in His kingdom: "That ye may eat and drink at
my table in my kingdom, and sit on thrones judging the twelve tribes of
Israel" (Lk 22:30). In the forty days after His resurrection what did He
teach His apostles? Luke 24:44 says that He explained to the disciples
on the road to Emmaus all the things written in the law of Moses, and
in the prophets, and in the psalms, "concerning me." It is a very common
idea today that Jesus explained to them all about the church He was
about to establish, but this is not what the Bible says. He taught them
about things "pertaining to the kingdom of God" (Ac 1:3). The examination of the first seven verses of Acts will show that the apostles were not
thinking of the church nor a "universal kingdom of God." They were

thinking about the kingdom promised to Israel—and Jesus didn't correct them. This is in spite of the fact that Israel had rejected her King and His offer of the kingdom. He didn't say there was not going to be a kingdom, nor that the kingdom was going to be given to the church, but that it was not for them to know the *times* or *seasons* when the kingdom would be restored to Israel (1:6-7).

TEACHING MINISTRY CONCERNING THE CHURCH

Jesus promised His disciples before He was crucified that when the Holy Spirit came He would teach them all things, bring things to their remembrance, guide them in all truth, and show them things to come (Jn 14:26; 16:12-13). The reason that He gave for not teaching them before His death was that they were not ready. It was not until the day of Pentecost that the Holy Spirit came.

TEN DAYS TO PENTECOST

The apostles, with the exception of Judas who had committed suicide, stayed in Jerusalem in an upper room, where eventually about 120 disciples gathered. "These all continued with one accord in prayer and supplication, with the women, and Mary the mother of Jesus, and with his brethren" (Ac 1:14). They didn't stay in this upper room all the time because they "were continually in the temple, praising and blessing God" (Lk 24:53).

During this interval Matthias was chosen to replace Judas. Peter quotes from Psalm 109:8, "His bishoprick let another take" (Ac 1:20), which probably refers to his ruling over one of the twelve tribes of Israel as promised in Luke 22:29-30.

The apostles had a temporary ministry in the early days of the church, mostly concerned with teaching (Ac 2:42; 5:42; 6:2). There was no permanent office of apostleship in the church and, upon the death of the original twelve apostles, no one was elected or appointed to fill their office. In Acts 15, about twenty years after the church was founded, James, the half brother of Jesus, seemed to be the leader in the church in Jerusalem, and he was not one of the twelve apostles.

DISCIPLES AND APOSTLES

Two years before His death, Jesus chose His twelve apostles from among His many disciples. There is a distinction between the two: a disciple is a learner, student or follower, while an apostle is one who is sent forth on a special commission. It must be decided from context what the commission is. Mark 3:13-15 gives three reasons why Jesus appointed the twelve apostles: (1) that they might be with Him, (2) so they could be sent forth to preach, and (3) to have authority to cast out demons. When He sent them out two by two on the fourth Galilean tour, He told them the message that they were to preach: "The kingdom of heaven is at hand." Jesus gave the apostles power to authenticate their message through sign-miracles, which included power to heal all manner of sickness and to raise the dead (Mt 11:1-8).

AN EXPANDED MINISTRY OF WITNESSING

After Jesus' resurrection, they were given a new commission: "Go ye therefore, and teach all nations, baptizing them in the name of the Father, and of the Son, and of the Holy Ghost: teaching them to observe all things whatsoever I have commanded you: and, lo, I am with you alway, even unto the end of the world [age]" (Mt 28:19-20). Mark 16:15 adds "to every creature." "But ye shall receive power, after that the Holy Ghost is come upon you: and ye shall be witnesses unto me both in Jerusalem, and in all Judea, and in Samaria, and unto the uttermost part of the earth" (Ac 1:8). But this commission was not only for the twelve apostles; it was for Christians in general.

SUMMARY

The kingdom was promised and prophesied in detail in the Old Testament, but some major developments and revelations were given in the ministry of Christ:

1. John the Baptist, who began his ministry in the summer of A.D. 26, first preached that the kingdom of God was at hand (Lk 16:16). Jesus and the disciples also proclaimed this message.

2. Late in the fall of A.D. 28, after His rejection by the religious leaders of Israel, Jesus gave the kingdom of heaven parables. They revealed that (1) there would be a period of time between the time the kingdom was offered until it would be set up, (2) evil workers would continue to oppose it until it is established, (3) there would be a judgment at the end of the age, and (4) the establishment of the kingdom would follow this judgment.

3. Jesus revealed that the reason the kingdom would be delayed was that the King would be rejected and killed, but He would rise again from the dead and ascend to the Father.

4. In the interval between His first and second coming, Christ promised to build His church.

5. At Christ's return the nations will be judged and His kingdom established.

11

God's Two Programs

THE BOOK OF ACTS is the book of transitions. The offer of the kingdom was begun in A.D. 26 with John the Baptist's ministry (Lk 16:16), but the first offer was rejected and the King crucified. After Pentecost the first reoffer of the King and His kingdom was made by Peter. The kingdom cannot be received without the King; they go together. The reoffer continues until nearly the close of the book of Acts (see Fig. 10).

Only as the epistles are studied is the true nature of the church revealed. Christ had promised the church in Matthew 16, but He had never explained its character or nature. God had a second program, the church, operating concurrently with the reoffer of the kingdom unto Israel. The character of the new program is more clearly revealed or understood after the King and His kingdom are again rejected by the Jews.

This can be illustrated by a mother cooking supper. On the top of the stove, she is frying chicken, which can be seen by anyone looking into the kitchen. She has promised her family the chicken, and they are expecting it. After frying it, she opens the oven and takes out an apple pie. The pie has been baking all of the time and may have even added to the enticing smells of the kitchen, but any hungry visitor in the room would not have been aware of it until she opened the oven door and took it out. In the same way, the nature and purpose of the church are not understood at first, for the Jews were looking for the kingdom.

The witness to Christ the Saviour-King by His apostles and the early church was used in the furtherance of both programs. The details of the relationship that exists between the church, Israel, the Gentiles, the covenants, the kingdom, and Abraham are given later in the New Testament epistles.

SIGN-MIRACLES AND THE KINGDOM

Jesus performed many sign-miracles as He offered the kingdom to Israel, for these were His credentials. In the period of the Acts the same

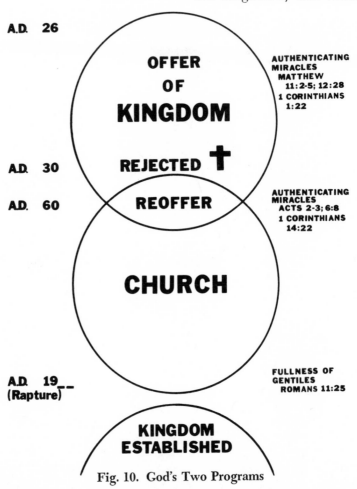

Fig. 10. God's Two Programs

type of sign-miracle was being performed by the apostles as the kingdom was reoffered to Israel. With the rejection of the kingdom by the nation at home and the Jews of the dispersion, the sign-miracles ceased.

Herman A. Hoyt says:

> The signs and wonders of the early Acts period were those promised in Old Testament prophecy of the kingdom, and similar to those found in the ministry of Christ. There were the outpouring of the Spirit at Pentecost (Acts 2:1-4, 16-18); healing of the sick (Acts 3:1-10; 19:11-12; Isa. 35:1-10); physical wonders (Acts 4:31; 8:39; 16:26; Joel 2:28-32); judgment upon sinners (Acts 5:1-11; 12:23; 13:11; Ezek. 11:13); miraculous visions (Acts 7:55; 9:3, 10; 11:5; Joel 2:28-32); and direct angelic ministry (Acts 5:19; 10:3; 12:7; John 1:51; Heb. 1:6).[1]

In speaking about the first thirty years of church history, Sir Robert Anderson in his book *The Silence of God* says, "My contention is that the Acts, as a whole, is a record of a temporary and transitionary dispensation in which blessing was again offered to the Jew and again rejected."[2] His explanation concerning the purpose of the sign miracles is that they were "to accredit the Messiah to Israel, and not as generally supposed, to accredit Christianity to the heathen."[3]

One would not question God's ability to perform miracles in any age in response to faith or prayer or because of His own desires.

Anderson points out that when Paul stood before Nero, the era of sign-miracles had closed. The miracles of Acts 28:8-9 "are chronologically the last on record, and the later epistles wholly silent respecting them."[4]

The writer of the book of Hebrews also confirms the fact that Christ's pronouncement that He was the Messiah and the kingdom of God was at hand was confirmed by miracles (Heb 2:3-4). It is important to see that there is a relationship between the sign-miracles and the kingdom rather than associating them with God's second program, the church. (Of course, this doesn't mean that God can't perform miracles in any age.) God's program for the church in this age will continue until "the fulness of the Gentiles be come in" (Ro 11:25).

Now let us return to Pentecost and see the development of these two programs as recorded in the book of Acts.

PENTECOST

Pentecost was one of the three national feasts which all able-bodied male Jews were required to attend in Jerusalem. The Bible says there were Jews attending from all over the known world—from Mesopotamia in the east to Rome in the west, from Asia Minor or modern-day Turkey in the north to Africa in the south. The key to understanding all the recorded proclamations of the apostles to the nation of Israel is the renewed offer of the kingdom. Jesus performed sign miracles to authenticate His first offer of the kingdom and brought prophesied kingdom conditions before the very eyes of the people. With the reoffer of the kingdom, God fulfilled other prophecies by the miracles He performed.

THE COMING OF THE HOLY SPIRIT

The people wanted to know what was happening to the disciples at Pentecost. Peter explained, "This is that which was spoken by the prophet Joel," referring to Joel 2:28-32 which describes the pouring out of the Holy Spirit. Peter didn't mean that this was the fulfillment of Joel's prophecy, for when this prophecy is fulfilled there will be signs in nature and it will happen before the great and notable day of the Lord (Ac 2:19-20), but this was the same thing—the pouring out of the Holy Spirit. The Lord Himself also promised the Holy Spirit (Jn 14:16-17; Ac 1:5), as did John the Baptist (Lk 3:16) and Ezekiel (36:27). Three signs accompanied the giving of the Holy Spirit:

1. There was a sound as of a rushing mighty wind. Jesus in John 3:8 compared the Spirit of God to the wind.

2. Cloven tongues as of fire sat on each of them. John the Baptist had foretold this in Luke 3:16. The burning bush and the fiery pillar in the Old Testament revealed God's presence.

3. The 120 spoke with other tongues or languages as the Spirit gave them utterance, so that all present heard the gospel in their own language. The confusion of tongues at Babel was a result of sin. Eventually in the restoration of all things, man will be able to communicate once again in one language (Zep 3:9). This also foreshadowed the coming ministry of the believers as they carried the gospel in all languages to every part of the world.

PETER'S MESSAGE—REOFFER OF THE KING

These miraculous signs had a startling effect on the people, and a great crowd gathered. Peter preached unto them about Jesus Christ. The main points of his message were the following:

1. Jesus of Nazareth was approved by God by the very miracles, wonders and signs which God did by Him among them.

2. With wicked hands they had crucified Him.

3. God raised Him from the dead.

4. David had prophesied concerning Him, calling Him Lord, Holy One, and Christ. He would be the King "to sit on his throne" (Ac 2:30).

5. David prophesied of Christ's resurrection (2:31).

6. Jesus has been exalted to the right hand of God (2:33).

7. Jesus has sent forth the promise of the Holy Ghost which they see and hear (Ac 2:33; Jn 7:39).

8. His final accusation is that they have committed the greatest crime of all time—they have crucified their Messiah the King. The people were pricked in their hearts and wanted to know, "What shall we do?"

"Then Peter said unto them, Repent, and be baptized every one of you in the name of Jesus Christ for the remission of sins, and ye shall receive the gift of the Holy Ghost. For the promise is unto you, and to your children, and to all that are far off, even as many as the Lord our God shall call" (Ac 2:38-39). This verse has been misunderstood and misapplied throughout the centuries. The first thing to notice is the question asked: "What shall we do?" They did not ask, "What is the least we can do and be saved?" Verse 40 says, "And with many other words did he testify and exhort, saying, Save yourselves from this untoward generation." In the counsel and instruction given to new believers in the remainder of this chapter, they participated in prayer, Bible study, breaking bread, worship, and fellowship with other Christians. In verse 38, Peter only mentions one other activity after repentance—baptism.

The word "repent" means to change one's mind. In this verse it is a command in the second person plural. The word "be baptized" is also a command, but it is in the third person singular, so it could be translated, "Repent, all of you, and (he that does repent) be baptized in the name of Jesus Christ." Peter had just pointed out to them that they had crucified the Lord for blasphemy because He had said that He was the Son of God. Now they are to "change their mind" and receive Him for what He said He was, the very Son of God, the promised King (Ac 2:30), and publicly take their stand for Him by being baptized in His name. John's baptism of repentance before this had been connected with their changing their mind about their sinful lives and turning to a life of holiness in expectation of the coming Messiah and their national ministry as a kingdom of priests. The repentance asked for here is related to the particular sin of rejecting their Messiah, for they cannot receive the kingdom without the King.

Directly connected with the command to repent, Peter gives two resulting promises. The first is "for the remission of sin." Luke uses this expression "remission of sins" several times. In Luke 1:77 it is connected with *salvation:* "To give knowledge of salvation unto his people by the remission of their sins." In Luke 24:47 it is connected again with *repentance:* "And that repentance and remission of sins should be preached in his name among all nations, beginning at Jerusalem." In Acts 10:43 remission is connected with *faith* or *belief:* "To him give all the prophets witness, that through his name whosoever believeth in him shall receive remission of sins." See also Romans 3:25; Hebrews 9:22; 10:18. The general teaching of Scripture does not make forgiveness dependent upon baptism.

The second promise is the gift of the Holy Spirit. Both promises are contained in the new covenant and are given to others beside those who are present at Pentecost: their children, those in the dispersion, and as many as the Lord God should call.

PETER'S SECOND SERMON—REOFFER OF THE KINGDOM

After the healing of the crippled man at the gate of the temple, Peter says, "The God of Abraham, and of Isaac, and of Jacob, the God of our fathers, hath glorified his Son Jesus; whom ye delivered up, and denied him in the presence of Pilate, when he was determined to let him go" (Ac 3:13). He acknowledged that they did it in ignorance but says that it was prophesied that Christ should suffer. But God raised up Jesus and it is through faith in His name that this man was healed.

His call unto them now is to repent: "Repent ye therefore, and be converted, that your sins may be blotted out." (Note that no mention is made of baptism being a requirement of having sins blotted out.)

The American Standard Version renders Acts 3:19-21:

> Repent ye therefore, and turn again, that your sins may be blotted out, that so there may come seasons of refreshing from the presence of the Lord; and that he may send the Christ who hath been appointed for you, even Jesus: whom the heaven must receive until the times of restoration of all things, whereof God spake by the mouth of his holy prophets that have been from of old.

J. R. Lumby explains it as follows:

> *Repent ye therefore*) i.e. because you see the greatness of your offence.
> *and be converted*) literally, *turn again*, i.e. from the evil of your ways. The word *convert* has received much ongrowth of meaning since the A.V. was made. The same word is well rendered "a great number believed and *turned* unto the Lord."
> *when the times of refreshing shall come*) *hopos an* cannot be translated *when* the times . . . *shall* come, but *that* the times . . . *may* come. These particles indicate a purpose, the accomplishment of which still lies in doubt. So the Apostle's argument is, Repent, that your sins may be blotted out, *that in this way* (i.e. by your penitence) the times of refreshing *may* come. The particles are rendered in this sense Acts 15:17, "that the residue of men might (better *may*) seek after the Lord."
> *and he shall send*) The construction is continued from the previous verse. Read, *and that he may send*.
> In the rest of this verse both the order of the words and the reading of the *Tex. Rec.* is different from that of the best MSS. The sentence should read: *the Christ which was appointed for you, even Jesus.* Not only is this the more authoritative reading but it agrees with the proofs which St. Peter presently cites (v. 25), "Ye are the children of the covenant which God made with our fathers." The Christ, the Messiah, had been appointed and promised unto the Jewish nation, and now the promise of the covenant is fulfilled in Jesus.
> *whom the heaven must receive*) and retain, as we are witnesses that He has been taken up into heaven.
> *until the times of restitution*) Better, *restoration of all things*, i.e. at Christ's second coming.[5]

The word translated "restitution" is from the same word translated "restore" in Acts 1:6. This word is only used these two times in the Bible and refers to the restoration of Israel back in the land and the restoration of all things when the curse of sin is finally lifted. This phrase is referring to the same thing as the previous verse where it says "the times of refreshing." The Old Testament prophets repeatedly referred to this restoration when Israel would come under the full privileges and provisions given in the Abrahamic and other covenants in the kingdom.

It cannot be overlooked that with this offer there was the promise that if Israel would repent, Jesus would return. The fact that God foreknew Israel's rejection of this offer does not keep it from being a bonafide offer. When they finally did reject His offer, He revealed His gracious plan for the church. There is little profit in contemplating what would have happened if the Jews had accepted. That is like asking, "What would have happened if Adam had never sinned?" or "What would have happened if the Jews had received Messiah and not crucified Him" God foreknew the end from the beginning and planned accordingly.

The apostles and other believers continued to preach that Jesus was the Messiah and many signs and wonders were performed by the apostles (Ac 5:12). Even though the apostles were thrown in prison, beaten, and threatened, "daily in the temple, and in every house, they ceased not to teach and preach Jesus Christ" (5:42).

The antagonism of religious Israel reached a climax in Jerusalem with the martyrdom of Stephen, one of the seven chosen to help in the ministry among the widows. He preached in the synagogues and performed wonders and miracles among the people (6:8-9).

JESUS MANIFESTING HIMSELF THROUGH HIS NEW BODY

One of the most outstanding examples of God the Son revealing Himself through His new body, the church, is in the trial and martyrdom of Stephen. Notice the many similarities between the sufferings and sayings of Christ and the martyrdom of Stephen: Acts 6:10 and Matthew 22:46; Acts 6:11 and Matthew 26:65; Acts 6:13-15 and Matthew 26:59; Acts 6:14 and Matthew 26:61; Acts 7:58 and John 19:17-20; Acts 7:59 and Luke 23:46; and Acts 7:60 and Luke 23:34.

This was a pivotal point for religious Israel at Jerusalem. They had refused to believe that Jesus was their Messiah or Saviour-King and had rejected the reoffer of the King and His kingdom. No other miracles are recorded at Jerusalem.

THE GEOGRAPHICAL OUTREACH

The pattern of the ministry followed the basic plan of Acts 1:8. Pentecost occurred in A.D. 30. Jesus said, "Ye shall be witnesses unto me,"

1. "both in Jerusalem"—the first five years' activities centered around the city of Jerusalem until the stoning of Stephen in A.D. 35.

2. "and in all Judea, and in Samaria"—the activities for the next ten years were in these two areas but reaching as far as Antioch.

3. "and unto the uttermost part of the earth"—from about A.D. 45 to the close of Acts in A.D. 60. During these fifteen years the gospel extended from Antioch to Rome. They include Paul's three missionary journeys and his imprisonment. Notice the progressive steps: five, ten, fifteen, and thirty years (see Fig. 11).

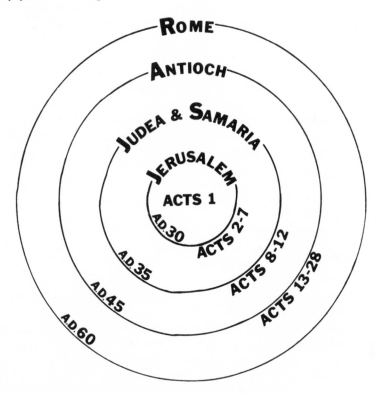

Fig. 11. Geographical Outreach

BELIEVERS ARE SOWN IN JUDEA AND SAMARIA

Persecution drove the witnesses out into Judea, Samaria, and on toward Antioch. "Therefore they that were scattered abroad went every where preaching the word" (Ac 8:4). The literal meaning of the words "were scattered" is "sown as seed." From the human standpoint it looked as though evil was winning, but this is another example of God overruling evil for good. As the believers went forth, they carried the Word everywhere.

The Samaritan people were a mixed race, but some of their ancestors had been Israelites. Philip went to Samaria and preached and they listened to him. "But when they believed Philip preaching the things concerning the kingdom of God, and the name of Jesus Christ, they were baptized, both men and women" (8:12). The King and His kingdom were a vital part of Philip's message.

Acts 10 records the visions and ministry of Peter to the house of Cornelius which occurred about A.D. 40, ten years after Pentecost. Cornelius was a Roman army officer, a Gentile. Peter said, after his vision, "Of a truth I perceive that God is no respecter of persons: but in every nation he that feareth him, and worketh righteousness, is accepted with him. The word which God sent unto the children of Israel, preaching peace by Jesus Christ: (he is Lord of all:) that word, I say, ye know, which was published throughout all Judea, and began from Galilee, after the baptism which John preached; how God anointed Jesus of Nazareth with the Holy Ghost and with power: who went about doing good, and healing all that were oppressed of the devil; for God was with him" (10:34-38). He explained about Jesus' death and resurrection and then gave the promise: "To him give all the prophets witness, that through his name whosoever believeth in him shall receive remission of sins" (10:43).

While he was yet speaking, the Holy Spirit fell upon them and one of the same signs appeared that had occurred at Pentecost—the people spoke in other languages. This foreshadows the unity of the nations of the world under the rule of the King of kings when they all shall speak one language (Zep 3:9).

While most of the attention was centered upon Judea and Samaria, there was other activity outside of the nation proper: "Now they which were scattered abroad upon the persecution that arose about Stephen travelled as far as Phenice, and Cyprus, and Antioch, preaching the word to none but unto the Jews only. And some of them were men of Cyprus and Cyrene, which, when they were come to Antioch, spake unto the Grecians, preaching the Lord Jesus. And the hand of the Lord was with them: and a great number believed, and turned unto the Lord" (Ac 11:19-21). When the word got back to Jerusalem, Barnabas was sent to Antioch.

TO THE UTTERMOST PART

With Paul's missionary journeys the gospel went out from the new center of evangelism at Antioch. There is an order that can be traced "to the Jew first and also to the Gentile." As they went from place to place, if there was a synagogue, they would go to the synagogue first. The Bible only records the briefest outlines of the messages they preached, but in Antioch of Pisidia they told how God fulfilled the promises made unto Israel and had raised up Jesus, a Saviour, from the seed of David. They quoted from Psalm 2, which describes God's King as His Son and promises the forgiveness of sins through Him. While some Jews responded, most were bitterly opposed and Paul said, "It was necessary that the word of God should first have been spoken to you: but seeing ye put it from you, and judge yourselves unworthy of everlasting life, lo, we turn to the Gentiles" (13:46).

After going as far as Derbe, they started retracing their route and as they went back through the towns, "confirming the souls of the disciples, and exhorting them to continue in the faith, and that we must through much tribulation enter into the kingdom of God" (14:22). When they returned to Antioch in Syria they reported how God had "opened the door of faith unto the Gentiles" (v. 27), but nothing is recorded about the response of the Jews.

THE COUNCIL AT JERUSALEM

Some Jews in Judea came up to Antioch and said, "Except ye be circumcised after the manner of Moses, ye cannot be saved" (15:1). This caused a lot of dissension and Paul and Barnabas went down to Jerusalem to talk to the apostles and elders about this question. The Pharisees were insisting that the Gentiles become Jewish proselytes.

Peter testified that God had used him to take the gospel to Gentiles "and put no difference between us and them, purifying their hearts by faith" (15:9). Salvation is by faith, not law-keeping. James said,

> Simeon hath declared how God at the first did visit the Gentiles, to take out of them a people for his name. And to this agree the words of the prophets; as it is written; After this I will return, and will build again the tabernacle of David, which is fallen down; and I will build again the ruins thereof, and I will set it up that the residue of men might seek after the Lord, and all the Gentiles, upon whom my name is called, saith the Lord, who doeth all these things (15:14-17).

It was probably at the council of Jerusalem that the distinct program of the church began to be understood. A. C. Gaebelein says:

> Note in verses 14-17 the four important steps:
> 1. God visits the Gentiles, to take out of them a people for His name. This is the purpose of the present age. The called people constitute the church, the body of Christ.

2. After this I will return. This means the second Coming of Christ. When the Church is completed and all the members added to that body, Christ comes again, first, as subsequently revealed, for His saints and then with them.

3. The Restoration of Israel follows after His Return. The Tabernacle of David will be built again and will be set up.

4. Then all the Gentiles will seek after the Lord.[6]

The final decision at Jerusalem was that Gentiles did not have to become Jews to be saved and were not under the law or Mosaic covenant.

SECOND MISSIONARY JOURNEY

Paul followed the same pattern on his second missionary journey; he went to the Jews first wherever he could find them. There was some response, especially at Berea (17:11-12). But the opposition by the Jews at Corinth was especially strong, and Paul "testified to the Jews that Jesus was [the] Christ. And when they opposed themselves, and blasphemed, he shook his raiment, and said unto them, Your blood be upon your own heads; I am clean: from henceforth I will go unto the Gentiles" (18:5-6).

THIRD MISSIONARY JOURNEY

At Ephesus, "he went into the synagogue, and spake boldly for the space of three months, disputing and persuading the things concerning the kingdom of God" (19:8).

This announcement and the preaching of the kingdom were authenticated by sign-miracles. "And God wrought special miracles by the hands of Paul" (19:11). Returning to Rome, Paul stopped to see the Ephesian elders and said, "And now, behold, I know that ye all, among whom I have gone preaching the kingdom of God, shall see my face no more" (20:25).

Upon his return to Jerusalem, it was the Jews from Asia who caused the riot which resulted in Paul's arrest (21:28). After his arrest he gave his testimony to the multitudes as to how he met his Messiah—Jesus. They listened until he told about his ministry to the Gentiles (22:21-22), and then they wanted to kill him.

PAUL TAKEN AS A PRISONER TO ROME

When Paul arrived in Rome he called the chief Jews together and explained why he was a prisoner and his desire to talk to them. Some believed Paul and some didn't. Arguing among themselves, they departed, but not before he told them, "Be it known therefore unto you, that the salvation of God is sent unto the Gentiles, and that they will hear it" (28:28). Notice that he did *not* say that the kingdom would be taken away from them and given unto the Gentiles. Paul continued to dwell in his own rented house in Rome for two years, "preaching the kingdom of God, and teaching those things which concern the Lord Jesus Christ, with all confidence, no man forbidding him" (28:31). Both the Jews in the homeland and those in the dispersion had rejected the reoffer of the kingdom, and about ten years later God's judgment fell upon them. Jerusalem was destroyed by the Roman army of Titus, and Jewish refugees were scattered far and wide.

Hoyt says:

> There was growing opposition in relation to the teaching concerning the King and His kingdom as in the period of the Gospels. The Sadducees were against Christ (Acts 4:1-4). The Pharisees were divided (Acts 5:33-39). A great persecution arose against the church (Acts 7:51-8:1). Jewish riots were incited in opposition to Christ (Acts 22:22-23; 23:10-12). And at last there was but one thing to do and that was to turn to the Gentiles in view of the national rejection on the part of Israel (Acts 13:43-48; 18:5-6; 19:8-9; 28:17-31).[7]

PROGRESS OF THE KINGDOM PROGRAM

The outline of the kingdom program is as follows:

1. offer of the kingdom—A.D. 26
2. rejection of the King and the kingdom—A.D. 30
3. reoffer of kingdom at Pentecost—A.D. 30-35
4. rejection of the King and the kingdom at Jerusalem at Stephen's death—A.D. 35
5. Preaching in the dispensation—A.D. 35-60
   a. Jesus the Christ, the Saviour-King, and His kingdom
   b. God's plan for the Gentiles (Ac 15:14-17)

For thirty years Israel at home and abroad continued to reject Jesus as the Saviour-King and His offer of the kingdom. So the kingdom was delayed, postponed, or held in abeyance until that time in the future when Israel will turn to their Messiah. Because of this rejection by Israel, the character of the visible church emerged.

Because of our place historically, it is hard for us to understand how little the early believers understood about the church. Nothing had been revealed in the Old Testament concerning the church, so it is only in the light of the New Testament epistles that we understand the significance of the newly formed assemblies of believers.

"SELF-CONSCIOUSNESS" OF THE CHURCH

Psychologists say there is a period of time before a baby has a "self-consciousness" in relation to his own body. As he grows older, he finds his toes or his ears and plays with them, and gradually the realization comes that they are a part of him. Similarly, although the early Christian Jews continued to worship in the temple and to attend the synagogues, they also began to realize that there was something unique about themselves as Christians. Sometimes they separated voluntarily, and at other times they were forcefully put out of the synagogue. While there was a uniqueness about them (Ac 5:12-14), there is no evidence at first that the Jewish Christians in the land of Israel considered themselves any more than a faithful remnant.

When Paul's party started retracing its steps on the first missionary journey, they appointed elders in each of the assemblies and committed them unto the Lord. Gradually it became apparent that because of the rejection by the Jewish nation, God was taking out a people for His name. When this is accomplished, He will restore Israel under her covenants (Ac 15:14-17; Ro 9–11). Paul also testified that he was sent unto the Gentiles "to open their eyes, and to turn them from darkness to light, and from the power of Satan unto God, that they may receive forgiveness of sins, and inheritance among them which are sanctified" (Ac 26:18).

The book of Acts only hints at the relationship of these new assemblies to the kingdom, but in Paul's epistles to the churches this is revealed. He wrote 1 and 2 Thessalonians on his second missionary journey but they do not explain very much about the nature of the church. It is in 1 Corinthians, written on the third missionary journey in about A.D. 57, that the apostle describes the church as the body of Christ and a temple. In Galatians, written in about A.D. 57, Paul reveals the relationship between the church and Christ and Abraham.

In Romans in A.D. 58, he explains how Israel as a nation has been temporarily set aside. God is calling out a people from the Gentiles, and they are being grafted into the root stock of the promised line of the seed (Gen 3:15; Ro 11:16-24). Gentiles have been included in the line of the seed before by marriage, for example, Rahab and Ruth, but now they are placed into the royal line by being "in Christ." It is still possible for individual Jews to be saved, but a judicial blindness has come upon Israel "until the fulness of the Gentiles be come in" (Ro 11:25).

During his Roman imprisonment, Paul wrote letters to the Ephesians and Colossians and gave additional information concerning the body of Christ and its relationship to Christ the head. From the scriptural evidence it is hard to see how the early believers could have understood very much about the nature and makeup of the church before these epistles were written approximately at the close of the Acts period, or about A.D. 60, a generation after Pentecost.

The kingdom continued to be preached all through the book of Acts (1:3, 6; 8:12; 14:22; 19:8; 20:25; 28:23, 31), but the stress was no longer that the kingdom was "nigh," as it had been when Jesus was present. The rejection of their Messiah and the judgment that had fallen upon national Israel brought up some important questions concerning the kingdom, and the book of Hebrews was given to answer these questions.

THE NATURE OF THE CHURCH

The church by name is a called-out assembly but it is also described by different figures. Several references describe it as a building or house (1 Pe 2:5; Eph 2:20-21; 1 Co 3:16); a body (1 Co 12:27), and perhaps as a bride (2 Co 11:2; Eph 5:21-31; Rev 19:6-9), but never as the kingdom.

SUMMARY

1. The book of Acts records the progress of God's two programs: the offer of the kingdom and the formation of the church.

2. The apostles and early Christians were used in both programs.

3. God used sign-miracles to authenticate the offer of the kingdom.

4. The church was born on the feast of Pentecost.

5. In Peter's second sermon he promised that if Israel would repent, God would send back King Jesus who would then establish His kingdom.

6. By about A.D. 35 at the stoning of Stephen, the religious rulers in the homeland had again rejected Jesus as the Messiah and His offer of the kingdom.

7. There is a progressive movement out from Jerusalem to Samaria, Antioch and Rome as the kingdom is proclaimed to the Jews in the dispersion, the gospel is preached to Jew and Gentile, and churches are established.

8. By A.D. 60, a generation after Pentecost, the Jews in the dispersion had also failed to respond to the reoffer of the kingdom. The nature of the church was revealed in more detail in 1 Corinthians and Ephesians.

12

God's Purpose and Plan for the Church

GOD'S PLAN can be divided into two parts: today and in the future kingdom. The church today is involved in many activities, and some churches have been rightly accused of majoring in the minors. Three basic divisions are in God's program for the church today:

1. evangelizing the world
2. manifesting Christ before the world
3. training or discipling believers for the present and future age

WORLD EVANGELISM

Jesus told His disciples just before He ascended into heaven, "Go ye into all the world, and preach the gospel to every creature" (Mk 16:15). The good news, that long-promised redemption, is now offered to all: "and that repentance and remission of sins should be preached in his name among all nations, beginning at Jerusalem" (Lk 24:47). The nucleus of 120 believers formed on the day of Pentecost into the church by the Holy Spirit is the starting point. It is God's plan that the church would be used in its own growth, that through its members the gospel would be preached in the power of the Holy Spirit and with Spirit-given abilities or gifts. The different ministries are seen in Ephesians 4:11-12: "And he gave some, apostles; and some, prophets; and some, evangelists; and some, pastors and teachers; for the perfecting [equipping] of the saints, for the work of the ministry, for the edifying [building up] of the body of Christ." The pattern is this: as people are evangelized and respond to the gospel, they, through the ministry of the church, are trained or equipped so they can enter the same ministries. This results in the building up of the body of Christ both numerically and spiritually.

People are called out from among all nations, with no distinction now as to nationality. This is to continue until "the fulness of the Gentiles be come in" (Ro 11:25). When the body of Christ is complete, Christ will proceed with the next step in His program of destroying or undoing the work of the devil (1 Jn 3:8).

CHARACTERISTICS OF EARLY CHURCH EVANGELISM

It was at least A.D. 45 before any of the New Testament was written. Yet, churches were established, and sometimes after only a very short visit. They flourished and grew without a New Testament or without importing highly trained leaders. Five reasons help us to understand their success: (1) Paul and the other evangelists gave the people the key to understanding the Old Testament or its Greek translation—Jesus was *the Christ*, (2) a reliance upon the gifts and teaching ministry of the Holy Spirit, (3) an emphasis upon the second coming of Christ, (4) a lack of concern about buildings and property in which to meet, (5) they realized the Christian life was a new and different way of life (Ac 9:2).

MANIFESTING CHRIST BEFORE THE WORLD

Fallen mankind's knowledge of God is perverted. Jesus came to this earth, took on a human body, and lived among mankind so that we could learn what God is like. Just before Jesus' death, when Philip wanted Him to show them the Father, He said, "He that hath seen me hath seen the Father" (Jn 14:9). Jesus now indwells believers (Col 1:27; Jn 14:23) and they are being changed into the image of Christ "from glory to glory, even as by the Spirit of the Lord" (2 Co 3:18). Jesus is now manifesting Himself unto the world through His new body, the church.

TRAINING BELIEVERS FOR THE FUTURE

We must remember that this age is not the end; it is the workshop for the golden age. This training and discipling have a very important use in this age in the evangelization of the world, but they also have a direct bearing upon the future.

In the Garden of Eden, man rebelled against God's order, wanting to act independently of God. Israel found that they didn't have the ability to keep God's requirements given in the Mosaic covenant. Under the benefits of the new covenant the Christian has been given the indwelling Holy Spirit and God has performed a work of grace in his heart through the new birth. During this age he is being trained to walk under the direction of the Holy Spirit (Gal 5:16). This is a walk of faith in which believers are to learn to trust the Lord for all things: strength, guidance, provision, and abilities.

TWO KINDS OF TESTING

Two different Greek words are used in the New Testament for testing. *Teirazo* is testing with the hope or expectation that the thing tested will break down. It is sometimes used in the solicitation or suggestion to do evil. At other times a thing is tested to discover what is good or evil in it or to bring out the character.

Dokimazo is used of a test that is made with the expectation and hope that the object tested will pass the test, or similarly, it is the testing of someone or something for the purpose of approving it. It is this second word that is used in James 1:3 and 12.

God never tempts us to do evil, but He does test us (Ja 1:13). Satan, however, has many tricks and devices. God, who allows tests to come so that our faith may be approved, limits the power of Satan so that we do not have to fall into sin (1 Co 10:13) but can have victory in Jesus Christ (1 Co 15:57; Phil 4:13). The "divers temptations" spoken of by James in James 1:2 have the idea of a great variety. For example, your faith may be tried in poverty, illness, the death of a loved one, riches, health or the vigor of life, social advancement, fame, or the denial of fame.

Your tests may be your reactions to the environments of life around you. For example, will you trust the Lord to help you in your social life or relations with the opposite sex; at examination time when the temptation is to cheat; when the dirty story is told or profane language used; when there is friction within the family or misunderstanding or problems at work; when you choose your TV programs; when there is a lack of co-operation within the Sunday school or church?

Trials are beneficial because every trial puts faith to the test, thus not only proving the genuineness of our faith but also helping us grow. In a very real sense the exercise of faith can be compared to the exercise of muscles. Exercise does not destroy muscles; it develops their skill and strength. James says that the trying of your faith produces patience, or literally, patient endurance or the ability to stand up under a load. In the exercise of faith we learn to stand up and not give way to insult, praise, laziness, worry, gossip, failure, misunderstanding or fame. In other words, Christ desires that our testing will develop in us the capacity to carry a great load in life without it stopping or depressing us.

We are given the opportunity to exhibit this faith in God in each trial, so we are to rejoice and consider each trial as a challenge to our faith, recognizing that each victorious trial moves us toward the goal of "Christ-likeness."

An End to Spiritual Growth?

In Luke 16 the Lord shows that there is no opportunity or second chance after death. If you don't receive the Saviour in this life, you will not be given a chance in the next. There seems to be a parallel regarding spiritual growth, for in the parable of the pounds, Jesus said that rewards would be given unto servants according to their faithfulness, and that there would be a loss of reward for the unfaithful (Lk 19:11-28). The rewards mentioned in this parable are responsibilities, or the rule over cities. (The various kinds of rulership are discussed later.) This rulership will be in the resurrection body when we will no longer have the sin nature and be able to sin.

The twelve apostles were promised that they would rule over the twelve tribes of Israel. It seems significant that during the forty-day period between the resurrection and the ascension that Christ was instructing the disciples concerning the kingdom of God. There must have been special training and instruction which He wanted to give them while they were in this present body. If you have been turning testings into proven acts of faith, then you have been building your capacity for usefulness for both now and the eternal ages that follow.

It is a rather frightening thought, but nevertheless true, that if you have been "flunking the tests," you have been proving your uselessness for future service for the Lord. Ephesians 5:15-17 can literally be translated, "See then that ye walk carefully, not as fools, but as wise, buying up the opportunities, because these are evil days. Wherefore be not unwise, but understanding what the will of the Lord is." Since the will of the Lord is revealed in His Word, "study to shew thyself approved unto God, a workman that needeth not to be ashamed, rightly dividing the word of truth" (2 Ti 2:15), for "all scripture is given by inspiration of God, and is profitable for doctrine, for reproof, for correction, for instruction in righteousness: that the man of God may be perfect, throughly furnished unto all good works" (3:16-17).

There is no indication in Scripture that it will be possible to "play" your way through this life and then "get down to business" in the next life. So it seems correct to say that spiritual growth is determined by what we do in this life, and this in turn will determine our position with Christ in the ages that follow. Remember, we are talking about positions or rewards for Christians, and not salvation.

Testings of life take on an entirely different character when viewed in this light. Each testing can be viewed as (1) an opportunity to learn to trust Him, (2) an opportunity to display our faith in Him, (3) an opportunity to exercise spiritual gifts or abilities, (4) an opportunity to gain a better knowledge of God, (5) an opportunity for God to show Himself faithful—that He can be depended upon to keep His word and promises, that God's way is the best way, and that the creature should be dependent upon the Creator.

With each act of faith we get to know God a little better and learn to live in closer fellowship with Him. There are many related areas: worship, prayer, praise.[1]

THE RELATION OF THE CHURCH TO THE ETERNAL KINGDOM

God's program for the future of the church is expressed by Erich Sauer:

> The Kingdom of God in its form as the kingdom of glory will be the sphere of the active rule of the church: "Know ye not that the saints shall judge the world" (1 Cor. 6:2, 3): "Fear thou not, thou little flock, it is your Father's good pleasure to give you the kingdom" (Luke 12:32). The church is thus the ruling aristocracy, the official administrative staff, of the coming kingdom of God.[2]

Christians were chosen by God as kings and priests for this ministry (Rev 1:6), which brings us to the very difficult doctrine of election.

GOD'S ELECT

One of the doctrines that has caused many divisions among Christians is the doctrine of election. History, heresy, misconceptions and the misuse of terms have all contributed to the confusion. It is hard to believe that if a person were isolated on an island and studied by himself that he would come up with any of the usual elaborate systems. The following view is not presented for polemical purposes, but as an effort to make a contribution toward understanding this difficult doctrine and especially its relation to position and service in the kingdom. Our approach is to study the meaning of the word *election*, to briefly trace the biblical usage as it develops, to compare the usage in the Old and New Testament, and to trace some historical interpretations that have influenced our thinking.

The word *election* and its cognates, *elect*, *chose* and *chosen*, all mean practically the same thing and sometimes are translations of the same words. *Choosing*, whether referring to God or man, is directly related to an act of the will. No one would question the fact that God is not limited in His choices by anything outside of Himself. In contrast, man is sometimes limited by knowledge, power, ability, or some other restriction. Creation is a good example of the many choices that God made. There are all kinds of created beings: men, angels, animals, fish, etc. God could have chosen to create all creatures the same, but He didn't.

OLD TESTAMENT USES

The Old Testament abounds in examples of God electing or selecting for outward privileges. This electing can be divided into two classes: individual and corporate.

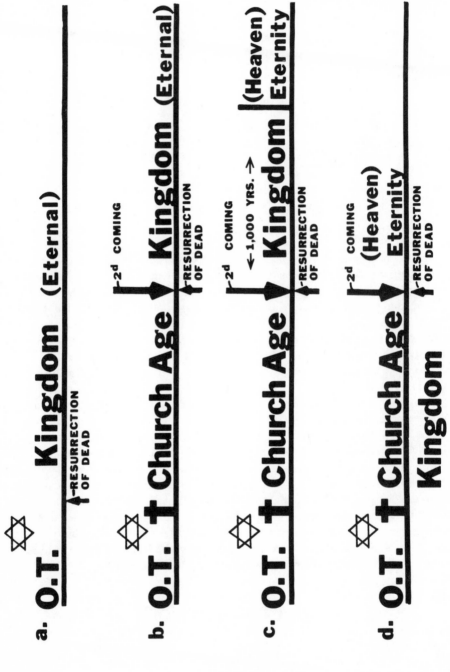

Fig. 12. Election and the Kingdom

INDIVIDUAL ELECTION

One of the most important recorded choices is God's selection of Abraham as the father of a new nation. Moses was chosen as a leader to deliver Israel (Ex 3:10; Ps 106:23); Aaron was chosen as God's high priest (Ps 105:26); and David was chosen as king (1 Sa 16:12; 20:30). Christ is also prophetically referred to as God's elect in Isaiah 42:1. All of these refer to ministry or outward privileges and not to salvation.

CORPORATE ELECTION

The nation of Israel is an example of corporate election: "For Jacob my servant's sake, and Israel mine elect, I have even called thee by my name: I have surnamed thee, though thou hast not known me" (Is 45:4). It was to this elect nation that the kingdom was offered, and the people were to be a kingdom of priests (Ex 19:5-6). (The six objectives of Israel's election are studied in chap. 3.) God also chose Judah as the ruling tribe of Israel (1 Ch 28:4).

The Old Testament Jew's general understanding of election can be diagrammed as line A in Figure 12:

1. They understood that they had been chosen (elected) as a special people, a nation of priests.

2. The Word of God has been committed to them (Ro 3:2).

3. The Messiah (represented by the star), was to be born of the Jews.

4. When the Messiah came, the dead would be raised and the kingdom established.

NEW TESTAMENT USES OF ELECTION

Some Jews were trusting that their family relationship or membership in an elect nation would automatically give them a place in the kingdom without repentance. But John the Baptist warned them, "And think not to say within yourselves, We have Abraham to our father: for I say unto you, that God is able of these stones to raise up children unto Abraham" (Mt 3:9). This verse illustrates the use of *election* in the New Testament, following the same pattern used in the Old Testament. There are both individual and corporate election, and being a member of a chosen (elect) nation does not guarantee individual election. Examples of individual election to ministry include apostles (Lk 6:13-16), the seventy witnesses (Lk 10:1), and missionaries (Ac 13:1-2). Some, such as the apostles, had eternal significance in the kingdom (Mt 19:28). An example of a corporate use is given in 1 Thessalonians 1:4, where the church is called elect. At this point it must be noted that election is used in ways other than election to eternal life.

Because of the rejection and crucifixion of their Saviour-King, elect Israel was temporarily set aside as a nation while God instituted a new program of election. He now is selecting from Jews and Gentiles a new assembly that He calls the church. When this is completed, He will come to the earth a second time, raise the righteous dead, and establish His kingdom. The elect of both the Old and New Testaments will have an important place (see line B in Fig. 12; details of the rapture of the church are studied in chap. 15).

THE KEY TO ELECTION

Peters says:

> This doctrine of the Kingdom in its covenanted aspect gives us *the key* to the doctrine of election. The language referring to election based (1) on the Divine Purpose relating to this Theocratic Kingdom; (2) on the Plan embraced in that Purpose, of gathering out a people,—whose character, etc., is predetermined—to whom it can be entrusted; (3) on the acceptance of the conditions by persons through which they come into the line of that purpose. The election then (a) is, *so far as God* is concerned, pre-ordained; such a people *will be gathered* (as even Moses predicted) for such a Kingdom of kings and priests to be established, and, as *God changes not*, it will most assuredly be carried into execution; (b) on the part of man, he comes in the line of the predestined order, or elect, or chosen, *just as soon* as he accords or falls in with the determined process of engrafting through faith in Jesus Christ.[3]

Ephesians 2:14 speaks of Christ breaking down the "middle wall of partition" between Jew and Gentile. Note that this is between Jewish and Gentile believers in Christ and not between the Jewish nation and Gentile nations. No Gentile nation has been chosen in place of the Jewish nation, for this would violate God's oath-given covenants. Israel as a nation rejected their Messiah, but in order that God's promise and His purpose to establish His kingdom on the earth might be fulfilled to the elect nation, He continues the election by incorporating Gentile believers. He requires a certain determined number for the accomplishment of His purpose: This is "that blindness in part is happened to Israel, until the fulness of the Gentiles be come in" (Ro 11:25).

This plan for the church and Israel is explained in Romans 9–11. Notice several important points:

1. This passage is dealing with the election of Israel, not the church (9:3-4).

2. It has to do with election to religious privileges rather than with personal salvation (9:4-5).

3. It speaks of both national and individual election (9:4, 6-7).

4. The consequences are earthly: election is not said to be to heaven or hell.

5. This chapter reveals that corporate or national election does not save individuals. National election is to national privileges, but each individual person needs salvation, and Paul was burdened for his Jewish brethren.

6. This passage records and explains the fall and restoration of Israel (because they rejected their Messiah). They are being chastised in this age (Deu 28:63-68; Ac 13:46; 18:6).

7. All Israel is not the true Israel—the unbelieving ones are excluded from the ministry and privilege (Ro 9:6) as well as eternal life (9:31-32).

8. Isaac and Jacob were elected for the privilege of being the pathway of the seed from which Christ was born (9:7-13).

9. God overrules evil for His own purpose. Pharaoh is an example. Exodus says that on occasion God hardened Pharaoh's heart, and that at other times he hardened his own heart. God hardened his heart by letting him exercise his own will, which became a little harder each time he resisted God. The word *fitted* in Romans 9:22 can be translated in the middle voice to read, "What if God, willing to show his wrath, and to make his power known, endured with much longsuffering the vessels of wrath [who have] *fitted* [*themselves*] to destruction."

10. Whether for Jew or Gentile, righteousness always comes by faith (9:30-32).

UNITED WITH CHRIST

God does not just arbitrarily give away what He promised by an oath to give to Israel. By faith we are identified with Christ in His death, burial, and resurrection (Ro 6:3-4). "For if we have been planted together in the likeness of his death, we shall be also in the likeness of his resurrection" (6:5). The words *planted together*, from a biological word in Greek, are used to mean grafted into or joined with Christ. Because of our position in Christ, who is God's Elect (Is 42:1), corporately we are also called elect (1 Pe 1:2; Ro 8:33; 2 Ti 2:10; Titus 1:1; Col 3:12). And because of this union with the living Christ, we are said to be chosen "in him" (Eph 1:4). This is positional truth. We are *not* said to be chosen and "put *into* him." Because of our position "in him" we receive these blessings. Both individual Jew and Gentile are being added to His body, the church. We have unique privileges as "the body of Christ" and in Christ as "the seed of Abraham" (Gal 3:6-9, 14, 16, 18).

The word *predestination* in its various forms only appears four times in the Bible (Ro 8:29-30; Eph 1:5, 11). It is always used in connection with the saved and tells about the special character of blessing that is theirs:

"to adoption," "to the praise of his glory," or "conformed to the image of his Son."

Herbert Lockyer says,

> What must be borne in mind is the fact that predestination is not God's predetermining from past ages who should and who should not be saved. Scripture does not teach this view. What it does teach is that this doctrine of predestination concerns the future of believers. Predestination is the divine determining the glorious consummation of all who through faith, and surrender become the Lord's. He has determined beforehand that each child of His will reach *adoption*, or "son-placing" at his resurrection when Christ returns. It has been determined beforehand that all who are truly Christ's shall be conformed to His image (Rom. 8:29; Eph. 1:5).[4]

THE MEANING OF ADOPTION

The word *adoption* means literally "son-placing." W. E. Vine says that it "signifies the place and condition of a son given to one to whom it does not naturally belong."[5] It carries with it the idea of full rights and privileges as an heir.

The adoption of Christians is necessary for two reasons. First, so that they may legally inherit and share the covenant promises, for they cannot just appropriate Israel's possessions. Second, to prove the faithfulness of God. He proves this in two ways: (1) by providing a seed to inherit the promises and (2) by keeping His covenants.

THE PLAN OF ADOPTION

How is adoption accomplished? Peters clearly explains:

> The plan of adoption is simple: Abraham was justified by faith, the election was bestowed upon him in virtue of that faith, and hence those who believe in the promised seed being also justified by faith, are brought into living union with Christ ("the King of the Jews"), and through Him become the adopted children of Abraham who was of like faith. Hence the apostle in Galatians 3 tells us (v. 7), "Know ye therefore, that they which are of faith, the same are the children of Abraham." But why become the children of Abraham? Because, as he shows, verses 14-18, the promises and inheritance are given through him, and we must be related to Abraham in order to receive and inherit the same. Therefore he goes on and insists that this very essential relationship is established in and through Jesus Christ, and (v. 28-29), adds: "for ye are all one in Christ Jesus. And if ye be Christ's, then are ye Abraham's seed, and heirs according to promise." Thus those (ch. 4:5) receiving "the adoption of sons," become united and identified with Christ, who is the chief inheritor under the Abrahamic covenant, we become co-heirs with Him. This marvellously simple arrangement, introducing mercy and grace to us Gentiles, preserves the covenanted promises intact and confirms them.[6]

All believers are given the Holy Spirit. Also called the Spirit of adoption (Ro 8:15), He produces in believers the realization of sonship and the attitude belonging to sons.

THE CONSUMMATION OF ADOPTION

Adoption is spoken of as being a present reality, yet it is also in the future for it includes the redemption of the body. The living will be changed and those who have fallen asleep will be raised (Ro 8:23). Galatians points out "that the heir, as long as he is a child, differeth nothing from a servant, though he be lord of all; but is under tutors and governors until the time appointed of the father" (4:1-2). Israel was under the tutorship of the law (3:24), but Christ came "to redeem them that were under the law, that we might receive the adoption of sons" (4:5).

In the introduction to his gospel, John says, "He came unto his own, and his own received him not. But as many as received him, to them gave he power to become the sons of God, even to them that believe on his name" (1:11-12). Several words are translated *power* in the New Testament. The word used here means *authority*. It is by the very authority of Christ that we become sons of God. It's hard to understand all that is involved, but 1 John 3:1-2 says, "Behold, what manner of love the Father hath bestowed upon us, that we should be called the sons of God: therefore the world knoweth us not, because it knew him not. Beloved, now are we the sons of God, and it doth not yet appear what we shall be: but we know that, when he shall appear, we shall be like him; for we shall see him as he is." Positionally in the sight of God, we are now sons of God, but the final consummation of adoption awaits the coming of Christ and the redemption of the body (Ro 8:23). The Romans had a ceremony in which the rights were officially given to a son.

A BLESSING OF ABRAHAM UNTO ALL THE FAMILIES OF THE EARTH

In Genesis 12:3 God promised Abraham that "in thee shall all families of the earth be blessed." This blessing will be in at least these three ways:

1. Jesus Christ, the seed of Abraham, died for the sins of the whole world (1 Jn 2:2). He offers salvation unto all who will believe (Jn 3:16).

2. The blessing is extended to the whole world in this age as He calls out individuals "for his name" (Ac 15:14-17) through the ministry of the church.

3. Blessing will flow to all people of the world in the future as Israel and the engrafted church serve in Christ's kingdom (Ex 19:6; 1 Pe 2:9; Ro 11:24; Rev 1:6).

God always chooses a few in order that all or many may be blessed through their service (Gen 12:1-3; 2 Sa 7:16; 1 Ti 2:1-7). Richard Wolff says:

> The election of Israel did not limit God's world-wide purposes to one single nation. On the contrary, this choice was a means to implement his grace and mercy toward all nations. Far from justifying narrow nationalism and pride, election is a call to service and responsibility.[7]

MAKING YOUR CALLING AND ELECTION SURE

Election is definitely connected to the kingdom: "Wherefore the rather, brethren, give diligence to make your calling and election sure: for if ye do these things, ye shall never fail: for so an entrance shall be ministered unto you abundantly into the everlasting kingdom of our Lord and Saviour Jesus Christ" (2 Pe 1:10-11). Christians make their calling and election sure by building into their lives through spiritual growth the traits mentioned in 2 Peter 1:5-8. They receive an abundant entrance in contrast to the believer mentioned in verse 9 who has even forgotten that he "was purged from his old sins." Assignments to positions in the kingdom are studied later, but kingdom ministries explain this verse and the expression "many be called, but few chosen" in Matthew 20:16; 22:14 (cf. Rev 17:14).

DENIAL OF A LITERAL KINGDOM

When men began to doubt that Christ would return and literally reign in His kingdom, this doubt began to confuse their interpretation of election and other doctrines. Many people today deny that there will be a millennial kingdom. They are called amillennialists, which means "no millennium." John Walvoord points out the important early influence that Augustine has had upon the thinking of the church:

> Augustine's concept of the millennium is not difficult to grasp nor are the major facts subject to dispute. Augustine conceived of the present age as a conflict between the City of God and the City of Satan, or the conflict between the church and the world. This was viewed as moving on to the ultimate triumph of the church to be climaxed by a tremendous struggle in which the church would be apparently defeated, only to consummate in a tremendous triumph in the second coming of Christ to the earth. Augustine held that the present age of conflict is the millennium. . . . Augustine, however, also held to a future millennium, to round out the seven millenniums from Adam which he held comprised the history of man. This future millennium, he held, was not literal but is synonymous with eternity—a use of the number in a symbolic sense only. . . . In Augustine, therefore, we have specific and concrete teaching on the millennium. There is no future millennium in the ordinary meaning

of the term. The present age is the millennium; Satan is bound now; when Christ returns the present millennium will close, the future millennium or eternity will begin.[8]

Because Augustine confused two points: (1) the present age with the kingdom and (2) eternity and a nonliteral millennium, he also confused the biblical concept of election. He recognized that immortality and other promised kingdom blessings were not being enjoyed by the church (which he called the kingdom), so he transferred these kingdom blessings of the elect to eternity. In this way eternal life became the *object* of election. But this puts the emphasis in the wrong place. In order for the elect to fulfill their ministries in the eternal kingdom, they must have eternal life. (Death is the curse of sin.) Eternal life makes possible the performing of an elected ministry and the enjoying of promised blessings, rather than it being the object of election (see line D in Fig. 12).

Peters says that the doctrine of predestination to salvation sprang out of a misapprehension and erroneous interpretation of the history of the kingdom of God on earth, transferring what belonged only to such a kingdom "to eternal religious relationship."[9]

THE INFLUENCE OF AUGUSTINE

Augustine not only influenced the Roman Catholic Church, but Protestant leaders as well. Such leaders as Calvin, Luther and Melanchthon are all properly classified as amillennial. In the city of Geneva, Switzerland, Calvin put into practice the ideas he had drawn from the *City of God*. He believed that the civil government should enforce the laws of the church. For the last nine years of his life, his authority went unchallenged. The idea of the spiritual kingdom, represented by the church and his denial of a literal reign of Christ upon the earth, was transmitted to the Calvinistic denominations: the Reformed churches and Presbyterian churches, with influence upon the Baptist, the Church of England, and many other groups. Remember, because Christ's kingdom is eternal, it is necessary that those who participate in it as rulers have eternal life, but eternal life is a gift given to those who have been saved by placing their faith in Christ.

Today premillennialists have once again expressed their faith in a literal millennial kingdom (see line C in Fig. 12). Usually they overemphasize the millennium (line B is the more correct view). There is some carryover of Augustinian thinking, for some consider the church as a "spiritual" kingdom of God. But this is a misuse of the word *kingdom* because God has one kingdom in prophecy, and His Son will establish and rule over it.

In summarizing the relation of this difficult doctrine to the kingdom, remember: (1) election is used individually and corporately; (2) it is also used in ways other than election to eternal life; (3) there is often a direct relation to the kingdom as some believers are chosen for positions or ministries; and (4) each usage must be studied in context to determine the meaning.

SUMMARY

1. God's plan for the church today is to evangelize the world, manifest Christ before the world, and train believers.

2. The believer's training is to prepare him for ministry in the eternal kingdom.

3. This kingdom ministry will be as kings and priests unto God (Rev 1:6).

4. The Bible teaches both an individual and corporate election.

5. The doctrine of the kingdom is the key to understanding the doctrine of election.

6. The elect of the New Testament is continuation of the elect of the Old Testament through their union with Christ.

7. Because of this union with Christ, believers are adopted or "placed as sons" and receive full rights and privileges as sons of God.

13

The Book of Hebrews and the Kingdom

THE BOOK OF HEBREWS was written about one generation after Pentecost and shortly before Israel was invaded by the Roman armies who destroyed Jerusalem and the temple in A.D. 70. Hebrews answers some questions which would naturally come to the mind of the Jews who had become Christians.

When the nation Israel crucified and rejected their Messiah, God had opened the door of faith unto the Gentiles and many had responded. In 1 Corinthians, Ephesians, Galatians, Romans, and other New Testament epistles, God had revealed something of the nature and privilege of the church. The question then arising in the mind of the Jews was: "What about the nation of Israel and its rich heritage: the sacrificial system, the priesthood, the tabernacle and temple worship, the covenants—especially the Mosaic covenant? What about the relationship of these to the kingdom? How do all these things fit together?"

The answer is that everything centers around Christ— the key who explains the past and the future. In a series of contrasts, Hebrews shows the superiority of the person and ministry of Christ. The heritage of the Hebrew people was very rich and dear to their hearts, but the book of Hebrews puts it in proper perspective. The institutions were not in their final form, "for the law having a shadow of good things to come, and not the very image of the things" (10:1). They all pointed toward the future and the fulfillment that we have in Christ. Notice the following comparisons:

1. Christ is superior to the prophets because of His work, His ministry, and His person (He is the revelation of God).

2. Christ is superior to the angels. He is God, and they are His ministers.

3. Christ is superior to Moses, who is a servant in God's house. Christ is the Head over His own house.

4. Christ is superior to Joshua. He will lead His people into a more perfect rest.

5. Christ is superior to Aaron. His priesthood is of a higher order. He is a perpetual and perfect High Priest.

6. Christ's ministry is in a superior sanctuary, the true tabernacle.

7. Christ ministers through a better covenant, for the new covenant has better promises.

8. Christ's sacrifice—the sacrifice of Himself—is a better sacrifice.

THE SCARLET THREAD OF REDEMPTION

Although we are primarily interested in the new light which the book of Hebrews sheds on the kingdom of Christ, note that eighteen things are said about His redemptive work: 1:3; 2:3, 9, 14-15, 17; 5:9; 7:27; 8:12; 9:12, 15, 23, 26, 28; 10:1, 14, 19.

CHRIST THE HEIR (CHAPTER 1)

Hebrews 1:2 proclaims that Christ, "by whom also he made the worlds [literally, the ages]" is heir of all things. He not only created all things (Jn 1:1-3), but He planned the very ages, including the time when He "purged our sin," and the coming time when it will be said, "Thy throne, O God, is for ever and ever: a sceptre of righteousness is the sceptre of thy kingdom" (Heb 1:8). He has been identified by God the Father as His Son (1:5) and anointed by God the Holy Spirit for this ministry (Heb 1:9; Mt 3:16). The angels of God are His ministers. They are to worship Him and minister unto those who shall be heirs of salvation (Heb 1:6-7, 14).

WARNING—MISSED BLESSINGS (CHAPTER 2)

"Therefore we ought to give the more earnest heed to the things which we have heard, lest at any time we should let them slip" (Heb 2:1). This was the first of a series of warnings given by the writer of Hebrews. The picture in this verse can be compared to someone drifting down a stream in a boat without oars. They are warned that they should not drift on by these things. (The literal idea is that *they* are drifting rather than the promises.)

As an example, he points to the children of Israel in the wilderness. The Mosaic covenant, given through the instrumentality of angels, brought a judgment for its transgression and disobedience. The adult generation that came out of Egypt perished, with the exception of Joshua and Caleb, so they did not enter the land nor into the ministry as a kingdom of priests. If this was true under the old covenant, how can the people of this age escape the same judgment if they neglect the "so great salvation" promised by Christ in the age to come?

SO GREAT SALVATION

The writer of Hebrews warns against neglecting this "so great salvation" (Heb 2:3). The word *salvation* is the great and inclusive word of the Scripture, as C. I. Scofield says in his reference Bible.[1] It includes all Christ's work in undoing the works of the devil (1 Jn 3:8), this includes the lifting of the curse upon creation, and the glorious future that He has planned for His own. While salvation is a present possession of believers, there is a future aspect spoken of in the Scriptures. See Romans 13:11; 1 Peter 1:5; Hebrews 9:28, and 2:3-5, which relates this to the coming kingdom of Christ.

THE WORLD IN SUBJECTION

In the beginning God created man in His own image and put him over all other created things. He said, "And let them have dominion over the fish of the sea, and over the fowl of the air, and over the cattle, and over all the earth, and over every creeping thing that creepeth upon the earth" (Gen 1:26). When Adam sinned, the curse of sin came upon the earth and upon Adam, breaking his dominion of the earth. "For the creature [creation] was made subject to vanity, not willingly, but by reason of him who hath subjected the same in hope" (Ro 8:20). But the hope of this creation is given in the next verse: "Because the creature [creation] itself also shall be delivered from the bondage of corruption into the glorious liberty of the children of God. For we know that the whole creation groaneth and travaileth in pain together until now" (8:21-22).

Where does man fit into this? Quoting the psalmist, the writer to the Hebrews says, "Thou madest him a little lower than the angels; thou crownedst him with glory and honour, and didst set him over the works of thy hands: thou hast put all things in subjection under his feet. For in that he put all in subjection under him, he left nothing that is not put under him. But now we see not yet all things put under him" (2:7-8). Man does not have complete dominion over the earth at the present time, but he will under Christ's leadership. It is through His death upon the cross that He will lead "many sons unto glory" (Heb 2:10) and destroy the devil and all his works (Heb 2:14; 1 Jn 3:8). Christ will recover all that has been lost through sin. In order to do this "he took on him the seed of Abraham" (Heb 2:16; cf. Gal 3:16). Christ Himself becomes the one who fulfills the covenant promises made unto Abraham. He is the *Promiser* and the *promise*.

THE HEAVENLY CALLING (CHAPTER 3)

Christians have a heavenly calling. They are called as kings and priests unto God (Rev 1:6), Jesus Christ Himself being the High Priest (Heb 3:1; 10:21) and King of kings (Rev 19:16).

CHRIST'S HOUSE

In the Davidic covenant, God promised David, "And thine house and thy kingdom shall be established for ever before thee: thy throne shall be established for ever" (2 Sa 7:16). The use of the word *house* here refers to a ruling family. Christ is superior to Moses because Moses was only a servant in God's house. God called the children of Israel out to be His own ruling nation: "And ye shall be unto me a kingdom of priests, and an holy nation" (Ex 19:6). Christ, as a greater Son of David, has His own house or ruling family. We have the legal right to reign with Him because we are united to Him by faith (Gal 3:14; Ro 8:17). "But Christ as a son over his own house; whose house are we, if we hold fast the confidence and the rejoicing of the hope firm unto the end" (Heb 3:6). Note that this verse gives a qualification for those who would participate in Christ's reign as a member of His house.

This high calling as priests and kings unto God can be forfeited, and some people confuse these forfeited ministries with salvation. But salvation depends upon the finished work of Christ and is an eternal redemption (Heb 9:12), while a Christian's faithfulness or lack of faithfulness will determine his rewards and ministry in the future ages (1 Co 3:11-15). Hebrews 3 compares the wilderness experience of the Israelites with the promises of serving with Christ. The children of Israel were saved in Egypt by their faith, as shown in placing the blood of the Passover lamb. Even though they saw God's miracles, the plagues, the destruction of the armies of Pharaoh, ate of the manna that He provided, and drank of the water from the rock, they still hardened their hearts. God taught them about Himself through the law, the priesthood, the tabernacle, the offerings, and the feasts—but to no avail. "Wherefore I was grieved with that generation, and said, They do alway err in their heart; and they have not known my ways" (3:10). God's judgment was: "So I sware in my wrath, They shall not enter into my rest" (3:11).

REST (CHAPTER 4)

Canaan foreshadowed a future rest, but what is this rest? It is not heaven. It does not refer, primarily, to the deeper Christian life because such a life was a prerequisite for entrance into the land.

The word *rest* used in Hebrews 3:11, 18 refers to a rest in the land as described in Deuteronomy 12:9-10: "For ye are not as yet come to the rest and to the inheritance which the LORD your God giveth you. But when ye go over Jordan, and dwell in the land which the LORD your God giveth you to inherit, and when he giveth you rest from all your enemies round about, so that ye dwell in safety." Note that in this rest there was safety from all their enemies. Rest was mentioned again as God gave the Davidic covenant (2 Sa 7:11). This rest foreshadows the glorious rest prophesied by Isaiah: "And in that day there shall be a root of Jesse, which shall stand for an ensign of the people; to it shall the Gentiles seek: and his rest shall be glorious" (11:10).

The Israelites under Joshua never really entered into that rest. (The word translated "Jesus" in Heb 4:8 should be "Joshua." It is the Greek translation of the Hebrew name Joshua. The context shows it refers to Joshua the leader of Israel.)

Some four hundred years after Joshua led the Israelites into the land, David prophesied about a coming rest that had its origin before the foundation of the world (Heb 4:3). In Hebrews 4:9 he is quoted, "There remaineth therefore a rest to the people of God." The exhortation that follows says, "Let us labour [be eager, diligent] therefore to enter into that rest, lest any man fall after the same example of unbelief" (4:11). The word translated "unbelief" in this verse means "unpersuaded" or "disobedient."

The Lord is seeking those to share in His reign who will trust Him and "know his ways," and those who are hardened by the deceitfulness of sin and unbelief are disqualified. He desires a joyful unwavering confidence in Himself (3:6, 14), by which we become partakers of this heavenly calling and members of His ruling house (3:1, 6, 14).

Remember, we are not members of the body of Christ because we hold something fast to the end. This is not a condition of salvation; we are saved by grace through faith. Eternal life is a gift given to those who receive Jesus Christ as their personal Saviour. Nothing can separate us from the love of God which is in Jesus Christ (Ro 8:35-39).

While all Christians have eternal life through Christ, all will not reign with Him: "If we suffer, we shall also reign with him: if we deny him, he also will deny us" (2 Ti 2:12). Romans 8:17 continues the same theme: "Joint-heirs with Christ; if so be that we suffer with him, that we may be also glorified together."

The unbelief of Israel in the wilderness was failure to believe God's promises, especially as they applied to the Canaan rest. God does not demand perfection or sinlessness, but the proper attitude of heart. A provision for discipline and training for the child of God, to qualify him for this inheritance, is explained in Hebrews 12.

IF THEY SHALL FALL AWAY (CHAPTERS 5–6)

Through the ages Hebrews 6 has been a battleground for commentators, some of whom have used it as proof that a Christian can lose his salvation. Their opponents quickly point out that if by sin you can lose your salvation, then Hebrews 6:4-6 would teach that it is impossible ever to regain it. But most people who teach that salvation can be lost by sin also teach that it can be restored unto them again by repentance.

Others teach that this passage is used to distinguish between real believers and mere professors of faith. This distinction is pointed out in other passages of Scripture (e.g., Ja 2) but does not seem to be the purpose here.

In Hebrews 5:12-14 the writer is concerned about Christians who have not grown spiritually because they have not applied the Word of God, which they know, to their lives. After warning and exhorting, he says, "And we desire that every one of you do shew the same diligence to the full assurance of hope unto the end" (6:11). This is the same type of exhortation given earlier in the book, where he promised them that they were members of Christ's ruling house "if we hold fast the confidence and the rejoicing of the hope firm unto the end" (3:6). He promised that believers were partakers or joint-participators with Christ "if we hold the beginning of our confidence stedfast unto the end" (3:14), and exhorted them to labor to enter into that Canaan rest "lest any man fall after the same example of unbelief" (4:11). Now in 6:12 he says, "That ye be not slothful, but followers of them who through faith and patience inherit the promises." Abraham is then cited as one who received the promise by faith (6:13-15). This particular promise was Isaac, the seed promised to Abraham. Chapter 11 gives many other examples of those who exercised faith.

FIVE BLESSINGS

A warning is given to the babes mentioned in 5:11-14, who have received five blessings but have not, by reason of use, had their senses exercised thereby:

1. They were once enlightened.
2. They tasted of the heavenly gift.
3. They were made partakers of the Holy Ghost.
4. They tasted the good Word of God.
5. They tasted the powers of the world (age) to come.

The word "tasted" used here is the same word used in 2:9 where it says Jesus tasted death for every man. These benefits are really a paraphrase or a commentary upon the benefits of the new covenant. The warning given is similar to that given in chapter 4 concerning the lack of faith of the children of Israel in the wilderness. After seeing all His miracles and provision in bringing them out of Egypt, they refused to believe that God could take them into the promised land. In chapter 6 the babes still need the milk of the Word because they have never grown spiritually. When they fail to trust Him and doubt His promises concerning their present life and future ministry, "they crucify to themselves the Son of God afresh, and put him to an open shame" (6:6). They are saying by their actions that He is an imposter, one who cannot be trusted, even as their fathers had said that Jesus was an imposter and not the true Messiah.

Using an illustration from nature, the writer compares their reaction to God's grace to rain falling upon the earth. Some herbs are fruitful and profitable, while others bear only thorns and briers and are rejected. But a word of encouragement is given: "But, beloved, we are persuaded better things of you, and things that accompany salvation, though we thus speak. For God is not unrighteous to forget your work and labour of love, which ye have shewed toward his name, in that ye have ministered to the saints, and do minister" (6:9-10). He is not questioning their salvation, but encouraging them to be diligent not slothful and bring forth fruit unto the very end that they might inherit the promises—the promises of reigning with Christ in His kingdom (6:11-12).

FAITH IN COMING THINGS (CHAPTER 11)

"Now faith is the substance of things hoped for, the evidence of things not seen" (11:1). This chapter has often been called "Heroes of Faith." In a paraphrase of verse 1, their "faith gave substance to coming things." R. E. Neighbour has drawn up an interesting parallel of the Old Testament saints mentioned:

> Abel—the faith that saw the blood shed on Calvary by our Saviour.
> Enoch—the faith that saw the coming of the Lord.
> Noah—the faith that saw the Great Tribulation.
> Abraham—the faith that saw the New Jerusalem.
> Sarah—the faith of a begetting of an innumerable abiding nation.
> Abraham (twice mentioned)—the faith of the coming resurrection.
> Isaac and Jacob—the faith of Israel's future inheritance.
> Moses—the faith that saw a day of rewards for the saints.
> Rahab—the faith that saw the crumbling thrones of nations—the Gentiles.
> A large number of saints who saw the better resurrection.[2]

Two classes of heroes are cited in this chapter: those victorious over their trials through faith (vv. 33-35), and those who were victors but not victorious (vv. 35-39).

THE TRAINING OF SONS (CHAPTER 12)

As chapter 12 opens, the training of a son is compared to a race, Jesus Christ being the example. The proof of the Lord's love is that He will chasten or discipline every son whom He receives (v. 6) so He can triumphantly lead these "sons unto glory" (2:10). Anyone who does not receive the training and discipline of the Lord is not a true son but an illegitimate one (12:8). The Lord's disciplining is not judicial but "for our profit, that we might be partakers of his holiness" (12:10). And even though it may not be a happy experience, it "yieldeth the peaceable fruit of righteousness unto them which are exercised thereby" (12:11).

WRONG ATTITUDES

While God's discipline is meant for training purposes, four improper attitudes are given: (1) despising the chastening or rebelling against what God is trying to do (12:5); (2) fainting—like a child crying because of his discipline but not being sorry for his errors (v. 5); (3) bitterness—resenting God's correction and the lack of freedom to have your own way (v. 15); and (4) despising the birthright—placing no value upon this right to rule.

Those who fail to respond to the training of the Lord are compared to Esau: "Lest there by any fornicator, or profane person, as Esau, who for one morsel of meat sold his birthright" (12:16). Esau later changed his mind but it was too late: "For ye know how that afterward, when he would have inherited the blessing, he was rejected: for he found no place of repentance, though he sought it carefully with tears" (v. 17). This should be a warning to Christians today that they cannot ignore or rebel against the Lord's training and then at the end of their life repent and expect to receive a place of honor in the kingdom.

Israel repented after first heeding the message of the ten spies and desired to go into the land, but God did not permit them. If this was true under the old covenant, think how much more important it is under the new covenant for those who are called to the heavenly Jerusalem. "Wherefore we receiving a kingdom which cannot be moved, let us have grace, whereby we may serve God acceptably with reverence and godly fear" (12:28).

SUMMARY

1. Christ is the Heir of the kingdom.
2. Promised blessings can be missed.
3. Christians have a heavenly calling in the ruling house of Christ.
4. The rest promised by Christ will be in His kingdom.

5. Believers need to grow in the faith by exercising or putting to use the things they have learned from God's Word.

6. The life of faith is the only one that will please God.

7. God disciplines and trains all His true sons.

8. Those who fail to respond to the Lord's training will suffer loss of rewards and/or positions of ministry.

14

The Kingdom in the Epistles and the Revelation

ALTHOUGH THE EPISTLES contain "church truths," the theme of the kingdom can be traced through them also, giving them unity. Peter lists five things that the epistles have in common:

> "They all agree (1) in expressing faith and hope in the covenants and prophecies; (2) in Jesus as the Messiah; (3) in a complete fulfillment of both covenant and prophecy at the Second Advent; (4) in locating the covenanted Messianic Kingdom in the future Second Coming of Jesus; and (5) in urging all to accept Jesus as the promised Messiah, so that they may become qualified to enter into His coming Kingdom."[1]

THE KINGDOM IN ROMANS

The introduction to Romans states that Jesus was "made [out] of the seed of David according to the flesh" (1:3), a fulfillment of the Davidic covenant. Chapters 1–3 state that salvation is obtained by faith, that the gospel is the power of God unto salvation, and that it is needed by both Jew and Gentile, "for all have sinned."

In chapter 4, justification by faith is explained, and Abraham and David are shown to be examples of those who were justified by faith apart from works or ordinances. Abraham is called the "heir of the world" (v. 13). By faith we become his children and heirs with him: "Therefore it is of faith, that it might be by grace; to the end the promise might be sure to all the seed; not to that only which is of the law, but to that also which is of the faith of Abraham; who is the father of us all" (v. 16). Because we are justified and have peace with God through our Lord Jesus Christ, we "rejoice in hope of the glory of God" (5:2), which will be revealed in Christ's kingdom. Because of the eternal life and grace which we have in Christ, we shall "reign in life" by Him (5:17).

Chapters 6 and 7 show that because we have been united with Christ we should not live in sin nor serve sin but should walk in a newness of life. Chapter 8 declares us to be "joint-heirs with Christ" (v. 17), looking forward to a time when believers will be glorified with Him and the curse on creation is to be lifted "because the creature [creation] itself also shall be delivered from the bondage of corruption into the glorious liberty of the children of God. For we know that the whole creation groaneth and travaileth in pain together until now" (vv. 21-22).

In chapter 9 Paul shows the sevenfold privilege of Israel "who are Israelites; to whom pertaineth the adoption, and the glory, and the covenants, and the giving of the law, and the service of God, and the promises; whose are the fathers, and of whom as concerning the flesh Christ came, who is over all, God blessed for ever. Amen" (vv. 4-5). He also speaks of the calling out of Gentiles "even us, whom he hath called, not of the Jews only, but also of the Gentiles" (v. 24). He argues that those who are heirs with Jesus Christ are "children of the promise" (vv. 8, 26). This includes both Jew and Gentile.

Chapters 10 and 11 answer the question of who shall be saved and explain "that if thou shalt confess with thy mouth the Lord Jesus, and shalt believe in thine heart that God hath raised him from the dead, thou shalt be saved" (10:9). The author also explains about the judicial blindness that has come upon Israel and about the calling out and the grafting in of the Gentiles into the root. The root appears to be Christ (15:12). This will continue "until the fulness of the Gentiles be come in" (11:25). The final restoration of national Israel is also promised.

Chapters 12–16 give practical directions for Christian living, with exhortations about Christ's second coming and His fulfillment of the promises made to the fathers. "And again, Esaias saith, There shall be a root of Jesse, and he that shall rise to reign over the Gentiles; in him shall the Gentiles trust" (15:12). The idea of this section is to serve Him now in holiness but with an expectant heart looking for His return.

In a discussion about doubtful things and the eating of meat, Paul said, "For the kingdom of God is not meat and drink; but righteousness, and peace, and joy in the Holy Ghost" (14:17). Our rewards in the kingdom will not be based upon a legalistic approach concerning meat and drink, but by righteousness. Jesus said, "But seek ye first the kingdom of God, and his righteousness; and all these things shall be added unto you" (Mt 6:33). The righteousness, holiness, and peace of the Spirit-filled life will bring reward.

THE KINGDOM IN THE CORINTHIAN EPISTLES

First Corinthians tells us that when Christ returns we will be rewarded for faithful service (3:11-15). Consequently we should be faithful stewards (4:2-5).

Some in the Corinthian church were acting proud and puffed up and Paul said, "Now ye are full, now ye are rich, ye have reigned as kings without us: and I would to God ye did reign, that we also might reign with you" (4:8). They were acting as if they were already ruling as kings, and Paul wistfully was looking forward to that day when the saints would be reigning with Christ.

Paul continues his exhortation to the proud in 4:18-19 and then says, "For the kingdom of God is not in word, but in power" (v. 20). They could pretend that they were important, but the real test was whether they really had the power, and he asked them whether they would rather have him come with a rod and discipline them to show his power or come in love.

Because of the Christians' future position as judges in the kingdom, the Corinthians were told not to go before heathen judges to settle their differences: "Do ye not know that the saints shall judge the world? And if the world shall be judged by you, are ye unworthy to judge the smallest matters? Know ye not that we shall judge angels? How much more things that pertain to this life?" (6:2-3).

Some, because of their conduct, will prove themselves unfaithful and unfit and will not inherit a place of ministry in the kingdom: "Know ye not that the unrighteous shall not inherit the kingdom of God? Be not deceived: neither fornicators, nor idolaters, nor adulterers, nor effeminate, nor abusers of themselves with mankind, nor thieves, nor covetous, nor drunkards, nor revilers, nor extortioners, shall inherit the kingdom of God" (6:9-10). This does not refer to eternal life but to any place of responsibility in Christ's kingdom. He is speaking of a habitual way of life rather than individual acts of sin (see Gal 5:21).

In chapter 15, the great resurrection chapter, Paul points out that those who rule with Christ will be in their resurrection bodies: "Now this I say, brethren, that flesh and blood cannot inherit the kingdom of God; neither doth corruption inherit incorruption" (v. 50).

Peters explains:

> It is expressly asserted that "*flesh and blood cannot inherit the Kingdom of God.*" *To inherit* a Kingdom, if it has any propriety of meaning, undoubtedly denotes *the reception of kingly authority or rulership* in the Kingdom—for thus it is also explained by parallel passages which follow. But this Kingdom—this rulership with Jesus—cannot be inherited by mortal men, it requiring immortal beings who resemble the mighty Theocratic King; for the heirship with Jesus, the identity of associated rule, the unspeakable honor, etc., which can only safely be confided to persons previously prepared for it; the duration, the perfection, design, and results of the reign—*all demand* this previous resurrection and glorification.[2]

The Davidic covenant demanded an immortal Ruler, one not subject to death, because He was to rule forever. The same is true of His joint-heirs. The church, while in flesh and blood, only awaits the promises. Believers look forward with anticipation to the time that they will possess the kingdom according to promise.

Looking to the far distant future when the kingdom of God will assume its eternal character after all of Christ's enemies and even death itself have been destroyed, Paul says, "Then cometh the end, when he shall have delivered up the kingdom to God, even the Father; when he shall have put down all rule and all authority and power" (v. 24). This is not the end of the kingdom, but a unity of rule so that "God may be all in all" (v. 28).

Second Corinthians carries the same theme forward in appealing to our holiness, faithfulness and love as we wait the coming of the Lord. Because, "therefore if any man be in Christ, he is a new creature [creation]: old things are passed away; behold, all things are become new" (5:17).

THE KINGDOM IN GALATIANS

The gospel of Christ is summarized in Galatians 1:4, "Who gave himself for our sins, that he might deliver us from this present evil world, according to the will of God and our Father." He prepares us for the kingdom and the eternal ages that follow by giving us His very own life (2:20). Paul again cites Abraham as one who "believed God, and it was accounted to him for righteousness" (3:6). Then he makes a point of saying, "Know ye therefore that they which are of faith, the same are the children of Abraham. And the scripture, foreseeing that God would justify the heathen [Gentiles] through faith, preached before the gospel unto Abraham, saying, In thee shall all nations be blessed. So then they which be of faith are blessed with faithful Abraham" (3:7-9). Christ has redeemed us from the curse of the law "that the blessing of Abraham might come on the Gentiles through Jesus Christ; that we might receive the promise of the Spirit through faith" (3:14). Christ is "the seed" of Abraham, and because of our union with Him, we are joint-heirs with Him. "For ye are all the children [sons] of God by faith in Christ Jesus. And if ye be Christ's, then are ye Abraham's seed, and heirs according to the promise" (3:26, 29).

In chapter 5 the works of the flesh are contrasted with the walk in the Spirit and, after listing a long list of sins, Paul again warns "that they which do [practice, continual action in the Greek] such things shall not inherit the kingdom of God" (v. 21).

The important thing is not to try to obtain righteousness by keeping ordinances but to be "in Christ" and a "new creature" (6:15).

THE KINGDOM IN EPHESIANS

The key thought in the book of Ephesians is "in Christ." The plan of God reveals that believers, because of their position in Christ, are to be adopted or placed as sons with full rights and privileges (1:5). "That in the dispensation of the fulness of times he might gather together in one all things in Christ, both which are in heaven, and which are on earth; even in him" (1:10). It is in Christ that we have obtained an inheritance. We have already received the earnest or down payment of our inheritance, the Holy Spirit (1:11, 14). We are assured of this inheritance upon the redemption of the body (Eph 1:14; Ro 8:23). In Ephesians 1:18 he exhorts them to understand about this high calling. Christ has been exalted above all, "not only in this world [age], but also in that which is to come" (1:21).

In chapter 2 Paul gives a flashback into the spiritual history of the Ephesians and then points out that they are to be "trophies of grace" in the ages to come so that "he might shew the exceeding riches of his grace in his kindness toward us through Christ Jesus" (v. 7).

He contrasts the Ephesians' position in the past and in the future: "That at that time ye were without Christ, being aliens from the commonwealth of Israel, and strangers from the covenants of promise, having no hope, and without God in the world: but now in Christ Jesus ye who sometimes were far off are made nigh by the blood of Christ" (vv. 12-13). He has taken from the Jews and from the Gentiles, and He is going "to make in himself of twain one new man . . . that he might reconcile both unto God in one body by the cross" (vv. 15-16).

In this new body they now have a new relationship: "Now therefore ye are no more strangers and foreigners, but fellowcitizens with the saints, and of the household of God" (v. 19). In their new position "in Christ" they come under the covenant promises as taught in Galatians 3:14. It is now revealed "that the Gentiles should be fellowheirs, and of the same body, and partakers of his promise in Christ by the gospel" (Eph 3:6). This is not talking about all Gentiles but only those of this age who are "in Christ." Paul closes chapter 3 with a little prayer in which he mentions the glory of Christ throughout the ages to come.

Chapters 4–6 give many practical exhortations in the light of the high calling in Christ Jesus. In 4:1 Paul exhorts them "that ye walk worthy of the vocation wherewith ye are called." Cautioning them not to grieve the Holy Spirit by sinning, for they are sealed by Him unto the day of redemption (4:30), he exhorts them to walk as followers of God and to live holy lives. Then he warns them, "For this ye know that no whoremonger, nor unclean person, nor covetous man, who is an idolater, hath any inheritance in the kingdom of Christ and of God" (5:5). This is practically the same exhortation given in 1 Corinthians 6:10 and Galatians 5:21. People who live a life of open, habitual sin will forfeit their inheritance in the kingdom of God. Remember, this is not talking about salvation, but the privilege in having a part in the reign of Christ's kingdom.

THE KINGDOM IN PHILIPPIANS

A prominent subject in Philippians is the coming day of Jesus Christ (1:6, 10; 2:16; 3:20; 4:5). When Christ returns to set up His kingdom, His glory will be revealed—a contrast to His first coming in humility. At the second coming He will be exalted "that at the name of Jesus every knee should [shall] bow, of things in heaven, and things in earth, and things under the earth" (2:10). Paul, who was in prison at the time he wrote this, looked forward to the time of resurrection and the coming of the Lord "who shall change our vile body, that it may be fashioned like unto his glorious body, according to the working whereby he is able even to subdue all things unto himself" (3:21). We should remember our "high calling of God in Christ Jesus" (3:14) and that "our conversation [citizenship] is in heaven" (3:20). There are many activities in which a Christian can become involved, some profitable and some not. Rewards will be given when Christ returns for His own. Paul said of the Philippian believers, "Therefore, my brethren dearly beloved and longed for, my joy and crown" (4:1). Several crowns are mentioned in Scripture, and Paul considered these believers as his crown.

THE KINGDOM IN COLOSSIANS

In Colossians, Paul gives thanks to the Father who has "made us meet to be partakers of the inheritance of the saints in light: who hath delivered us from the power of darkness, and hath translated us into the kingdom of his dear Son" (1:12-13). Because of our position in Christ, we are, *positionally*, already in the kingdom of Christ. For as Philippians says, "our citizenship" is in heaven with Him (3:20, margin). This positional truth is expressed of believers *now* being in Christ in heavenly places (Eph 2:6).

First John 3:8 says that Jesus came to destroy or undo the work of the devil. Sin has brought enmity between man and God. Colossians 1:20 says, "And, having made peace through the blood of his cross, by him to reconcile all things unto himself; by him, I say, whether they be things in earth, or things in heaven." When Christ returns we will be sharing in His glory: "When Christ, who is our life, shall appear, then shall ye also appear with him in glory" (3:4). The Colossians are exhorted to a holy and fruitful life because "knowing that of the Lord ye shall receive the reward of the inheritance: for ye serve the Lord Christ" (3:24). God will reward His faithful, but "he that doeth wrong shall receive for the wrong which he hath done: and there is no respect of persons" (3:25).

There are two ways in which the unfaithful will receive the reward of their unfaithfulness: first, in this life through the governmental principle of reaping what they sow (Gal 6:7); second, they will suffer future loss, as in the parable of the pounds (Lk 19:11-26). In Colossians 4:10-11 Paul mentions his companions while in prison and describes them as "these only are my fellowworkers unto the kingdom of God."

THE KINGDOM IN THE THESSALONIAN EPISTLES

The predominant theme in the Thessalonian letters is the return of the Lord and the events accompanying it. The believers are charged "that ye would walk worthy of God, who hath called you unto his kingdom and glory" (1 Th 2:12). At His coming there will be crowns, or rewards, given (2:19), the dead in Christ will be resurrected, and living believers will be caught up to meet the Lord in the air (4:14-17). The day of the Lord, as prophesied in the Old Testament, is coming upon the unbelieving world unexpectedly (5:2-3). But believers are promised that they are not appointed unto wrath (1:10; 2:16; 5:9).

While the first epistle emphasizes the Lord's coming for His church, the second epistle tells more about His coming in power and glory to put down His enemies and establish His kingdom. Paul exhorts them that they "may be counted worthy of the kingdom of God" (2 Th 1:5, 11). He corrects a misunderstanding, for some thought that the day of the Lord had already come. That day will not come until three things happen: (1) a falling away or apostasy from the faith; (2) the man of sin is revealed; (3) the restraining influence on evil is removed (2:3, 6-7).

Meanwhile he says, "And the Lord direct your hearts into the love of God, and into the patient waiting for Christ" (3:5).

THE KINGDOM IN THE PASTORAL EPISTLES

In 1 Timothy Paul refers to Jesus as the King eternal (1:16-17). After many personal instructions, he ends his first epistle with the exhortation, "that thou keep this commandment without spot, unrebukeable, until the appearing of our Lord Jesus Christ: which in his times he shall shew, who is the blessed and only Potentate, the King of kings, and Lord of lords" (6:14-15).

Second Timothy is the last letter Paul wrote before his death, and the theme of the kingdom appears many times throughout this short epistle. "If we suffer, we shall also reign with him: if we deny him, he also will deny us" (2:12). This verse, in its context, is obviously not talking about believers losing their salvation, but parallels Romans 8:17 where suffering *for* Christ qualifies believers as joint-heirs *with* Christ. It gives one the privilege of reigning with Him (cf. Ac 14:22).

Christians, both those who have died and those who are living at His return, will be called before the judgment seat of Christ, where they will be rewarded (2 Ti 4:1, 8). "I charge thee therefore before God, and the Lord Jesus Christ, who shall judge the quick and the dead at his appearing and his kingdom" (4:1). At that time rewards will be given: "Henceforth there is laid up for me a crown of righteousness, which the Lord, the righteous judge, shall give me at that day: and not to me only, but unto all them also that love his appearing" (4:8). Even though Paul faced death, he faced it with confidence: "And the Lord shall deliver me from every evil work, and will preserve me unto his heavenly kingdom: to whom be glory for ever and ever. Amen" (4:18).

In writing to Titus, he reminds him that the grace of God has not only brought salvation, but also is teaching or training Christians how to live in this present world (2:11-12), so that they will be prepared for the next age: "Looking for that blessed hope, and the glorious appearing of the great God and our Saviour Jesus Christ" (v. 13).

After speaking of the mercy of God in saving and regenerating the believer, he refers to the purpose of God, "that being justified by his grace, we should be made heirs according to the hope of eternal life" (3:7).

The book of Philemon has no direct reference to the kingdom.

THE KINGDOM IN JAMES

James begins his epistle by explaining that the purpose of trial or temptation is to proof-test the Christian's faith in order to build patient endurance in the believer and bring him to maturity. The victorious will be rewarded (1:12). In chapter 2 he warns them not to be respecters of persons, pointing out that it is those who are rich in faith who are the heirs of the kingdom (v. 5). In the last chapter he asks them to "be patient therefore, brethren, unto the coming of the Lord" (5:7).

THE KINGDOM IN 1 PETER

Christ promised Peter that he would rule with Him over one of the twelve tribes of Israel (Mt 19:28). Realizing the importance of the kingdom in the plan of God, Peter calls believers in this age "pilgrims," or "strangers," addressing his epistle to the "strangers scattered," which can be literally translated, "chosen pilgrims sown-as-seeds." God has a plan for this age in which believers are to carry the gospel to every creature. He has sown them as seeds throughout the world, and in the process He is also training them for the age to come.

Peter swings back and forth between the two views: present responsibilities and conduct, and future reward. He encourages them by reminding them of "an inheritance incorruptible, and undefiled, and that fadeth not away, reserved in heaven for you" (1:4). While salvation is a present possession of believers, yet there is a future aspect which will be received when all things are restored under the reign of Christ (1:5, 9-11). Believers have a very exalted position: "But ye are a chosen generation, a royal priesthood, an holy nation, a peculiar people; that ye should shew forth the praises of him who hath called you out of darkness into his marvellous light" (2:9; cf. Ex 19:5-6). The new position is in marked contrast with the old relationship to God before salvation (1 Pe 2:10; Eph 2:12, 19). Because they are strangers and pilgrims, Peter says for them to "abstain from fleshly lusts, which war against the soul" (2:11). Throughout the book, Peter often mentions "suffering and glory." Christ first suffered, and then He was glorified by the Father. Believers are promised that if they are partakers of Christ's suffering, then they will also share His glory (4:13; 5:1), and that He will reward His faithful (5:4).

THE KINGDOM IN 2 PETER

Peter tells believers to give diligence to build good qualities in their lives because, if they do, "an entrance shall be ministered unto you abundantly into the everlasting kingdom of our Lord and Saviour Jesus Christ" (2 Pe 1:11). Peter is very confident that the kingdom of the Lord will be glorious, because he, with James and John, was given a preview of the majesty and glory of the Lord when they saw Him on the mount of transfiguration (1:16-18). In the last days many wicked and false teachers will arise, but their judgment is sure. The day of the Lord will bring judgment upon the wicked and the ungodly, and the very ends of earth will see the fire of God's judgment (3:7, 10, 12). But he looks beyond this to a future time: "Nevertheless we, according to his promise, look for new heavens and a new earth, wherein dwelleth righteousness" (3:13). The exact time that these fires of judgment occur is studied in a later chapter.

THE KINGDOM IN THE EPISTLES OF JOHN

John, who was concerned that believers know how to walk in fellowship with God, also warned of the Antichrist who will come in the last times (1 Jn 2:18, 22; 4:3). He looked forward to the coming of the Lord, which he called a purifying hope (3:2-3). He explains that Christ's ministry was for this purpose: "The Son of God was manifested, that he might destroy [undo or put to naught] the works of the devil" (3:8).

THE KINGDOM IN JUDE

The word *kingdom* is not used in the book of Jude, but he does speak of the Lord's return with "ten thousands of his saints" (v. 14). He prophesies that ungodly mockers will come in the last times (v. 18), and when Christ comes He will judge the ungodly just as surely as God judged Sodom and Gomorrah. Jude closes with a little benediction: "To the only wise God our Saviour, be glory and majesty, dominion and power, both now and ever. Amen" (v. 25). This will be fulfilled in Christ's kingdom.

THE KINGDOM IN THE REVELATION

The book of Revelation is a closed book to most Christians. They do not understand it for several reasons, but two things will help them. First, the kingdom must be given its proper place. McClain says, "The last book of the Bible is preeminently *the book of the kingdom of God* in conflict with, and victory over, the kingdoms of this world. With this general viewpoint most commentators would agree, regardless of differences over principles and details of interpretation."[3] He lists the many occurrences of words connected with the kingdom: throne, kingdom, crown, reign, power, rule and judge. The majority of these words are used in connection with the kingdom of God.

The second aid is to study it in close connection with the other prophetic passages in the Bible, especially the Old Testament. The book of Daniel is very important.

In his introduction, John says that God has revealed to him things that are going to come to pass. He identifies Jesus Christ as the "prince of the kings of the earth. Unto him that loved us, and washed us from our sins in his own blood, and hath made us kings and priests unto God and his Father; to him be glory and dominion for ever and ever. Amen" (1:5-6).

The threefold division of the book is given in 1:19, "Write the things which thou hast seen, and the things which are, and the things which shall be hereafter." Chapters 2 and 3 are messages to seven churches in Asia Minor, while chapters 4—19 describe the events that will take place immediately before the establishment of the kingdom. John said, "I was in the Spirit on the Lord's day" (1:10), which can be translated, and probably should be rendered "I was in the Spirit in the Day of the Lord."

"The day of the Lord" is an Old Testament term. Chapter 20 tells briefly of the first thousand years of Christ's reign in His kingdom, and chapters 21 and 22 describe the new heavens and the new earth and the New Jerusalem.

THE MESSAGES TO THE CHURCHES

Christ's message to the churches revolved around two main ideas: present conduct and future rewards. It is difficult to know exactly what these rewards mean: "eat of the tree of life," "not be hurt by the second death," "eat of the hidden manna," "given a white stone with a new name," "clothed in white raiment," "be made a pillar in the temple of God," and a new relationship with God in the new Jerusalem. However, they do speak of fellowship and blessing because of our relationship with Christ and by virtue of the fact that we are overcomers (2:7, 11, 17; 3:5, 12). Two promises are directly related to the kingdom of Christ: "And he that overcometh, and keepeth my works unto the end, to him will I give power [authority] over the nations: and he shall rule them with a rod of iron; as the vessels of a potter shall they be broken to shivers: even as I received of my Father" (2:26-27; cf. Ps 2:9). And again, "To him that overcometh will I grant to sit with me in my throne, even as I also overcame, and am set down with my Father in his throne" (3:21). Both these verses refer to sharing the rule of Christ. If all believers were overcomers, these exhortations would not make sense. The warnings and promises could be summarized, "Christian, it does make a difference what you are doing now. Faithfulness will be rewarded and appointments may be gained from this present life."

The remainder of the book is studied in more detail in later chapters.

SUMMARY

The epistles teach that

1. Jesus is the Messiah, the Saviour-King, Heir and promised seed of the covenants.

2. He will return to the earth
   —to judge His enemies
   —to establish His kingdom
   —to resurrect the righteous dead
   —to reward His followers

3. Entrance into the kingdom is obtained by receiving Jesus as the promised Messiah.

4. Positions in the kingdom and other rewards will be awarded to believers according to faithfulness of service.

15

Preliminary Events Before the Kingdom

SEVERAL IMPORTANT EVENTS must take place before Christ establishes His kingdom. He will come again the second time

1. *to receive His own.* This includes all living believers, or the church.

2. *to resurrect the dead believers.* First He will come for the dead "in Christ"; later on He will raise the Old Testament believers and the believers who have died during the tribulation.

3. *to judge.* Christians will be judged for rewards at the judgment seat of Christ. Living Gentiles and Jews will be judged at the close of the tribulation period, and tribulation martyrs and Old Testament saints probably will be judged at the beginning of the millennium.

4. *to restore the Davidic kingdom.* He will defeat all of His enemies and establish the kingdom according to promise.

After Christ comes back to meet the church in the air, and before His return to set up His kingdom, there will be a counterfeit kingdom set up by Satan and headed by a counterfeit Christ.

When the church is removed, the judgments described in the Old Testament as belonging to the day of the Lord will begin. In the New Testament this is called the great tribulation, during which there will be war, famine, disease, signs in nature, and special judgments of God poured out upon the earth. It will climax in the great Battle of Armageddon when the nations of the world under the Antichrist will be arrayed against God, and Jesus Himself will descend with the armies of heaven and destroy them.

THE SECOND COMING FOR HIS OWN

Jesus promised His disciples that He would return a second time: "In my Father's house are many mansions: if it were not so, I would have told you. I go to prepare a place for you. And if I go and prepare a place for you, I will come again, and receive you unto myself; that where I am, there ye may be also" (Jn 14:2-3). The manner of His coming for His own is explained in detail in Paul's writings: "Behold, I shew you a mys-

149

tery; We shall not all sleep, but we shall all be changed, in a moment, in the twinkling of an eye, at the last trump: for the trumpet shall sound, and the dead shall be raised incorruptible, and we shall be changed" (1 Co 15:51-52).

In 1 Thessalonians 4:17 Paul gives some additional details. Christ is not going to return all the way to earth; we are going to meet Him in the air. "Then we which are alive and remain shall be caught up together with them in the clouds, to meet the Lord in the air: and so shall we ever be with the Lord."

Students of prophecy often call this the rapture of the church. Charles Ryrie explains:

> Living believers will be changed and "caught up to be with the Lord." The word "caught up" means to "seize" or to "snatch," and this verb, in Latin, is the term from which we get the English word "rapture." Strictly speaking, the word *rapture* means the act of conveying a person from one place to another, and is properly used of the taking of living persons to heaven. Paul used it of his own experience of being caught up into the third heaven (II Cor. 12:4). However, we use the term, "rapture of the Church" loosely to include all that happens at Christ's coming, including not only the change in living Christians but also the resurrection of dead believers. The term "rapture" implies whatever change is necessary to fit mortal bodies for immortal existence in heaven. Though the method of this change is nowhere explained, Paul clearly believed that it is possible to have such a metamorphosis without experiencing the dissolution caused by death.[1]

Fig. 13. Comings of Christ

THE COMINGS OF CHRIST AND THE SEVENTIETH WEEK OF DANIEL

The relation of the advents of Christ are easy to understand if seen in relation to the seventieth week. In Figure 13, C1 (beside the star) stands for His birth at Bethlehem. C2a stands for the rapture of the church— when He meets them in the air. C2b stands for His second coming to establish His kingdom.

RAPTURE BEFORE THE TRIBULATION

The Bible promises, "For God hath not appointed us to wrath, but to obtain salvation by our Lord Jesus Christ. Who died for us, that, whether we wake or sleep, we should live together with him. Wherefore comfort yourselves together . . ." (1 Th 5:9-11).

It is again important to emphasize the fact that the tribulation or day of the Lord is the day of His wrath. This wrath of God sets the period apart from all other days and gives the tribulation its characteristics. "For the the great day of his wrath is come; and who shall be able to stand?" (Rev 6:17); "Behold, the day of the Lord cometh, cruel both with wrath and fierce anger" (Is 13:9); "That day is a day of wrath" (Zep 1:15).

Other verses emphasize that the church will not pass through this wrath of God: "Much more then, being now justified by his blood, we shall be saved from [the] wrath through him" (Ro 5:9); "From heaven . . . even Jesus, which delivered us from the wrath to come" (1 Th 1:10).

In the message to the church at Philadelphia, Jesus said, "Because thou has kept the word of my patience, I will also keep thee from the hour of temptation, which shall come upon all the world, to try them that dwell upon the earth" (Rev 3:10).

CONTRASTS BETWEEN THE TRANSLATION OR RAPTURE AND THE COMING TO ESTABLISH THE KINGDOM

Some people believe that there will be only one aspect of the Lord's return. John Walvoord shows an interesting contrast between these two aspects of the Lord's return:

These can be stated as (a) translation; (b) coming to establish His kingdom:

(a) Translation of all believers;	(b) no translation at all.
(a) Translated saints go to heaven	(b) translated saints return to the earth.
(a) Earth not judged;	(b) earth judged and righteousness established.
(a) Imminent;	(b) follows definite predicted signs including the tribulation.
(a) Not in the Old Testament;	(b) predicted often in the Old Testament.
(a) Believers only;	(b) affects all men.
(a) Before the day of wrath;	(b) concluding the day of wrath.
(a) No reference to Satan;	(b) Satan bound.

These contrasts should make it evident that the translation of the church is an event quite different in character and time from the return of the Lord to establish His kingdom, and confirms the conclusion that the translation takes place before the tribulation.[2]

CHRIST COMES TO RESURRECT BELIEVERS

Christ has conquered death (1 Co 15:54), so it has no claim over those whom He has redeemed. Believers of all ages have looked forward by faith to the promises of the age to come: "These all died in faith, not having received the promises, but having seen them afar off, and were persuaded of them, and embraced them, and confessed that they were strangers and pilgrims on the earth" (Heb 11:13). "And these all, having obtained a good report through faith, received not the promise: God having provided some better thing for us, that they without us should not be made perfect [complete]" (vv. 39-40).

THE ORDER OF RESURRECTION

Revelation 20 divides the resurrection into two parts: The first resurrection is of believers; the second resurrection is of the lost. First Corinthians 15 gives further details: "For as in Adam all die, even so in Christ shall all be made alive. But every man in his own order: Christ the firstfruits; afterward they that are Christ's at his coming. Then cometh the end, when he shall have delivered up the kingdom to God, even the Father; when he shall have put down all rule and all authority and power" (vv. 22-24).

The word "order" in this verse is a military word. Imagine a parade going by with each group of soldiers in its proper place. From this passage we can see there are three basic groups:

1. Christ the firstfruits
2. they that are Christ's
3. those at the end (the close of the thousand years), the lost

Other portions of Scripture expand the second group into three more divisions:

1. the dead in Christ (members of the church)
2. the tribulation saints
3. the Old Testament saints

In Figure 14, R1a stands for Christ the firstfruit; R1b stands for the dead in Christ; R1c stands for the tribulation and Old Testament saints; R2 stands for the unsaved dead of all ages.

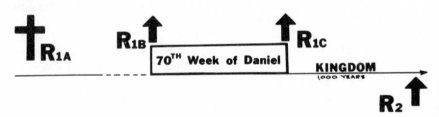

Fig. 14. Resurrections

DEAD IN CHRIST RESURRECTED

The first thing the Lord will do when He returns for His own (Fig. 14, R1b) will be to resurrect the "dead in Christ." At the time of death, the soul and spirit are separated from the body: "And it came to pass, that the beggar died, and was carried by the angels into Abraham's bosom: the rich man also died, and was buried; and in hell [hades] he lifted up his eyes, being in torments" (Lk 16:22-23). This verse shows that the lost soul goes immediately into hades, but for the Christian the Lord has prepared something else: "Therefore we are always confident, knowing that, whilst we are at home in the body, we are absent from the Lord: (For we walk by faith, not by sight:) We are confident, I say, and willing rather to be absent from the body, and to be present with the Lord" (2 Co 5:6). The Bible speaks of the *body* of the believer as sleeping (1 Co 15:51). It is the *body* that Christ is coming back to resurrect. When the Lord returns He will bring back the dead "in Christ" with Him. With a commanding shout the Lord will resurrect the members of His church who have died; then the living and the dead will be caught up together to meet the Lord in the air (1 Th 4:16-17).

TRIBULATION SAINTS RESURRECTED

The basic passage for the resurrection of the tribulation saints (Fig. 14, R2c) is in Revelation 20:

> And I saw thrones, and they sat upon them, and judgment was given unto them: and I saw the souls of them that were beheaded for the witness of Jesus, and for the word of God, and which had not worshipped the beast, neither his image, neither had received his mark upon their foreheads, or in their hands; and they lived and reigned with Christ a thousand years. But the rest of the dead lived not again until the thousand years were finished. This is the first resurrection. Blessed and holy is he that hath part in the first resurrection: on such the second death hath no power, but they shall be priests of God and of Christ, and shall reign with him a thousand years (vv. 4-6).

This resurrection takes place at the close of the tribulation period and the beginning of the millennium.

OLD TESTAMENT SAINTS RESURRECTED

At the completion of the seventieth week of Daniel or the great tribulation, the Old Testament saints (Fig. 14, R2c) will be raised:

> And at that time shall Michael stand up, the great prince which standeth for the children of thy people: and there shall be a time of trouble, such as never was since there was a nation even to that same time: and at that time thy people shall be delivered, every one that shall be found written in the book. And many of them that sleep in the dust of the

earth shall awake, some to everlasting life, and some to shame and everlasting contempt (Dan 12:1-2).

CHRIST RETURNS TO JUDGE

One reason Christ is going to return to the earth is to judge, "for the
Father judgeth no man, but hath committed all judgment unto the Son"
(Jn 5:22). Many people misunderstand what the Bible teaches about
judgment. As W. E. Blackstone says,

> We often hear post-millennialists use the expression "general judgment"
> thereby conveying the idea of some future day in which all mankind will
> simultaneously appear before God to be judged.
> The expression is not in the scriptures. Premillennialists believe that
> the judgment is general, *only* in the sense that all are judged—but *not all
> at the same time.*[3]

There is a universal belief in the world that man is accountable for the
things he does; this agrees with the Bible. Another common idea is that
everything a person has done will be examined; if he has done more good
things than bad, he will be saved. This idea is false and utterly contrary
to what the Scriptures teach, for salvation is a free gift received by those
who have put their faith in Jesus Christ: "For by grace are ye saved
through faith; and that not of yourselves: it is the gift of God: not of
works, lest any man should boast" (Eph 2:8-9). Because God is holy and
just He will judge all men, but He will not judge all alike because each
man or group of men will be judged on a proper and just basis. The saved
will be judged on a different basis from the lost. Believers will receive
rewards or loss of rewards according to their works (1 Co 3:14-15), while
the unsaved will be punished according to what they have done (Rev
20:12).

Fig. 15. Judgments

THE ORDER OF THE JUDGMENTS

Of the many judgments mentioned in Scripture, five are shown on the
chart in Figure 15. Others mentioned in Scripture include: self-judgment
of sin by believers, the great tribulation, the flood, and the ten plagues
in Egypt. J1 represents the sins of the believer, J2 represents the works
of the believer, J3 represents living Jews and Gentiles at the close of the

great tribulation, J4 represents the works of the Old Testament and tribulation saints, and J5 represents the unsaved dead of all ages. The five judgments will each be classified according to four different aspects: (1) time, (2) place, (3) subject, and (4) result.

THE THREEFOLD JUDGMENT OF A CHRISTIAN

Each believer will have a threefold judgment: as a sinner, as a son, and as a servant.

1. The believer's judgment as a *sinner* took place at the cross when Christ, as his substitute, paid the penalty for his sin (1 Pe 2:24).

2. As a *son* in the household of God, he is judged or disciplined in this life. Hebrews 12:8-11 teaches that God chastens all of His sons, but this is so that they will bring forth the peaceable fruit of righteousness or learn from their discipline. If the son judges his own sin and confesses it (1 Jn 1:9), then God will not have to judge him, "for if we would judge ourselves, we should not be judged. But when we are judged, we are chastened of the Lord, that we should not be condemned with the world" (1 Co 11:31-32). The purpose of this judgment is for training and is not judicial in character.

3. The works and conduct of a believer as a *servant* will be judged by Christ. This includes our motives (Ro 14:10; 15:1, 7), our ministry (1 Co 3:11-15), our use of our money (2 Co 8:9; 9:6). The result of this judgment is either rewards or loss of rewards.

THE SINS OF THE BELIEVER

The judgment (Fig. 14, J1) of the believer's sins is already passed.
Time: A.D. 30
Place: the cross of Jesus Christ
Subject: the sins of the world
Result: death for Christ, but justification for the believer. "Who his own self bare our sins in his own body on the tree, that we, being dead to sins, should live unto righteousness: by whose stripes ye were healed" (1 Pe 2:24; cf. 3:18; Gal 3:13; 2 Co 5:21; Heb 9:26; 1 Jn 2:2).

THE JUDGMENT OF THE BELIEVER'S WORKS

Because the believer's sins have already been judged at the cross and the penalty paid, the believer's works can now be judged for rewards or loss of rewards (Fig. 14, J2).
Time: when Christ comes
Place: before the judgment seat of Christ (in the air?)
The Greek word translated *judgment seat* is *bema*. In the Grecian

games there was a seat on which the umpire or judges sat. Contestants were called before this seat where the reward was given to the winner.

Subject: works of the believer. The believer's life will come up for review only from the time he was born into the family of God. The works that are built upon the foundation—Jesus Christ—will be judged (1 Co 3:11).

Results: There is a threefold purpose in the believer's judgment: (1) vindication, (2) rewards, (3) assignments in the kingdom. "For we must all appear before the judgment seat of Christ; that every one may receive the things done in his body, according to that he hath done, whether it be good or bad" (2 Co 5:10).

> For other foundation can no man lay than that is laid, which is Jesus Christ. Now if any man build upon this foundation gold, silver, precious stones, wood, hay, stubble; every man's work shall be made manifest: for the day shall declare it, because it shall be revealed by fire; and the fire shall try every man's work of what sort it is. If any man's work abide which he hath built thereupon, he shall receive a reward. If any man's work shall be burned, he shall suffer loss: but he himself shall be saved; yet so as by fire (1 Co 3:11-15).

VINDICATION

Christians are often misunderstood by fellow Christians. "But why dost thou judge thy brother? Or why dost thou set at nought thy brother? For we shall all stand before the judgment seat of Christ" (Ro 14:10). The Christians at Corinth were even going to law with one another, and Paul reproved them (1 Co 6:2-3).

"Therefore judge nothing before the time, until the Lord come, who both will bring to light the hidden things of darkness, and will make manifest the counsels of the hearts: and then shall every man have praise of God" (4:5).

The world often unjustly accuses Christians. Stephen, the first martyr, was accused of being a blasphemer, yet the Bible says he was a man full of faith and the Holy Spirit (Ac 6:5). When all the facts are known and the motives of the heart are revealed, then believers will be cleared of all false charges and misunderstandings. The wicked will be judged for the mistreatment of believers (Rev 20:12). Christians are not to try to avenge themselves: "Recompense to no man evil for evil. Provide things honest in the sight of all men. If it be possible, as much as lieth in you, live peaceably with all men. Dearly beloved, avenge not yourselves, but rather give place unto wrath: for it is written, Vengeance is mine; I will repay, saith the Lord" (Ro 12:17-19).

God's ways with believers will be vindicated, and we'll understand why He permitted certain things to happen. As Peters explains,

> God's equity is vindicated by this reign of the saints. We do not now allude to the restoration of forfeited blessings, for this has been mentioned before, but to the simple fact that the very place, here on earth, which was the scene of the saint's pilgrimage, the Church's struggle, the martyr's suffering, the believer's fight of faith under trial, shall become the witness of the saint's elevation, the Church's honor, the martyr's triumph, the believer's reign. God's justice and grace have crowned all with the kingship and priesthood, thus vindicating His assurances of ultimate uplifting in the very earth where humiliation was experienced in reliance upon His Word. It is no small thing that the saints shall be kings where they once were poor and needy; that they shall be happy Princes where once they suffered; that they shall be rejoicing Nobles where once they sorely wept and prayed; and triumphant Rulers where once they were tempted, tried, persecuted, and afflicted. When this reigning is thus experienced, God's ways will be vindicated before the enraptured saints and an astonished world.[4]

REWARDS

Exactly what form the rewards of the believer will be is not disclosed. Two different words are used for *crown* in the New Testament. One is the diadem or crown of imperial authority (Rev 19:12), while the other is the victor's crown given to the winners after the games and was usually made of laurel leaves. These victors' crowns are mentioned as rewards for believers.

The New Testament speaks of five different crowns: (1) *the crown of life* or martyr's crown (Ja 1:12; Rev 2:10); (2) *the crown of glory* or the pastor's crown (1 Pe 5:2-4); (3) *the crown of rejoicing* or the soul-winner's crown (1 Th 2:19-20; Phil 4:1); (4) *the crown of righteousness*, which is for those who love His appearing (2 Ti 4:8); (5) *the incorruptible crown* or victor's crown, which is given to those who "keep their body under" (1 Co 9:25-27).

Elsa Raud says, "Each of the promised crowns is for the believer who reflects the life of Christ in his own life. Each crown has a condition tied to it, but each condition is a character requirement."[5]

The requirement for the incorruptible crown is to manifest the *self-control* of Christ, while the crown of rejoicing is given to those who demonstrate the *love of Christ for souls*. The crown of righteousness is given for those who live the *faithful, dedicated life as did Christ* who said, "I have come to do the will of him who sent me." The crown of glory will be given to the true shepherds who have the *heart* of Christ, who is the good Shepherd of His sheep. The crown of life is given to those who are *faith-*

ful even unto death, even as the good Shepherd giveth His life for His sheep.

Undoubtedly there will be definite rewards for different kinds of service, but the descriptions of the crowns reveal certain characteristics of the rewards that make them different from any earthly reward: *incorruptible* —they will last and endure in contrast with laurel leaves which will wilt and decay (1 Co 9:25); *righteousness*—this shows the character of the reward and it corresponds with the nature of the giver (2 Ti 4:8); *life*— the quality or nature of the reward that comes from the living God in contrast to the reward or wages of sin (Ja 1:12; Rev 2:10; cf. Ro 6:23), which is given to those who are faithful under trial, even to the point of death; *glory that won't fade*—this is a glory that comes from the God of glory and is given to those who are faithful in their service to God's own (1 Pe 5:4); *rejoicing*—this will bring joy and is given to those who are soul-winners whose concern is in the welfare of others.

ASSIGNMENT TO POSITIONS IN THE KINGDOM

"In making arrangements for His everlasting Kingdom, God works for perfection," says Rand. "He will grant no honor, nor authority in His Kingdom without complete fitness to exercise it. In this truth we discover that our daily life holds a relation to our future inheritance."[6]

Walvoord adds:

> The principle is laid down that those who are faithful will be given larger spheres of service. Hence, in eternity the rewards Christians will receive for faithful service here will be in the form of privileged service in Christ's eternal Kingdom. Just as the members of athletic teams in our colleges are chosen on the basis of their showing in practice, so in heaven Christians who have been faithful in their time of testing on earth will be allotted places of service accordingly in the eternal state. These rewards will be much like a diploma at graduation exercises in any school. Although students may differ in their academic achievements and some graduate with more honors than others, all receive recognition for what they have done. Graduation is a time of rewards, not a punishment, and although some students might regret that they had not done better, the emphasis seems to be on the happy note of achievement.[7]

JUDGMENT OF THE LIVING NATIONS

This judgment includes only those who survive the tribulation (Fig. 4, J3). We will consider Israel and the Gentiles separately.

Subject: Israel.

Time: At the close of the tribulation period.

Place: On the earth (Zec 14:4; Eze 20:34-38).

Results: Only the believers will be allowed to enter into Christ's kingdom (Jn 3:3). All rebels will be purged (Eze 20:37-38; Ro 11:26-27).

Subject: The Gentile nations.

Time: At the close of the tribulation period, probably following Israel's judgment (Mt 25:31-46).

Place: On the earth (Mt 25:31-32).

Result: The basis of judgment is according to the treatment they gave His brethren the Jews, especially the 144,000 witnesses sent out during the great tribulation. These went out bearing the good news of Christ and of the kingdom. Jesus said if they despised them or heard them not, it was the same as if they had despised Him (Jn 13:20; Lk 10:16; Mt 25:31-46). This is also a fulfillment of a promise that God gave to Abraham in Genesis 12:3, "And I will bless them that bless thee, and curse them that curseth thee: and in thee shall all families of the earth be blessed." Those who received the message are allowed to enter into Christ's kingdom, but those who reject the message "shall go away into everlasting punishment: but the righteous into life eternal" (Mt 25:46).

JUDGMENT OF OLD TESTAMENT AND TRIBULATION SAINTS

Subject: The Old Testament believers and those who died during the tribulation (Fig. 15, J4).

Time: After Christ returns (Dan 12:1-3; Rev 20:4).

Place: Probably on the earth.

Result: Rewards will be given and assignments made in the kingdom (Rev 20:4-6).

JUDGMENT OF THE UNSAVED DEAD OF ALL AGES

Subject: The unsaved dead of all ages (Fig. 15, J5). They are resurrected and are judged at one time.

Time: After the kingdom has been established for one thousand years (Rev 20:5, 7).

Place: Before the great white throne (20:11).

Result: Eternal punishment (20:15).

SUMMARY

1. Christ returns for His church before the great tribulation period.

2. After the rapture, the living and dead believers "in Christ" making up the true church will be judged before the *bema* seat of Christ.

3. The tribulation martyrs and Old Testament believers will be resurrected and judged at the beginning of the kingdom.

4. Believers have a threefold judgment as sinners, sons and servants.

5. Believers' sins were judged at the cross.

6. Believers' judgment as sons is in this life and is for training purposes.

7. Believers' judgment as servants is for vindication, rewards and assignments in the kingdom.

8. The unsaved dead of all ages are resurrected and judged at the end of the millennial era.

16

Conflicting Programs

DURING THE SEVENTIETH WEEK of Daniel, immediately before the establishment of Christ's kingdom, many events will take place. They fall in three main categories:

1. the establishment of Satan's counterfeit kingdom
2. God's worldwide program of evangelism
3. God's judgment upon unbelieving mankind (the day of the Lord)

SATAN'S COUNTERFEIT KINGDOM

The black thread of sin, having originated with Satan, winds its way through history. Satan is a creature (Eze 28:13-15), not "another god." Originally he was the "anointed cheribim that covereth," having a special place by the throne of God. He was created perfect, but he fell into sin (28:15) after pride and the desire to put himself in the place of God led to his rebellion against his Creator (28:17; Is 14:12-14). Lacking the power to create, Satan has attempted to persuade, trick and trap other creatures of God into giving allegiance to him. A large number of angels (now called demons) rebelled with him, perhaps as many as one-third of the angelic host (Rev 12:4).

God created Adam to have dominion over the world. But when Adam fell to temptation, he placed himself under Satan's power, and Satan stole his title of "prince of this world." Jesus Himself called Satan by this title (Jn 14:30). Since the fall, all sinners have been under the power of the devil. "And you hath he quickened, who were dead in trespasses and sins: wherein in time past ye walked according to the course of this world, according to the prince of the power of the air, the spirit that now worketh in the children of disobedience" (Eph 2:1-2; cf. Jn 8:44; 2 Co 4:3-4; 1 Jn 3:8, 10, 12; 5:19). Satan was defeated at the cross, and his power broken. His supreme goal, for which he fights with all his power, is to achieve on earth the total dominion and universal adoration of all mankind.

161

THE ANTICHRIST

In the end time there will arise a super man through whom Satan will exercise his mighty power. He will come under the guise of "the Christ" when in reality he is a false Christ. The word *Antichrist* has a twofold meaning: one who is opposed to Christ, and a substitute Christ. The title is used only in the writings of John, who uses it in a threefold sense: (1) of the person Antichrist (1 Jn 2:18); (2) of the spirit of Antichrist (1 Jn 4:3; and (3) of the antichrists (plural) (1 Jn 2:18, 22; 2 Jn 7); he is also called the man of sin (2 Th 2:3); the son of perdition (2 Th 2:3); a god (2 Th 2:4); the wicked one (literally *the lawless one*) (2 Th 2:8); the beast (Rev 13:1-10); the little horn (Dan 7:8, 23-25); the prince that shall come (Dan 9:26-27); and the rider on a white horse (Rev 6:2).

THIRD MEMBER OF THE COUNTERFEIT TRINITY

The false prophet, the third member of Satan's counterfeit trinity (Rev 16:13), is the second beast of Revelation (13:11-18). In some ways he imitates and can be compared to the Holy Spirit.

1. The Holy Spirit glorifies Christ (Jn 16:14); the false prophet magnifies the Antichrist (Rev 13:12-16). Christ's human body was conceived by the Holy Spirit (Mt 1:20); the false prophet gives life (breath) to the image of the beast (Rev 13:15).

2. The Holy Spirit seals believers (Eph 1:13); the false prophet causes all to be sealed by the mark of the beast (Rev 13:12-18).

3. The Holy Spirit leads in the worship of God (Jn 4:23-24); the false prophet causes all to worship the Antichrist (Rev 13:12).

4. The Holy Spirit's ministry in this age comes from the Son (Jn 16:14); the false prophet received his authority from the Antichrist (Rev 13:12).

5. The Holy Spirit performed miracles to authenticate the Word of God (Ac 10:38; 1 Co 12:10-11); the false prophet will also perform miracles (Rev 13:14-15), but his power will undoubtedly come from Satan who is not all-powerful but who is powerful (see Job 2).

BABYLON, THE COUNTERFEIT KINGDOM

The name Babylon appears from Genesis to Revelation. It is with Nimrod, the founder of the first empire, that Babel (Babylon) is first mentioned.

> And Cush begat Nimrod: he began to be a mighty one in the earth. He was a mighty hunter before the LORD: wherefore it is said, Even as Nimrod the mighty hunter before the LORD. And the beginning of his kingdom was Babel, and Erech, and Accad, and Calneh, in the land of Shinar. Out of that land went forth Asshur, and builded Nineveh, and

the city Rehoboth, and Calah, and Resen between Nineveh and Calah: the same is a great city (Gen 10:8-12).

Nimrod's father was Cush, called Bel in secular history, who was the son of Ham. James Gray, in describing Nimrod says,

> But though he was a mighty hunter of beasts, he soon became a mighty hunter of men, for in the next verse we read about the beginning of his kingdom. Notice that this is the first reference to a "kingdom" we have met in sacred history, and that it is *his* kingdom, and not God's kingdom that is mentioned.
>
> The beginning of his kingdom was in the great cities of Babel (or Babylon), Erech, Accad, Calneh, and the rest. But not content with founding this kingdom, "he went forth into Syria"—which is the rendering of the Revised Version,—and builded Nineveh, and the following cities named. He was thus the founder of two of the greatest kingdoms the earth has known, Babylon and Assyria.[1]

Genesis 11 records the attempts of man to build a city and a tower whose top they thought would reach to heaven. God confused their tongues and scattered them abroad and the place was called Babel, which means confusion (Gen 11:5-9). René Pache says:

> The judgment of the tower of Babel is heavy with consequences. It marked the will of God to break the unity of the race given into the service of evil. After that, the nations are divided by language, prejudice, and distance. The Lord in this manner prevents the premature appearance of the Antichrist. As soon as the end of time arrives He will permit just once the unification of the entire world. The great long-awaited super man will arise.[2]

BABYLON AND THE CAPTIVITY

Under Nebuchadnezzar, Babylon reached its peak in power as a nation and God used it to bring judgment upon His Jewish people who were worshiping idols and committing all kinds of abominable acts. The book of Daniel gives a glimpse of the elaborate political structure of Nebuchadnezzar's kingdom: "Then Nebuchadnezzar the king sent to gather together the princes, the governors, and the captains, the judges, the treasurers, the counsellors, the sheriffs, and all the rulers of the provinces, to come to the dedication of the image which Nebuchadnezzar the king had set up" (3:2). Nebuchadnezzar required everyone to worship the great image which he set up, even as the false prophet will demand that all worship the image of the Antichrist that he will set up (Rev 13:15).

A glimpse of the culture of Babylon is given from the many different times that musical instruments are mentioned in connection with the idol worship (Dan 3:5). Nebuchadnezzar was very proud of his city and in the vanity of pride said, "Is not this great Babylon, that I have built for

The Kingdom of God Visualized

the house of the kingdom by the might of my power, and for the honour of my majesty?" (4:30). Secular records support his statement:

> Herodotus says the city was in the form of a square, one hundred and twenty stades (13 miles, 1,385 yards) on each side. It had two walls, inner and outer. The vast space within the wall was laid out in streets at right angles to each other, lined with houses three to four stories in height. He lists the following chief public buildings; (1) the temple of Bel, consisting of a tower, pyramidal in form, over eight stories, topped as a sanctuary. (2) the palace of the king. (3) the bridge across the Euphrates connecting the eastern and western sections of the city. Herodotus described the city as overwhelming in its size and magnitude.[3]

Babylon is used in a threefold sense in Scripture, especially in the book of Revelation:

1. political Babylon—the empire with universal power and influence

2. religious Babylon—one great religious system supported by a political power

3. commercial Babylon—with its cultural and economic and social controls

In all three phases these are developed to the utmost, but they are apart from and in opposition to God.

POLITICAL BABYLON

Nebuchadnezzar had a dream of a great image (2:2), which Daniel with the Lord's help interpreted for him. The dream showed that there would be four great empires succeeding each other: Babylon, Medo-Persian, Greece, and Rome.

In Nebuchadnezzar's dream he saw a stone smite the image and grow into a great mountain which filled the earth. Daniel explained that this is a kingdom which will be set up by the God of heaven (2:44). In chapter 7 the prophet records the visions he had concerning these same kingdoms: the Babylonian kingdom was a lion, the Persian a bear, the Grecian a leopard, and the fourth beast was an unnamed terrible beast.

When the Antichrist comes, his appearance will be a combination of these beasts: "And the beast which I saw was like unto a leopard, and his feet were as the feet of a bear, and his mouth as the mouth of a lion: and the dragon gave him his power, and his seat, and great authority" (Rev 13:2). The beast had seven heads and ten horns (13:1). The beasts in the vision of Daniel totalled the same number of heads and horns. The Babylonian lion, the Persian bear, and the terrible beast had one head each, but the Grecian leopard had four, making a total of seven. As to horns, the first three had none, but the last one had ten. This description also fits the dragon who had seven heads and ten horns (12:3), the one who gives the beast his power. Satan made a promise to Eve in the garden of Eden: "Ye shall be as gods." Erich Sauer turns this expression around and would say to the beast, "He shall be as—Satan, your god."[4]

The Antichrist's political power will extend over the area formerly occupied by the old Roman Empire and the territory occupied by these three previous empires. In the beginning he will have to fight for his power, but eventually he will be the most powerful force in all the earth:

> But in ever-increasing measure he will bring under his control the political, industrial, and commercial, as well as the religious and philosophical life of all the world. He will solve their civil and social problems, excite their enthusiasm, suppress their religions (II Thes. 2:4), and draw to himself their worship (Rev. 13:4). Finally, having obtained the summit of his power, he will dominate their whole outward and inward life in an imposing but at the same time God-defying manner (Rev. 13:7).[5]

RELIGIOUS BABYLON

The past generation has seen something new on the religious scene—a scramble of groups to unite. A driving compulsion seems to be bringing like and unlike religious groups together. When the true church is taken out of the world, a stampede will occur, one great unified religious system coming forth. The Antichrist will be given power over all kindreds, tongues and nations, and he will be worshiped (13:8, 12-15). But they will also worship the dragon, or Satan himself (13:4). They will admire the beast, partly because of his ability to make war, for they will ask, "Who is able to make war with him?" (13:4). Eventually he will set himself in the temple of God and say that he is God (2 Th 2:4). Religious liberty will be taken away from the people and they will be compelled on threat of death to worship the beast in a state religion (Rev 13:15). While the false prophet heads up religious Babylon (13:11-16), the system itself will be called the great harlot.

> So he carried me away in the spirit into the wilderness: and I saw a woman sit upon a scarlet coloured beast, full of names of blasphemy, having seven heads and ten horns. And the woman was arrayed in purple and scarlet colour, and decked with gold and precious stones and pearls, having a golden cup in her hand full of abominations and filthiness of her fornication: and upon her forehead was a name written, MYSTERY, BABYLON THE GREAT, THE MOTHER OF HARLOTS AND ABOMINATIONS OF THE EARTH (17:3-5).

Hislop, in his book *The Two Babylons* traces the Babylon mystery religion in Assyria, Egypt, Greece, Rome, India, and other Far Eastern countries:

The Chaldean mysteries can be traced up to the days of Semiramis, who lived only a few centuries after the flood, and who is known to have impressed upon them the image of her own depraved and polluted mind. That beautiful but abandoned queen of Babylon was not only herself a paragon of unbridled lust and lasciviousness, but in the Mysteries which she had a chief hand in forming, she was worshipped as Rhea, the great "mother of the gods."[6]

Semiramis was the wife of Nimrod and later gave birth to an illegitimate child. She said that it was Nimrod, her husband, who had been killed. In this way she was counterfeiting the virgin birth.

In contrast to what the harlot will have on her forehead, the high priest of God had "HOLINESS TO THE LORD" (Ex 28:36). At first the great harlot, or religious Babylon, will be carried about by the beast or political Babylon, but he will turn upon the harlot and destroy her (Rev 17:16). Under the guise of religion she will use her influence with the kings of the earth and, as most false religions today, she will practice her religion for economic profit: "For all nations have drunk of the wine of the wrath of her fornication, and the kings of the earth have committed fornication with her, and the merchants of the earth are waxen rich through the abundance of her delicacies" (18:13).

COMMERCIAL BABYLON

Political, religious and commercial Babylon will all be intertwined. Antichrist will so gain control over the commercial world "that no man might buy or sell, save he that had the mark, or the name of the beast, or the number of his name" (13:17). In Revelation 17, Babylon is no longer called a harlot but a great city—a city which symbolizes all of the economic and social world. Many churches and other religious systems are involved today in the business world, and some have multimillion-dollar holdings in businesses. Bible students are not agreed as to whether or not there will be a literal city rebuilt. Martin O. Massinger says,

> It appears that the prophetic teaching of the Scriptures is that there will yet appear on the banks of the Euphrates a great city. Ancient Babylon will rise again, flourish as an unspeakably wicked center of world commerce, only to be destroyed after a short time by a sudden judgment similar to that which befell Sodom and Gomorrah of old. This destruction of the center will quite naturally bring with it the collapse of world-wide commerce. The system will be without a headquarters. Or it is conceivable that at the same time that Babylon falls, the other great cities of the earth will fall likewise; for, after all, this is the time of the outpouring of the seventh bowl of the wrath of God upon the earth. And finally, the site of fallen Babylon will become "the hold of every foul spirit."[7]

THE FALL OF BABYLON

The sudden fall of Babylon can be compared to the fall of Jericho as God brought the children of Israel into the land to possess it (Jos 6:20-21). Babylon, at the time of Belshazzar, was considered an invincible city. But while the Babylonians were ridiculing the God of heaven and praising their idols in a drunken orgy, the Medes and Persians diverted the river and broke into the city, and Babylon fell.

The judgment that will fall upon this great city of the Antichrist will come in one hour (Rev 18:10), and the smoke of her burning will be seen afar off (18:18). The kings of the earth will mourn (18:9), and the merchants will weep (18:11). But those that escaped for fear will stand afar off (18:15). The sailors and those who have brought goods will stand afar off and cast dust on their head and cry over the city (18:17-19). A long list of her goods and services is given in Revelation 18:12-13. The last two things mentioned are slaves and souls of men, showing her utter depravity.

God's Program of Evangelism

The Antichrist will make war with the saints of God (13:7), but God will seal 144,000 witnesses, 12,000 each from the twelve tribes of Israel. Several cults today claim to be these witnesses but they are not. The 144,000 will be sealed in the tribulation period and will be from God's people Israel. The ministry of these witnesses was foreshadowed by the work of the twelve during the ministry of Christ when they were sent out two by two to proclaim the good news of the kingdom.

These 144,000 witnesses will go throughout the world and reap a harvest. John describes this response: "And after this I beheld, and, lo, a great multitude, which no man could number, of all nations, and kindreds, and people, and tongues, stood before the throne, and before the Lamb, clothed with white robes, and palms in their hands" (7:9). At the judgment of the living nations the people of the world will be judged according to their reception of God's witnesses and their message, and the way they treated them. It will be impossible for anyone to buy or sell without the mark of the beast (Mt 25:31-46).

ISRAEL PREPARED FOR THE KINGDOM

When the Messiah came to Israel the first time, they rejected Him. Before His return to the earth, God will prepare Israel as outlined in prophecy:

1. Israel will be refined through suffering (Eze 20:38; 22:21-22; Zec 13:8-9).

2. Israel is to be regathered and restored (Mt 24:30-31).

3. Israel will be made willing to be subject to Christ (Ps 110:1-3).

4. Israel will experience a national conversion and regeneration when they see Christ upon His return (Zec 12:10; Is 66:8).

MARRIAGE OF THE LAMB

In contrast to the beast and his harlot on earth, in heaven the Lamb and His wife are pictured. Almost all commentators agree that Jesus is the Lamb, but who is the bride and what is the significance of the wedding? The marriage of the Lamb is a very complicated subject to study.

The book of Hosea presents Israel as the unfaithful wife of Jehovah for she sought after false gods. She later is to be cleansed from her harlotry and restored to her place of blessing. The name *Jehovah* is used in the Old Testament for all members of the Godhead (Deu 6:4; the Father, Is 48:16-17; the Son, cf. Is 45:23 with Phil 2:10, and Is 6:1-5 with Jn 12:41; the Spirit, cf. Is 6:5, 9-10 with Ac 28:25-27). The Bible clearly shows that Jesus is the Lamb of God (Jn 1:29; 3:29; Mt 9:15; Rev 5:5-6). If too literal an interpretation is made, it will require Israel as being His first wife, and, prior to setting up His Kingdom, He takes a second wife.

To complicate matters, Israel is also called, in the same book of Hosea, a son of Jehovah: "When Israel was a child, then I loved him, and called my son out of Egypt" (11:1). Prophetically Hosea was speaking about Christ (see Mt 2:15). The first time the name "son" was used for Israel was with Pharaoh: "And thou shalt say unto Pharaoh, Thus saith the LORD, Israel is my son, even my firstborn" (Ex 4:22).

The terminology is even more confusing because Israel in her barren condition is spoken of as a widowhood (Is 54:4), yet Jehovah is her Husband (54:5). Jehovah promises that in a future time He will restore adulterous Israel and then make a new covenant with her (Ho 2:18).

In the parable of the marriage feast (Mt 22:1-14), Jesus said in verse 4, "All things are ready: come unto the marriage." How could all things be ready if the church is the bride and it is not begun until Pentecost? Also, the servants are sent out to bring in guests because those who are first invited proved themselves unworthy. The guests invited in this passage were the Jewish people of that day. The servants are not told to go out and get a bride, but guests. Wedding terminology is used to illustrate many things.

THE BRIDE

Chafer argues that Israel could not be the bride of Christ:

No small error has been proposed when it is claimed that Israel is the bride of Christ. It is true that Israel is represented as the apostate and repudiated wife of Jehovah yet to be restored. This, however, is far removed from the "chaste virgin" (cf. II Cor. 11:2) which the Church is, still unmarried to Christ. It is Israel that will be reigned over in the coming kingdom. But it is the promise to the Bride that she shall reign with Christ. Such a promise could not be addressed to those over whom Christ will reign.[8]

The church also has been unfaithful and the same argument could be used against it. James says, "Ye adulterers and adulteresses, know ye not that the friendship of the world is enmity with God? Whosoever therefore will be a friend of the world is the enemy of God" (4:4; see also 2 Co 11:2 and Rev 1, 3).

The book of Ephesians teaches that the church is the body of Christ, and in chapter 5 Paul's argument seems to be that because the church is His body, she also is His wife (vv. 25-33). The Bible stresses this same relationship between Adam and Eve: "And Adam said, This is now bone of my bones, and flesh of my flesh: she shall be called Woman, because she was taken out of Man. Therefore shall a man leave his father and his mother, and shall cleave unto his wife: and they shall be one flesh" (Gen 2:23-24). Most commentators consider the church as the bride, but, as shown, it is hard to be dogmatic about it.

Merrill Unger, commenting upon the marriage of the Lamb (Rev 19:6-10), says,

> It calls for honoring the Lamb, for this event is not said to be the marriage of the Bride, but "of the Lamb." The Bride, spoken of as "wife" to be, represents the N.T. Church (Jn. 14:3; I Thes. 4:13-17; Eph. 5:32). The figure of "wife" symbolizes the glorified Church joined to Christ her Head in royal administration and dignity in the kingdom. The figure of marriage symbolizes the outward, public consummation of the inner spiritual union between Christ and His Church (I Cor. 12:13; Rom. 6:3-4; Gal. 3:27; Eph. 5:25-27, 30; Rev. 21:9). The Bride making herself ready presupposes her being made fit by God through Christ (Col. 1:12) and having her works reviewed at the *bema* (judgment seat) of Christ (I Cor. 3:11-14; II Cor. 5:10). The Bride's robes prefigure the righteousness of Christ (Rom. 3:21-22), graciously given to her both by imputation and sovereignly on the basis of Christ's works ("righteous acts") performed in and through her (Phil. 2:13), 8 (ASV).[9]

MARRIAGE CUSTOMS

After looking at some of the problems, perhaps it would be best to consider the basic marriage customs in biblical times. Although they vary from the time of Isaac's marriage to the time of Christ, it is generally understood that there were four steps:

1. A marriage contract was usually signed about a year before the marriage.

2. The bridegroom went to get the bride and take her to his house (they both often had attendants that accompanied them).

3. In his home, the wedding supper was celebrated and guests were invited.

4. The bridegroom took the bride unto himself and the marriage was consummated.

Some have pointed out that there is a difference between the wedding ceremony which proclaims and announces the wedding and the wedding feast which celebrates it.

The Greek word *gamos* is translated "marriage" nine times and "wedding" seven times. Sometimes it refers to the wedding ceremony and at other times the wedding feast. In the parable of the ten virgins (Mt 25:1-13) it apparently is referring to the marriage feast. The virgins were to be guests, not the bride. Some have suggested that the wise virgins represent the faithful Jews during the tribulation period, especially the 144,000 witnesses.

THE CEREMONY

J. A. Seiss says that the wedding ceremony is Christ in the character of the Lamb and the mighty Kinsman-Redeemer, "formally acknowledging and taking to himself as co-partners of his throne, dominion, and glory, all those chosen ones who have been faithful to their betrothal, and appear at last in spotless and shining apparel of the righteousness of the saints, thence forward to be with him, reign with him, and share with him in all his grand inheritance, forever."[10]

If the wedding ceremony of the bride and the Lamb takes place in heaven at this time (Rev 19:7-8), the *most* people who could be included in the bride would be the saints of the Old Testament, the church, and part of the tribulation martyrs (Jews and Gentiles). But only members of the church would have their resurrection bodies to make ready and array in "fine linen." Probably the *least* people who could be included would be the church. But the text does not actually say that the wedding takes place at this time, although it implies it.

THE MARRIAGE SUPPER

Some believe the marriage supper will take place in heaven, while others feel that it will be in the millennial era of the kingdom. The word *bride* is also used in connection with the New Jerusalem and is considered in a later study. As seen from the above references, wedding terminology is used in several different ways to explain relationships and it is impossible to be dogmatic in each case as to its meaning. When one attempts to develop doctrine from the figurative use of this relationship, it only leads to confusion. We can say dogmatically that it refers to an intimate relation between God and His people.

Summary

1. Satan, his Antichrist, and false prophet will make up the unholy trinity.

2. Satan will establish a counterfeit kingdom during the great tribulation period.

3. His kingdom can be called "Babylon." It is used in a threefold sense: political Babylon, religious Babylon, and commercial Babylon.

4. The Babylonian system can be traced from Nimrod, its founder, to the Antichrist's kingdom.

5. God seals and uses a special force of 144,000 Jewish evangelists. Multitudes from all nations respond to their message.

6. Marriage terminology is used in many figurative ways in the Bible.

7. The bride of the Lamb is probably the church but may include other believers.

8. The marriage of the Lamb speaks of an intimate relationship between Christ and His people.

17

God's Judgment–The Great Tribulation

Several terms are used in the Bible describing the period preceding the establishment of the kingdom. They are not always used accurately by Bible students and they are not exact synonyms:

1. the seventieth week of Daniel
2. the great tribulation
3. the day of the Lord
4. the great and terrible day of the Lord
5. the time of Jacob's trouble
6. the day of Christ

See figure 16.

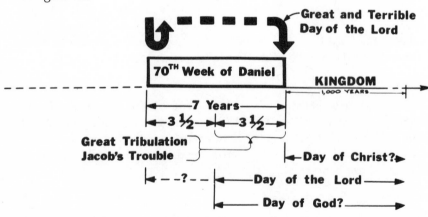

Fig. 16. Time Intervals

THE SEVENTIETH WEEK OF DANIEL

The seventieth week, or literally the seventieth seven, will be a period of seven years immediately preceding the establishment of the kingdom.

It will begin when Israel makes a covenant with the Antichrist, probably immediately after Christ returns for His church, but it doesn't have to. This seven-year period is divided into two portions of three and one-half years each (Dan 9:27).

THE GREAT TRIBULATION

While the term *tribulation* is often used for the entire seventieth week of Daniel, yet it probably more accurately refers to only the last three and one-half year period after the Antichrist breaks his covenant (Rev 6:17; 7:14).

THE DAY OF THE LORD

The expression "the Day of the Lord" is used many times in the Old Testament. One of the great themes of prophecy, it is first used in the Old Testament as the day when Jehovah went forth to fight for His people. The Old Testament prophets used it over and over to describe that time in the future when God will send judgment upon His enemies and establish His kingdom. It is used to include two ideas: judgment, and the kingdom age. Some catastrophic signs preceding the day of the Lord are given in Joel 3:14-16; 17-21; and yet other passages indicate that these signs are a part of the day of the Lord. Paul says the day will come as a thief in the night, or unexpectedly when people expect peace and safety (1 Th 5:2). But he says that the day of the Lord will not come before (1) an apostasy, (2) the removal of the hinderer, and (3) the revelation of the man of sin (2 Th 2:2-8). It's hard to tell exactly, but the day of the Lord begins at either the beginning of the seventieth week of Daniel or in the middle of it. The latter seems logical.

THE GREAT AND TERRIBLE DAY OF THE LORD

Joel and Malachi both refer to a "great and terrible day of the Lord" (Joel 2:31; cf. Mal 4:5), preceded by certain signs and the sending of Elijah (cf. Rev 11:3-6). This day is probably referring to the actual return of the Lord at the Battle of Armageddon. (It is terrible as far as His enemies are concerned.)

THE TIME OF JACOB'S TROUBLE

Jeremiah uses the expression "Jacob's trouble" to describe what will probably be the last three-and-one-half-year period when the Antichrist will break his covenant and the terrible persecutions will begin: "Alas! For that day is great, so that none is like it: it is even the time of Jacob's trouble, but he shall be saved out of it" (30:7).

"The day of Christ" is used seven times by Paul in connection with believers of this age. Some feel it refers to Christ's return for the church, however, Paul may have used it as a synonym for the day of the Lord in a specialized sense related to the church. The church will be caught out of the world before the judgments of the day of the Lord occur. The day of Christ may refer to the time when He returns to establish His kingdom, at which time the faithful, having received their rewards and assignments, will reign with Him.

THE JUDGMENTS OF GOD

The book of Revelation divides the judgments of the seventieth week of Daniel into three sections: the seal judgments, the trumpet judgments, and the vial (bowl) judgments. There are several interesting facts concerning the judgments of God in the Old Testament. In the judgment of the flood, God's people, as represented by Noah and his family, came out of the flood to a different earth, one in which nature had been changed. The believers who come through the great tribulation will enter a new earth in which the curse of sin will be lifted to a great extent.

At the destruction of Sodom by fire out of heaven, Lot escaped but all his possessions were destroyed. He is a good example of a carnal believer who escapes though "as by fire" but receives no reward (1 Co 3:15).

The ten plagues in Egypt foreshadow the great tribulation judgments. They came upon a people who were persecuting God's people Israel before they occupied the land the first time. The tribulation judgments will precede Israel's occupying the land in Christ's kingdom.

THE SEAL JUDGMENTS

The seal judgments will begin with the rider going forth on a white horse. This rider cannot be Jesus Christ because He is seen in heaven breaking the seals, and He doesn't begin His descent to the earth until Revelation 19. The rider, carrying a bow and wearing a victor's crown, is a military-political genius, the Antichrist. At first he will be able to establish his authority without war, but soon war will break out, followed by famine and death, and one-fourth of the earth's inhabitants will die (Rev 6:8). The fifth seal will be opened and a great host of martyrs seen. With the sixth seal will occur convulsions in nature, with earthquakes. The people will hide in the rocks of the mountains, realizing that this is the wrath of God, but they will not repent or want to face the Lamb (6:16-17).

THE TRUMPET JUDGMENTS

The trumpet judgments are additional judgments on and through nature, including earthquakes, lightnings, thunderings, hail and fire. One-third of the vegetation will be burned up. A great mountain burning with fire will be cast into the sea, killing a third of the sea creatures and destroying a third of the ships. This is probably the Mediterranean Sea. A third of the waters will become bitter and many men will die. The sun and moon will be smitten. There will be a plague of locusts which will have an unusual power to torment men, and men shall seek death and not find it (9:6). A great army will be loosed, and a third part of men will be killed by fire, smoke and brimstone (9:18). But even so, "the rest of the men which were not killed by these plagues yet repented not of the works of their hands, that they should not worship devils, and idols of gold, and silver, and brass, and stone, and of wood: which neither can see, nor hear, nor walk: neither repented they of their murders, nor of their sorceries, nor of their fornication, nor of their thefts" (9:20-21).

THE VIAL JUDGMENTS

The vial judgments are called the "seven last plagues; for in them is filled up the wrath of God" (15:1). As some of the plagues in Egypt in Moses' day were selective, the first vial also is selective and brings a grievous sore upon men who had the mark of the beast (16:2). The sea (Mediterranean?) will become blood, and every living thing in it will die. The sun will become hot and scorch men with its heat, causing them to blaspheme God, but they will not repent. A great darkness will come over the kingdom of the beast; the Euphrates River will be dried up. There will be lightnings and thunders and the greatest earthquake that has ever occurred. The great city will be divided into three parts with other cities falling, and isles and mountains shifting, and great hail coming out of heaven. After the last judgment Christ will return with the armies of heaven to smite the enemy (19:11-16).

The Terror of the Tribulation

In 1883 the volcano Krakatao erupted in Indonesia with an explosion that was heard 2,500 miles away. Tidal waves killed 35,000 people, and the outburst sent dust in the air around the world for nine years.

Only when we begin to imagine the accumulative effect of the tribulation judgments on nature, and the war, pestilence, famine, and demonic activity, do we begin to understand the terror of the tribulation. From the numbers given in the book of Revelation, it seems that perhaps as high

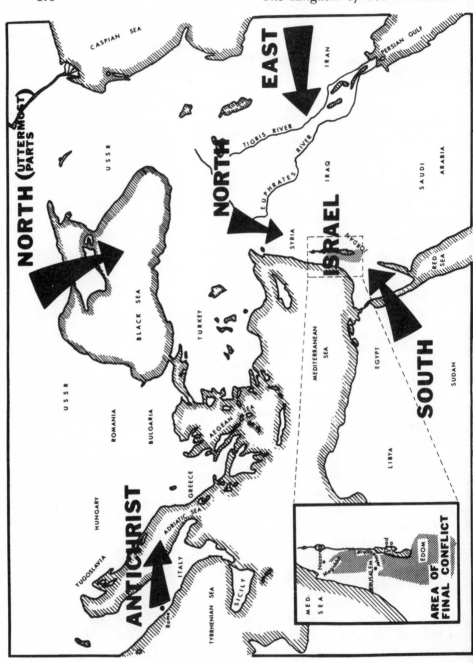

as two-thirds of the people of the world will be killed. L. M. Haldeman dramatically writes:

> We are led up to the Second Coming of Christ, not through the songs of chanting choirs, hymning the praise of an accepted Lord, but through trembling heavens and shivering earth. The sun and the moon are confounded, the sea and the waves roar; war, famine and pestilence are on the road, vieing with each other to fill the land with terror. Plagues and terrifying phenomena rush out at every angle; and there are voices and thunderings and lightenings and pillars of smoke. The underworld is opened and the spirits of the dead are stirred. Demons possess men and discordant cries from both men and demons fill the air. Honor and truth perish or flee away into the wilderness; wickedness and disobedience of the most lurid and sulphurous sort scorch the highways, expanding the trail of the Serpent over all things. Blood is the color of the hour; everything is red, cardinal red, crimson, gory, terrible. Judgment is heard in the heavens. Judgment on the earth. Denial of God the Father. Denial of God the Son; fear and the pit yawning as the mouth of a beast yawns. This is the pathway along which we are conducted to that moment when the heavens open and the Son of God comes forth as King of Kings, and Lord of Lords.[1]

WARS OF THE END TIME

Many wars will occur during the seventieth week of Daniel during the seal, trumpet and vial judgments. The Battle of Armageddon will really be the final climatic battle. Six main participants will be in the end-time conflicts besides the Lord and His armies from heaven (see Fig. 17):

1. Israel, who will be in the land
2. the northern confederation—Russia and her allies from the "uttermost parts of the north"
3. the king of the north—Syria
4. the king of the south—Egypt and perhaps some other African powers
5. the kings of the east
6. the ten-kingdom federation under the Antichrist—the end-time form of the old Roman Empire

ISRAEL IN THE SEVENTIETH WEEK OF DANIEL

In 1948 the Jewish nation was restablished in Palestine after 2,600 years. God promised, "That then the LORD thy God will turn thy captivity, and have compassion upon thee, and will return and gather thee from all the nations, whither the LORD thy God hath scattered thee" (Deu 30:3). Israel is to be regathered in the land, but at first they are in unbelief. Ezekiel is given a vision describing them as a valley of dry bones (chap. 37).

In the persecutions, warfare and judgments of the tribulation period, two-thirds of the Jews will be killed.

> And it shall come to pass, that in all the land, saith the LORD, two parts therein shall be cut off and die; but the third shall be left therein. And I will bring the third part through the fire, and will refine them as silver is refined, and will try them as gold is tried: they shall call on my name, and I will hear them: I will say, It is my people: and they shall say, The LORD is my God (Zec 13:8-9).

COVENANT WITH THE ANTICHRIST

According to Daniel 9:26-27, the prince (of the Roman Empire) will make a covenant with Israel for a seven-year period. He probably guarantees her safety in an attempt to settle the Middle East problem. Ezekiel 38 and 39 describe an invasion of Israel in the end time by Gog from the land of Magog. Five possible times for this invasion have been suggested:

1. before the seventieth week of Daniel (Mt 24:6)

2. at the beginning of the seventieth week, coinciding with the red horseman (Rev 6:4-8)

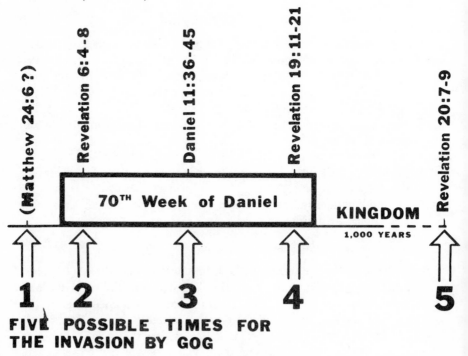

FIVE POSSIBLE TIMES FOR THE INVASION BY GOG

Fig. 18. Ezekiel 38-39

3. in the middle of the seventieth week of Daniel (Dan 11:36-45)
4. at the end of the seventieth week of Daniel (Rev 19:11-21)
5. at the end of the Millennial era (20:7-9; see Fig. 18)

INVASION BEFORE THE SEVENTIETH WEEK

While the invasion is to take place "in the latter years" (Eze 38:8), it is supposed to be at a time when the people of Israel are "at rest" and "dwell safely" in unfortified villages (v. 11). This seems unlikely to happen before the Antichrist makes his treaty with Israel, which will begin in the seventieth week. The destruction of Gog is to be a sign unto Israel and the Gentiles (39:7, 22) and appears out of place before the tribulation period.

INVASION IN THE MIDDLE OF THE SEVENTIETH WEEK

Probably the most popular position is that the invasion will take place in the middle of the seventieth week. Dwight Pentecost has a good outline of this interpretation:

1. Israel makes a false covenant with the beast and occupies her land in a false security (Dan. 9:27; Ezek. 38:8, 11).
2. Because of a desire for spoil at the expense of an easy prey, the King of the North, satanically motivated, invades Palestine (Ezek. 38:11; Joel 2:1-21; Isa. 10:12; 30:31-33; 31:8-9).
3. The Beast breaks his covenant with Israel and moves into the land (Dan. 11:41-45).
4. The King of the North is destroyed on the mountains of Israel (Ezek. 39:1-4).
5. The land of Palestine is occupied by the armies of the Beast (Dan. 11:45).
6. At this time the great coalition of nations takes place that forms one government under the Beast (Ps. 2:1-3; Rev. 13:7).
7. The Kings of the East are brought in against the armies of the Beast (Rev. 16:12), evidently as a result of the dissolution of the government of Gog.
8. When the nations of the earth are gathered together around Jerusalem (Zech. 14:1-3) and the valley of Jehoshaphat (Joel 3:2), the Lord returns to destroy all Gentile world powers so that He might rule the nations Himself. This is further described in Zech. 12:1-9; 14:1-4; Isa. 33:1-34; 5:17; 63:1-6; 66:15-16; Jer. 25:27-33; Rev. 20:7-10.[2]

Four weaknesses are in this position. No distinction is made between the king of the north and Gog. The king of the north of Daniel 11 was from Syria, while Gog is said to come from the "uttermost parts of the north" (literal translation of Eze 38:15; 39:2).

A second reason is that the king of the north (and king of the south) comes against the Antichrist, not against Israel (Dan 11:40). The Antichrist overruns their countries and *then* he occupies Israel (11:41). In contrast, Gog, from the uttermost parts of the north, invades Israel (Eze 38:8-9).

A third reason is that the Israelites will burn Gog's weapons for seven years (Eze 39:9), but at the same time Antichrist will begin his persecution of the Jews. Realistically the Jews would be using the weapons for defense rather than destroying them. It would also be hard to describe the middle of the tribulation as a time of "rest" with Israel dwelling safely in the land. At least the seal judgments will have occurred with their innumerable martyrs (Rev 6:9-11; 7:9-14).

The fourth reason for thinking that this is the wrong time is that for seven months all Israel will be burying the dead to cleanse the land, and then they will appoint burial parties to continue searching for bodies that have been missed (Eze 39:12-14). It doesn't seem that this would happen with Israel under the severe persecution of the Antichrist. At least the faithful remnant will have fled to the wilderness.

INVASION AT THE END OF THE SEVENTIETH WEEK

Another position is that the invasion will occur at the end of the seventieth week. Feinberg prefers this time, and it does have some advantages.[3] It would put the cleansing of the land and the destruction of weapons at the beginning of the kingdom, but Israel could not be at "rest" or dwelling safely in the land. In fact, Antichrist will be occupying the land (Dan 11:41). Another problem is that the world at that time is supposed to be under the rule of the Antichrist: "And it was given unto him to make war with the saints, and to overcome them: and power was given him over all kindreds, and tongues, and nations. And all that dwell upon the earth shall worship him, whose names are not written in the book of life of the Lamb slain from the foundation of the world" (Rev 13:7-8). Antichrist obviously is not Gog (even if Gog is identified as the king of the north), for Daniel 11:36-45 makes a distinction between Antichrist (the prince) and the king of the north. How can Antichrist be ruling over the world with Gog in opposition to him?

God's call to the animals to come feast on the dead in Ezekiel 39:17-20 and Revelation 19:17-18 does not have to be the same incident.[4] As history has recorded, this is nature's way of disposing of the large number of the dead.

The latter part of Ezekiel 39 speaks of the kingdom, but this does not mean that it must occur immediately after the animals are called to God's sacrifice. In chapters 34–39 the theme of the kingdom alternates with Israel's present captivity, judgment against Mount Seir, Israel's past sins, regathering in unbelief, and the invasion of Gog. Ezekiel again and again comes back to kingdom prophecies.

INVASION AT THE END OF THE MILLENNIUM

Most of the argument for this invasion happening at the end of the millennium comes from the similarity of the names, but the details in Revelation 20:7-9 are quite different: (1) Ezekiel places the time of the invasion in the "latter years" (38:8). John says that it is after a thousand years of Christ's kingdom (Rev 20:7), which is only the beginning of the *eternal* kingdom. (2) Gog's purpose is to come to take a prey while Satan gathers the armies to battle (Rev 20:8). (3) Gog's army is destroyed by earthquakes, fighting one another, pestilence, hailstones, and fire and brimstone (Eze 38:19-22). Satan's army is destroyed by fire from heaven (Rev 20:9). (4) Gog's destruction is a sign to Jews and Gentiles and seems inappropriate at the end of the millennium.

INVASION NEAR THE BEGINNING OF THE SEVENTIETH WEEK

The time which seems to fit the text better than others is the occurrence of the invasion near the beginning of the seventieth week.

1. It will occur at a time that Israel is dwelling at "rest" and in "safety" in the land, having made a treaty with the Antichrist, probably a mutual defense pact (Dan 9:27; Eze 38:8, 11).

2. Israel will have prospered and Gog will want to take a prey (Eze 38:12). He and his confederates will invade the land with a great army (Eze 38:15-16; Joel 2:1-21). This invasion probably will concide with the red horseman and take place early in the week (Rev 6:4).

3. This will anger God who will fight against Gog by:

   a. earthquake (Eze 38:19; Rev 6:12)

   b. confusion, fighting one another (Eze 38:21; cf. Gideon's victory over Midian, Judg 7:22)

   c. pestilence (Eze 38:22): the pale horseman (Rev 6:8)

   d. blood (Eze 38:22; Rev 8:7)

   e. rain and hailstones (Eze 38:22; Rev 8:7)

   f. fire and brimstone upon the army and on Magog (Eze 38:22; 39:6; Rev 8:7-8)

4. Gog will be destroyed upon the mountains of Israel (Eze 39:4).

5. Gog's destruction is to be a sign unto the nations that He is "the LORD, the Holy One in Israel" (Eze 39:7). By Gog's defeat, God will make His name "known in the midst of my people Israel" (v. 7). "So the house of Israel shall know that I am the LORD their God from that day and forward" (v. 22).

At the rapture of the church all believers will be caught out of this world. How will the 144,000 witnesses come to know the Lord? Some have suggested that because of the disappearance of true believers, Jews who have heard the preaching about the rapture will realize it is true and be saved. Others perhaps will turn to the Scriptures. This may be true, but it seems very reasonable that this miraculous intervention by God for His people will be what turns many of them to Him (vv. 7, 22).

6. For seven years they will use weapons of Gog for fuel, and salvage the spoils of war (vv. 9-10). During the last half of the seventieth week, they will not be able to buy or sell without the mark of the beast. They may also use them to defend themselves.

7. A valley, probably east of the Dead Sea, will be used for a mass grave. All Israel will spend seven months cleansing the land of the dead (vv. 11-13). Burial parties will be appointed to continue the work (v. 14). The animals and birds will help dispose of the bodies (vv. 17-20). At this time Israel is still governing their own land and at peace with the Antichrist.

8. Near the middle of the week the king of the north and the king of the south will fight against the willful king or the Antichrist (Dan 11:40), who in this battle will invade their countries and also enter "the glorious land" or Israel and occupy it (vv. 41, 45).

9. In the middle of the week the Antichrist will break his treaty, cause the sacrifices and worship in the temple to cease, and set himself up as god (Dan 9:27; 2 Th 2:4; Rev 13:8). This is a sign for Israel to flee (Mt 24:15-16) because at this time Satan will be cast out of heaven (Rev 12:9). Knowing that his time is short, with great wrath he will try to destroy the remnant of Israel (12:12, 17).

10. During the last half of the week, God will have two special witnesses (Rev 11:3-12). Although Israel will be regathered into the land, originally in unbelief, there will come a great awakening when they understand that Jesus is really their Messiah: "And I will pour upon the house of David, and upon the inhabitants of Jerusalem, the spirit of grace and of supplications: and they shall look upon me whom they have pierced, and they shall mourn for him, as one mourneth for his only son, and shall be in bitterness for him, as one that is in bitterness for his first-born" (Zec 12:10; see Ro 11:25-27).

11. The Antichrist will continue to invade his enemies. Edom, Moab and Ammon (modern Jordan) will escape, but Egypt will be occupied and the Libyans and Ethiopians subdued. His African campaign will be interrupted by rumors from the east and north (Dan 11:44).

12. With great fury he will go forth to destroy many. This may include

some of the fifteen Soviet republics of Russia (after the defeat of Gog) and the Far Eastern nations. This will probably continue most of the last three and one half years (Dan 11:44). Yet the Antichrist is recognized as the world ruler even though he may not control the world too well (Rev 13:7).

13. The kings of the east, along with the other world rulers, will be demonically influenced to gather together to battle with God at Armageddon. The demons will issue from the unholy trinity: Satan, the beast, and false prophet (16:12-16).

14. Christ will return to the earth with the armies of heaven and defeat His enemies (19:11, 14, 19).

Note that the campaign covers the entire land from the Valley of Megiddo in north central Palestine about ten miles south of Nazareth, through the Valley of Jehoshaphat (Joel 3:2, 12) which is east of Jerusalem, to Edom on the south (Is 34:5)!

VICTORY OVER THE ENEMY

The armies of the nations of the world will be gathered around Jerusalem when Christ returns:

> And I saw the beast, and the kings of the earth, and their armies, gathered together to make war against him that sat on the horse, and against his army. And the beast was taken, and with him the false prophet that wrought miracles before him, with which he deceived them that had received the mark of the beast, and them that worshipped his image. These both were cast alive into a lake of fire burning with brimstone. And the remnant were slain with the sword of him that sat upon the horse, which sword proceeded out of his mouth: and all the fowls were filled with their flesh (Rev 19:19-21).

Satan, the last member of this counterfeit trinity, will be imprisoned:

> And I saw an angel come down from heaven, having the key of the bottomless pit and a great chain in his hand. And he laid hold on the dragon, that old serpent, which is the Devil, and Satan, and bound him a thousand years, and cast him into the bottomless pit, and shut him up, and set a seal upon him, that he should deceive the nations no more, till the thousand years should be fulfilled: and after that he must be loosed a little season (Rev 20:1-3).

JUDGMENTS AND ESTABLISHMENT OF THE KINGDOM

The people who survive the tribulation will be judged; dead believers of the Old Testament age and tribulation martyrs will be resurrected and judged; and the kingdom established. The exact schedule is only hinted at.

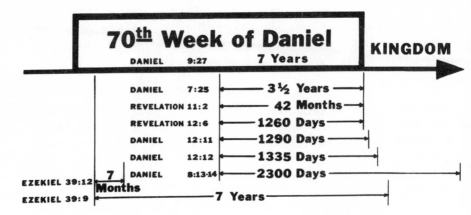

Fig. 19. Divisions of the Seventieth Week

OTHER DIVISIONS OF TIME

One of the difficulties in measuring time with Israel is that her monthly program of worship was measured by a lunar month of about 29½ days (29 days, 12 hours, 44 minutes, and 3½ seconds). But they measured daily and yearly time by the sun, which required a thirteen-month leap year about every three years. The last half of the seventieth week of Daniel has been marked off as a 3½ years, 42 months (evidently of 30 days), and 1,260 days (this evidently is a compromise between 42 lunar months of 1,239 days and 42 solar months of 1,276 days). But they all seem to refer to the same period of time. See figure 19.

Daniel mentions three other periods:

1. *1,290 days.* "And from the time that the daily sacrifice shall be taken away, and the abomination that maketh desolate set up, there shall be a thousand two hundred and ninety days" (Dan 12:11). This has been suggested as the time necessary for regathering and judging of living Israel and the Gentiles (Mt 24:31; 25:31-46) and the resurrection and judging of the Old Testament believers and tribulation martyrs (Dan 12:2; Rev 20:4).

2. *1,335 days.* "Blessed is he that waiteth, and cometh to the thousand three hundred and five and thirty days" (Dan 12:12). Perhaps this is the time that believers take their assigned positions and the kingdom is established (12:13).

3. *2,300 days.* "How long shall be the vision concerning the daily sacrifice, and the transgression of desolation, to give both the sanctuary and the host to be trodden under foot? And he said unto me, Unto two thousand and three hundred days; then shall the sanctuary be cleansed" (8:13-

14). Antichrist stops the sacrifices and defiles the tribulation temple in the middle of the week. A new temple, described in Ezekiel 40–44, will be built for the kingdom. It may be that these 1,040 days are used to build this temple before the resumption of the sacrifices (Eze 43:19-27).

SUMMARY

1. God's judgments in the seventieth week of Daniel are called by several names: the great tribulation, the day of the Lord, the great and terrible day of the Lord, and the time of Jacob's trouble. They are not exact synonyms.

2. There are three series of judgments: the seven seals, the seven trumpets, and the seven vials.

3. Six major important world powers are in the seventieth week: Israel, Antichrist (Western confederation), king of north, king of south, kings of the east, and Gog (from uttermost parts of the north).

4. Israel makes a treaty with the Antichrist and this starts the week.

5. The invasion of Gog probably takes place near the first of the week.

6. In the middle of the week Antichrist invades and occupies Israel, breaks his treaty, stops the sacrifices in the temple, and sets himself up as god.

7. At the end of the week, Christ returns and defeats the armies of the world gathered against Him.

8. The living Jews and Gentiles are judged by Christ; the Old Testament believers and tribulation martyrs are resurrected and judged; and the kingdom is established.

18

New Heaven and New Earth

WHEN WILL the new heaven and the new earth appear? To what extent will they be new? What is their relationship to the millennial kingdom? To the New Jerusalem? To heaven itself? Who will inhabit the new heaven and new earth and of what will their activities consist?

These and many more questions come to mind while searching the Scriptures concerning the new heaven and the new earth. The answers are all the more difficult because so few details are revealed. Therefore, one cannot be dogmatic concerning this great subject.

THE ORDER OF EVENTS AS USUALLY INTERPRETED

Students of prophecy usually outline the major events as follows: (1) Christ returns for His church, (2) the great tribulation period upon the earth, (3) the great Battle of Armageddon when Christ returns to the earth with the armies of heaven and defeats His foes, (4) the judgment of the living nations to see who will enter His kingdom, (5) the establishment of Christ's kingdom and His subsequent thousand-year reign, (6) the release of Satan and his final revolt, (7) Satan and his forces destroyed with fire from heaven, (8) the resurrection of the unsaved dead of all ages and their judgment before the great white throne, (9) at the same time the heavens and earth are renovated by fire, (10) the creation of the new heavens and new earth and the beginning of the eternal state.

A PROPOSED ORDER OF EVENTS

A direct relationship in biblical prophecy exists between the kingdom and the physical earth. The "new heaven and earth" describes the earth with the curse removed. An improper emphasis has been placed by many students of prophecy upon the first thousand years of Christ's kingdom. The general teaching of Scripture is that the kingdom is eternal, that it will last forever. It is not until chapter 20 of Revelation that the thousand-

186

IMPROPER MILLENNIAL EMPHASIS

BIBLICAL ETERNAL CONCEPT

Fig. 20. Duration of the Kingdom

year interval is marked off. Important events happen at that time, but they are not the end of the kingdom (see Fig. 20). After the thousand years are ended, the kingdom and the new heaven and new earth are seen in their final form. It appears from Scripture that the creation of the new heaven and the new earth is not accomplished in one step. This is a suggested order of events: (1) The judgments of the great tribulation are against ungodly men but they also bring about great changes in the earth. The fires of judgment spoken of in 2 Peter 3 are a part of the tribulation judgments. (2) At the Battle of Armageddon, Christ returns and defeats His foes. (3) Christ judges the living nations to see who will enter His kingdom. (4) The new heaven and new earth appear; there are dramatic changes in nature, among the mineral, vegetable and animal kingdoms. The earth is very much like the preflood era. (5) Christ establishes His kingdom. (6) After one thousand years, Satan and all the remaining evil men are judged by God with fire out of heaven and destroyed. It is at this time that the remainder of the curse on the earth is lifted and the new heavens and earth take on their final form.

The new heavens and earth are only mentioned in three books of the Bible: Isaiah, 2 Peter, and Revelation. The term, which seems to be used of a preliminary and final form, occurs first at the beginning of the millennium and again at the close of the millennium to describe the final form. In support of this usage of the new heavens and new earth, we will consider an eightfold argument: (1) the chronological order in the passages where they are mentioned, (2) what extent the earth is *new*, (3) the terms used to describe it, (4) the comparison of the gradual settling of the curse upon the earth in stages and its gradual lifting, (5) new creatures for a new creation, (6) the time and extent of the fires of judgment, (7) the significance of the one thousand years, and (8) God's promise to every living thing.

The first mention of the new heavens and new earth is in Isaiah 65:17, "For, behold, I create new heavens and a new earth: and the former shall not be remembered, nor come into mind." Verses 18-25, that immediately follow, refer to an earthly Jerusalem that God will create. It obviously is the millennial age because death is still present (65:20). There is no reason to say that verse 17 is after the millennium and then say verse 18 is a flashback into the millennium. A straightforward reading of the text says that in the new heavens and earth that God will create, He will create a new earthly Jerusalem. The dimensions of the city are given in Ezekiel 48:15-17, 30-35. Isaiah again mentions the new heavens and the new earth in 66:22-24, and again they are in a millennial context.

Peter in his second epistle also mentions the new heavens and the new earth: "Nevertheless we, according to his promise, look for new heavens and a new earth, wherein dwelleth righteousness" (3:13). This promise must refer to Isaiah's prophecy because that is the only recorded prophecy or promise concerning the new heavens and the new earth. Peter definitely connects it with the day of the Lord (3:10-12). He also uses the expression "the coming of the day of God." Some consider this as a term specifying some other time period such as the eternal age, but in its context it obviously is used as a synonym for the term "day of the Lord." Verses 10 and 12 are practically identical. His argument is that even though there are great and terrible fiery judgments coming upon the earth connected with the day of the Lord, believers are not to be distressed by this for they are to look for a new heavens and a new earth. The judgments of the tribulation period will destroy a major portion of the earth, yet the millennial kingdom is described as a place of beauty with the desert blossoming like the rose.

Revelation 20 speaks of the first thousand years of Christ's reign, during which time Satan is bound in the bottomless pit. Afterward Satan will be released and go out to deceive the nations. Like a magnet he will gather all the unbelievers together to battle God. But God will send fire down from heaven and destroy them (20:7-9). The devil will be cast into the lake of fire and brimstone, and the unsaved dead of all ages will be raised for judgment before the great white throne. It is not revealed where this judgment will take place. "And I saw a great white throne, and him that sat on it from whose face the earth and the heaven fled away; and there was found no place for them" (20:11). One must be careful to not read more into this verse than it says. One thing is certain: the place of judgment is far removed from the present heaven and earth. There is "no place for them" at the scene of judgment.

After discussing the judgment before the great white throne, John says, "And I saw a new heaven and a new earth: for the first heaven and the first earth were passed away; and there was no more sea" (21:1). He does *not* say that the new heavens and the new earth were created *at this time*. John has given other parenthetical passages in the book of Revelation in which he has flashed back to give the heavenly scene or the earthly, such as 10:1–11:14 and 12:1-5. In chapters 21–22 the new heavens and earth and New Jerusalem are described in their final form. Revelation 22:3 says, "And there shall be no more curse"; the curse is finally removed for sin has been purged. God destroyed sinful man and Satan with fire from heaven, and He removed them from the earth. Where there is no sin, there is no curse.

The argument from chronology is that in Isaiah the new heavens and the new earth are mentioned at the beginning of the millennial scene. Second Peter says the new heavens and earth follow the fiery judgments of the day of the Lord. Revelation says that the new heaven and earth are seen in their final form when sin has been purged and the curse is lifted.

WHAT DOES IT MEAN BY "NEW" HEAVENS AND EARTH?

Two words are translated "new" in the Greek New Testament: *neos* and *kainos*. Concerning the second word R. C. Trench says that it

> contemplates the new, not now under aspects of time, but of quality, the new, as set over against that which has seen service, the outworn, the effects or marred through age . . . (Luke 5:36) "a new garment," as contrasted with one threadbare and outworn; . . . "new wine-skins" (Matt. 4:17; Luke 5:38), such as have not lost their strength and elasticity through age and use; and in this sense . . . (II Peter 3:13), "a new heaven," as set over against that which was waxen old, and shows signs of decay and dissolution (Heb. 1:11-12). . . . It will follow from what has been said that *kainos* will often, as a secondary notion, imply praise; for the new is commonly better than the old; thus everything is new in the kingdom of glory, "the new Jerusalem" (Rev. 3:12; 21:2); the "new name" (2:17; 3:12); a "new song" (5:9; 14:3); "a new heaven and new earth" (21:1; cf. II Pet. 3:13); "all things new" (21:5). But this is not of necessity; for it is not always, and in every thing, that the new is better, but sometimes the old; . . . and the old wine (Luke 5:39), is better than the new.[1]

The idea throughout the Scriptures is that the earth will be changed, that there will be transition and not extinction. At the time of the flood the old world perished in the flood. The earth was changed in many ways after the flood receded, but it was the same earth (2 Pe 3:6). "Of old hast thou laid the foundation of the earth: and the heavens are the work of thy hands. They shall perish, but thou shalt endure: yea, all of them shall wax old like a garment; as a vesture shalt thou change them, and they shall be changed" (Ps 102:25-26). This is not *annihilation* but *change*. Hebrews 1:10-12 speaks of the heavens and earth perishing, but it also explains what it means by saying, "and they shall be changed."

Seiss explains:

> In those passages which speak of the passing away of the earth and heavens (see Matt. 5:18, 24, 34, 35; Mark 13:30, 31; Luke 16:17, 21, 33; II Peter 3:10; Rev. 21:1), the original word is never one which signifies termination of existence, but *parerchomai*, which is a verb of very wide and general meaning, such as to go or come to a person, place, or point; to pass, as a man through a bath, or a ship through the sea; to pass from one place or condition to another, to arrive at, to go through; to go into, to come forward as if to speak or serve. As to time, it means going into the past, as events or a state of things. That it implies great changes when applied to the earth and heavens is very evident; but that it ever means annihilation, or the passing of things out of being, there is no clear instance either in the Scriptures or in classical Greek to prove. The main idea is transition not extinction.[2]

In summary, the word "new" stands for quality and refers to an earth and heaven that have gone through a transition or a change which, according to context, is much superior to the previous heaven and earth.

DESCRIPTIVE TERMS OF THE KINGDOM

Four expressions in Scripture are directly related to the new heavens and new earth: (1) the regeneration, (2) the times of refreshings, (3) the times of restitution of all things, and (4) the deliverance of creation.

Regeneration. "And Jesus said unto them, Verily I say unto you, That ye which have followed me, in the regeneration when the Son of man shall sit in the throne of his glory, ye also shall sit upon twelve thrones, judging the twelve tribes of Israel" (Mt 19:28). Regeneration means a new birth, renewal or restoration.

The word "regeneration" is only used twice in the Scriptures: in Matthew 19:28 when it refers to the earth, and in Titus 3:5 when it speaks of the new birth of the Christian when he becomes a new creature.

Culver says:

> The time of the great coming conflagration is to be at the beginning of the Millennium, during the period immediately adjacent to that aspect of the second coming of Christ known as the revelation.

The great cosmic disturbances described shall consist of a limited renovation involving the death of all living wicked men at the revelation of Christ and such changes in the realms of inanimate material, of vegetable, animal, and human life as are necessary to produce conditions which the prophets declare shall prevail during the coming kingdom age. All this is best described, to use Jesus' own word for it, as a "regeneration."[3]

Times of refreshing, times of restitution of all things. "Repent ye therefore, and be converted, that your sins may be blotted out, when the times of refreshing shall come from the presence of the Lord; and he shall send Jesus Christ, which before was preached unto you: whom the heaven must receive until the times of restitution of all things, which God hath spoken by the mouth of all his holy prophets since the world began" (Ac 3:19-21). This looks to a time when all that has been lost through sin will be restored.

Deliverance of creation. Romans 8:23 states that the deliverance of creation will take place at the time of the redemption of our bodies: "And not only they, but ourselves also, which have the firstfruits of the Spirit, even we ourselves groan within ourselves, waiting for the adoption, to wit, the redemption of our body."

All of the above expressions begin with the second advent of Christ.

GRADUAL LIFTING OF THE CURSE IN STAGES

After Adam's sin the curse came upon the earth in stages. First there were thistles and thorns, and man was required to labor for his food. Even though the sentence of death was upon him, the average man still lived hundreds of years. Later great changes in nature took place at the time of the flood. Fear was placed in the hearts of animals toward man, and the life-span of man was shortened. At the Tower of Babel there was a confusion of tongues and man was scattered over the earth.

At the end of the tribulation period the earth will have undergone great judgments of fire. According to Old Testament prophecies, the millennial kingdom of Christ will be very different from the present earth. There will be changes in the mineral kingdom, the vegetable kingdom, and the animal kingdom. The life of man will be greatly extended, and disease will be practically unknown. The curse, to a large measure, will have been lifted, but there will still be sin and consequently there will still be death until the thousand years are over.

NEW CREATURES FOR THE NEW CREATION

"Therefore if any man be in Christ, he is a new creature [creation]: old things are passed away; behold, all things are become new" (2 Co 5:17). While the believer is a new creature, his old self is not annihilated;

he has the same body, soul and spirit, even the old sin nature. There is a promise that the body will be changed (1 Co 15:51-54), but Scripture does not say that believers *will be* new creatures *when* their bodies are changed but that at *present* they are new creatures. In the same way, when Christ begins His millennial reign, there will be a new heavens and a new earth, even though at that time they will not be in their final form. Yet, dramatic changes will have been made. The same expression is used for the new creatures and the new heavens and earth.

THE FIRES OF JUDGMENT

The basic passage concerning the fires of judgment is given in 2 Peter 3:5-13, where the apostle is talking especially against false teachers who reject God's prophecies. In verses 5 and 6 he says they forgot that great judgments came upon the world at the time of the flood and caused great changes. "Whereby the world that then was, being overflowed with water, perished" (v. 6). Obviously this first world was not annihilated, but it did undergo drastic changes.

2 PETER 3:7

"But the heavens and the earth, which are now, by the same word are kept in store, reserved unto fire against the day of judgment and perdition of ungodly men" (2 Pe 3:7). This verse can be paraphrased to read,

> The heavens that now are, and the earth, by the same creative word of power, have been stored with fire. These reservoirs of potential fire are being held in reserve for a day of settlement, the righting of the wrongs of the earth. Then will occur the utter destruction of the present system of wickedness dominating the earth.

The idea of the earth being "stored with fire" may refer to one of two things: a fiery center of the earth, as many scientists believe, or the inherent fire of the basic atomic structure of the earth. The one basic characteristic of the atomic bomb blast is its terrible fire. Some scientists describe the burning of the sun as a continual hydrogen bomb. Some of the description of judgment in the tribulation resembles atomic warfare (whether man-made or divine judgments).

The time of this judgment is important. It is connected with the "judgment and perdition [destruction] of ungodly men." Who are these ungodly men? They are those living on the earth in the tribulation period (Rev 9:20-21). Because of the present rate of population explosion it probably will include a majority or at least a large percentage of all men who have ever lived.

It will not be the unsaved dead of all ages, because this judgment before the great white throne will not take place on the earth (Rev 20:11). Neither the ungodly men nor the heavens and earth are annihilated, but they are both judged.

2 PETER 3:10-11

"But the day of the Lord will come as a thief in the night; in the which the heavens shall pass away with a great noise, and the elements shall melt with fervent heat, the earth also and the works that are therein shall be burned up. Seeing then that all these things shall be dissolved . . ." (2 Pe 3:10-11).

These verses include five descriptive phrases or ideas: (1) the day of the Lord, (2) the heavens shall pass away with great noise, (3) elements melt with fervent heat, (4) all things shall be dissolved, and (5) the earth and the works therein shall be burned up.

1. *The day of the Lord.* This is the time the judgments will occur. It begins in the middle of the seventieth week of Daniel and comes un-expectantly on the unbelieving world like "a thief in the night."

2. *The heavens shall pass away with a great noise.* The Greek root translated "shall pass away" is *parerchomai*. It is usually translated: come, come forth, go, pass, passover, or past transgress. It never means to annihilate but to pass over from one position in time or space to another.

3. *Elements melt with fervent heat.* Peter's description of this great judgment revolves around two key words: "dissolving" and "elements." The Greek word for elements, *stoicheion*, is used of the letters of the alphabet, first principles, first things in a series, and the elements of the earth. While the people of New Testament times did not have our present molecular theory, they did believe that the earth was made of certain basic ingredients. That appears to be what Peter is speaking of.

Aristotle, who lived 350 years before the birth of Christ, taught that nature was composed of four elements: fire, water, earth and air. The Greek word that is translated *elements* would have been interpreted by the readers of that day as referring to these four things and not to the chemical elements known to modern science. However, Peter's description of the fires may go beyond just the primitive use of the word and describe atomic warfare of the present age. The word *atom* has the idea of something that is indivisible. Scientists now know that the atom can be disintegrated since it is made up of various particles which are moving at a very rapid rate, with a tremendous amount of energy stored or contained in each atom. This has been demonstrated by the almost un-believable heat and power of the weapons of the atomic arsenal. Some have pointed out that fire is mentioned in the last plagues in the book of Revelation.

4. *All things shall be dissolved.* The word translated "dissolved" is the simple word *luo,* the verb stem Greek students use as a model to memorize the forms used in the various tenses. John the Baptist used this word when he said that he was not worthy to "unloose" the shoes of Jesus (Jn 1:27).

Seiss says:

> The *dissolving* of which Peter is made to speak, is really a deliverance rather than a destruction. The word he uses is the same which the Saviour employs where he says of the colt, "*Loose* him;" and of Lazarus when he came forth with his death wrappings, "*Loose* him, and let him go"; . . . and of the Devil, "He must be *loosed* a little season." . . . It is simply absurd to attempt to build a doctrine of annihilation on a word which admits of such applications. The teaching of the Scriptures is, that the creation is at present in a state of captivity, tied down, bound, "Not willing, but by reason of him who hath subjected the same in hope;" and the *dissolving* of all these things, of which Peter speaks, is not the destruction of them, but the breaking of their bonds, *the loosing of them,* the setting of them free again to become what they were originally meant to be, their deliverance. (Compare Romans 8:19-23). And as to the *flying* or *passing away,* of which John speaks, a total disappearance of all the material worlds from the universe is not at all the idea; for he tells us that he afterwards saw "*the sea*" giving up its dead, the New Jerusalem coming down "*out of the heaven,*" the Tabernacle of God established among men. . . .[4]

In commenting upon this passage, Wilbur M. Smith suggests the means by which this will be accomplished:

> We have the fundamental idea of *setting free that which has been bound.* Is this not exactly what we have in the release of atomic energy by the fission of the nucleus? What I am getting at is that when Peter said that at the end of this entire age there would be a great conflagration of the heavens and the earth, he expressed it in language that implied that the elementary particles of matter, which we call atoms, would be dissolved or released, or, as it were, their energies, hitherto imprisoned, set free; and that this will cause the fire. I do not mean by this that Peter here predicts the atomic bomb, but I do mean that *the principle involved in nuclear physics, which is at the basis of the atomic bomb, is the principle which Peter here sets forth.*[5]

5. *The earth and the works therein shall be burned up.* Manuscripts differ as to how the last part of 2 Peter 3:10 should read. The Nestle Greek Text translates it, "The earth also and the works therein shall be discovered." Other translations read, "be disclosed," "be laid bare," and "be detected." This probably refers to the judgment of nations in Mat-

thew 25:31-46. This is the preferred reading, for otherwise there is a conflict with Genesis 8:21.

2 PETER 3:12

Verse 12 is almost identical with verse 10. Some try to make "day of God" different from "the day of the Lord," but there is no reason to make a distinction. If one is made, when does it occur? There are no other uses of this phrase which in its context makes sense as meaning the same as the day of the Lord.

To summarize Peter's thoughts in this chapter, the day of the Lord will bring judgments to this world, the fires of these judgments will greatly change the earth but Christians ought not to worry because they have a promise: "Nevertheless we, according to his promise, look for new heavens and a new earth, wherein dwelleth righteousness" (2 Pe 3:13).

THE SIGNIFICANCE OF THE ONE THOUSAND YEARS

One thousand years are marked off in the eternal kingdom of Christ. Important things happen during and at the end of this period, but it should not be made to include more than it does. For this first thousand years Satan will be bound in the bottomless pit (Rev 20:2), and tribulation martyrs will reign with Christ (20:4), for they are a part of the first resurrection. The resurrection and judgment of the unsaved will take place at the end of the thousand years (20:5). The definite article appears in the Greek, so the expression should be "the" thousand years in verses 3, 5, 6 and 7. Revelation 20:6 does not mean that the tribulation saints will *only* reign a thousand years, but that they will reign with Him during this first thousand years (see Fig. 20).

As Culver explains,

> It is not an uncommon misconception among Premillennial believers that Christ's kingdom, the reign of Christ, and the reign of the saints are restricted to a one-thousand-year period. Revelation 20:4 ("and they lived and reigned with Christ a thousand years") and 20:6 ("they shall be priests of God and of Christ, and shall reign with him a thousand years") have been thought to teach that the reign of the saints and of Christ shall come to an end at the close of the Millennium. How foolish it is to cite these verses in proof of such an assertion is seen at once in a close look at verse four. "Lived" and "reigned" are both in the same person, gender, number, and tense in the Greek. There is no punctuation mark of any kind between them. Clearly, then, the thousand years modifies both the living of the saints and their reigning. To insist on a reign of only one thousand years on the basis of this verse would require equal insistence on a living of only one thousand years, which simply will not

do. And contrariwise, there are many passages which speak of the perpetuity of the reign of the saints in the kingdom of Messiah.[6]

John is next given a preview of the judgment before the great white throne: "And I saw a great white throne, and him that sat on it, from whose face the earth and heaven fled away; and there was found no place for them" (20:11). The apostle uses a figure of speech to personify heaven and earth as fleeing away. This does not say that they ceased to exist, nor does it explain what really happened to them. When flying in an airplane, one often has no sense of movement, but the ground will sometimes seem to be moving away. Perhaps John had this same sensation as he was carried to the judgment scene.

Revelation 20 closes with death and hell being cast into the lake of fire. "The last enemy that shall be destroyed is death" (1 Co 15:26). When sin is removed, the curse is removed, and the curse of sin is death.

The word "sea" is used in a variety of ways in Scripture. In Revelation 21:1 John has a vision of a new heavens and a new earth and he says, "And there was no more sea." Seiss thinks this means there was no more "old sea." It certainly does not mean that there will not be any more water, rivers, or lakes, for the Euphrates, the River of Egypt, and the Great Sea are used as boundaries to describe the promised kingdom. Certainly the earth will not be changed to such an extent that these boundaries would be unknown or meaningless.

When the final curse of death is lifted, the earth will return to a form similar to what it had in the days of the Garden of Eden. Some believe that there was a canopy of water vapor over the earth at that time (Gen 1:6-8; 2 Pe 3:5).

Culver summarizes the essentials of the teachings of the Scriptures on the millennium as follows:

> I. The Millennium is specifically (1) the period of time between the resurrection of the just and of the unjust, and (2) the period of Satan's imprisonment.
> II. The Millennium is further qualified as (1) an initial stage of the everlasting kingdom of Christ, (2) a period begun by the visible return of Christ in glory to judge and rule the nations, (3) a period closed by the final eradication of all evil from God's universe at the final judgment of the wicked, and (4) a period during which the saints of the first resurrection will be associated with Christ in His reign.[7]

To this we could add that at the close of the millennium the last of the curse is lifted from the earth as death is destroyed. The new heavens and earth are seen in their final form.

GOD'S PROMISE TO EVERY LIVING THING

The idea of a total baptism of the earth in fire has posed some real problems. Some have visualized the earth like a roasting marshmallow. If this is a true concept, *the big question is,* What does God do with the people on the earth? Although nothing is revealed, God could provide an ark of some kind, but this doesn't seem realistic because there will probably be billions of people on the earth. To avoid this problem, some have placed the baptism of the earth by fire at the end of the millennial kingdom. At this time the unsaved dead are raised for judgment before the great white throne, and they think of the saved as going to heaven. But this is just speculation. The strongest argument against this idea of a total baptism of fire is that it directly contradicts God's previous promise.

After Noah came out of the ark, he built an altar and offered a burnt offering unto the Lord: "And the LORD smelled a sweet savour; and the LORD said in his heart, I will not again curse the ground any more for man's sake; for the imagination of man's heart is evil from his youth; neither will I again smite any more every thing living, as I have done" (Gen 8:21). God doesn't just promise not to destroy mankind, but His promise is that He will not destroy again "every thing living."

While the earth undergoes great change, animal and vegetable life must continue in order for God to be true to His promise.

SUMMARY

The new heavens and earth are said to appear when Christ returns to establish His kingdom because:

1. Three of the four times they are mentioned in Scripture they are connected with the judgments preceding His kingdom or during the millennial era.

2. The word *new* (heaven and earth) has to do with *quality,* not *time.*

3. The descriptive terms—regeneration, times of refreshing, the times of restitution of all things, and the deliverance of creation—all are connected with Christ's second advent and are obviously descriptive of the new heavens and earth.

4. There was a gradual settling of the curse in stages, and a lifting by stages is indicated.

5. Even though we still have the old sin nature we are said now to be "new creatures." Also, even though the curse of death will still be upon the earth, it can be called a new creation or the new heavens and earth before the final lifting of the curse.

6. The fires of judgment, atomic or otherwise, of the tribulation are at

least the possible means of changing and freeing nature of most of the curse of sin so it can bring forth bountifully as promised.

7. The one thousand years are only the initial stage of the everlasting kingdom of Christ and not the end.

8. God promised never to destroy again all living things on the earth. So after one thousand years the new heavens and earth will be perfected instead of being destroyed.

19

Kingdom Conditions

CHRIST'S REIGN upon earth will affect every area of life in a large way. The good things which man has vainly sought for without God shall at last be poured out in the kingdom of His Son. One of the biggest changes will be with nature.

CONDITIONS OF NATURE

Man enjoys the beauty of nature, the flowers, the mountains, the rivers, and the seashore; but for all its beauty, creation is now under a curse. Christ came that He might destroy or undo the works of the devil (1 Jn 3:8). Through Him nature will be restored to the "good old days." The Bible says that man was created to have dominion over the earth (Gen 1:28; Heb 2:6-8). He was created by God and was to be subject to God, his Creator (Gen 2:6-17). In his original state he had fellowship with God (3:8). He was given life and had access to the tree of life (2:9, 16). Once all was peace. There were no weeds, destructive insects, storms, floods, earthquakes, hurricanes, deserts, wasteland, crop failures, nor famines. Animals and man lived at peace and in harmony with one another.

But through the temptation of Satan, sin came into the world through Adam (Ro 5:12). Sin changed things. Instead of life, we have death. Man, who was created out of the dust of the earth, is now to die and his body to return to dust (Gen 3:17-19). He is denied access to the tree of life (3:22, 24). Instead of fellowship with God, sin brought spiritual death or separation from God. Instead of being subject to God, man is now rebellious. Instead of having dominion over the earth, the earth is now cursed (Gen 3:17-19). Nature has been in turmoil and in a never ceasing struggle for survival, but God didn't create it this way. But now in the words of the Scripture, "We know that the whole creation groaneth and travaileth in pain together until now" (Ro 8:22). God made Adam as the king and gave him dominion over all, but through his sin the curse came upon creation. Mineral, vegetable and animal kingdoms were all cursed.

1. *The mineral kingdom:* "Cursed is the ground for thy sake" (Gen 3:17).

2. *The vegetable kingdom:* "Thorns also and thistles shall it bring forth to thee" (3:18). Before the curse, all Adam had to do was to dress and keep the garden (2:15), but after the curse he was told that he would earn his bread "in the sweat of thy face" (3:19).

3. *The animal kingdom:* The curse is placed upon the serpent in Genesis 3:14, but it was not until Noah came out of the ark that fear of man was placed in animals. "And the fear of you and the dread of you shall be upon every beast of the earth, and upon every fowl of the air, and upon all that moveth upon the earth, and upon all the fishes of the seas; into your hand are they delivered. Every moving thing that liveth shall be meat for you; even as a green herb have I given you all things" (9:2-3). Creation shall be delivered from this bondage "because the creature [creation] itself also shall be delivered from the bondage of corruption into the glorious liberty of the children of God. For we know that the whole creation groaneth and travaileth in pain together until now. And not only they, but ourselves also, which have the firstfruits of the Spirit, even we ourselves groan within ourselves, waiting for the adoption, to wit, the redemption of our body" (Ro 8:21-23). The curse on nature will be lifted, in a large measure, at the beginning of the millennial era, at the time of the "redemption" of the body.

1. *Mineral kingdom:* "The wilderness and the solitary place shall be glad for them; and the desert shall rejoice, and blossom as the rose. It shall blossom abundantly, and rejoice even with joy and singing: the glory of Lebanon shall be given unto it, the excellency of Carmel and Sharon, they shall see the glory of the LORD, and the excellency of our God. For in the wilderness shall waters break out, and streams in the desert. And the parched ground shall become a pool, and the thirsty land springs of water: in the habitation of dragons, where each lay, shall be grass with reeds and rushes" (Is 35:1-2, 6-7). The rain also will be in its season: "I will cause the shower to come down in his season; there shall be showers of blessing" (Eze 34:26).

2. *Vegetable kingdom:* "The tree of the field shall yield her fruit, and the earth shall yield her increase, and they shall be safe in their land, and

shall know that I am the LORD, when I have broken the bands of their yoke, and delivered them out of the hand of those that served themselves of them" (34:27). "Instead of the thorn shall come up the fir tree, and instead of the brier shall come up the myrtle tree: and it shall be to the LORD for a name, for an everlasting sign that shall not be cut off" (Is 55:13). "Behold, the days come, saith the LORD, that the plowman shall overtake the reaper, and the treader of grapes him that soweth seed; and the mountains shall drop sweet wine, and the hills shall melt . . . and they shall plant vineyards, and drink the wine thereof; they shall also make gardens, and eat the fruit of them" (Amos 9:13-14).

Because of the change in nature and the fruitfulness of the soil and peace upon earth there will be a material prosperity that the world has never known (Ps 72:16). Labor problems will be solved (Is 65:21-25; Amos 9:13-14; Eze 36:29-30).

3. *Animal kingdom:* There will be peace between animals and between man and animals. "The wolf and the lamb shall feed together, and the lion shall eat straw like the bullock: and dust shall be the serpent's meat. They shall not hurt nor destroy in all my holy mountain, saith the LORD" (Is 65:25). "The wolf also shall dwell with the lamb, and the leopard shall lie down with the kid; and the calf and the young lion and the fatling together; and a little child shall lead them. And the cow and the bear shall feed; their young ones shall lie down together: and the lion shall eat straw like the ox. And the sucking child shall play on the hole of the asp, and the weaned child shall put his hand on the cockatrice' den. They shall not hurt nor destroy in all my holy mountain: for the earth shall be full of the knowledge of the LORD, as the waters cover the sea" (Is 11:6-9; see also Ho 2:18).

The curse will be lifted from the mineral, vegetable and animal kingdoms and from the weather so there will be no storm or drought except as a disciplinary measure (Zec 14:16-19). There will be an increase of light: "Moreover the light of the moon shall be as the light of the sun, and the light of the sun shall be seven-fold, as the light of seven days, in the day that the LORD bindeth up the breach of his people, and healeth the stroke of their wound" (Is 30:26).

HEALTH CONDITIONS IN THE MILLENNIUM

Sickness is the work of the devil: "God anointed Jesus of Nazareth with the Holy Ghost and with power: who went about doing good, and healing all that were oppressed of the devil; for God was with him" (Ac 10:38). Jesus came to destroy the devil's works (1 Jn 3:8). Sin brought sickness into the world, and since Satan was the agent in the temptation, he is indirectly the cause of all sickness. Adam had been warned, "For in the day that thou eatest thereof thou shalt surely die" (Gen 2:17), or literally, "Dying ye shall die." While sin brings death (Ro 6:23), yet sickness and death are God's way of overruling evil for good. Because He did not want man to live forever in his sinful state (Gen 3:15), He provided a way of redemption.

Why are you sick? The world is spoiled by sin. Sickness may come from four different causes:

1. Some sickness comes from exposure to disease germs or virus.

2. Some sickness comes as a judgment of God, for example, the plagues in Egypt (Ex 9:8-10).

3. Some sickness comes to Christians as a discipline of God (1 Co 11:30). Paul spoke of his "thorn in the flesh" and the reason for it (2 Co 12:9).

4. Some sickness is attributed to the devil (Ac 10:38; Lk 13:11-13, 16; Job 2:3-7). However, the devil's power is limited by God, as seen in the story of Job.

Sickness can be directly attributed to Satan in four ways:

1. It may be for a purpose permitted by God, as in the case of Job.

2. It may be as a consequence of yielding to temptation. Many sins, such as social diseases and drug abuse, bring sickness.

3. One man's sins may bring sickness and suffering to an innocent one, such as a drunken driver or a hereditary disease.

4. Satan may lead us to break God's laws of physical health. However, all our ignorance shouldn't be blamed on Satan.

Satan is at war against God. If he can turn men away from God by prospering them or distressing them, he will do so. If he can afflict men and then win them over by removing the affliction, he will do this. Some miraculous cures come from him using this method of operation. In the kingdom age, though, Satan will be bound except for one brief interval before his final judgment.

Jesus came to remove the curse of sin, including sickness: "who forgiveth all thine iniquities; who healeth all thy diseases" (Ps 103:3), "but he was wounded for our transgressions, he was bruised for our iniquities: the chastisement of our peace was upon him; and with his stripes we are healed" (Is 53:5).

Healing in the atonement. There is healing in the atonement, the only question is when will its blessings be given to man. In His earthly ministry, Jesus demonstrated His power over all kinds of earthly diseases—blindness, deafness, leprosy and palsy—and brought kingdom conditions wherever He went. In the present age He heals at times in answer to prayer, but not every time (2 Co 12:9). During the church age God still uses sickness for His glory, giving men the opportunity to give or to receive the love of others and to see His faithfulness. In the kingdom age the curse of sickness and disease will be lifted. "And the inhabitant shall not say, I am sick: the people that dwell therein shall be forgiven their iniquity" (Is 33:24). "Then the eyes of the blind shall be opened, and the ears of the deaf shall be unstopped. Then shall the lame man leap as an hart, and the tongue of the dumb sing" (35:5-6).

Life lengthened. Life will be lengthened during the millennial kingdom era: "There shall be no more thence an infant of days, nor an old man that hath not filled his days: for the child shall die an hundred years old" (65:20).

There will be a tremendous increase in the birthrate: "And I will multiply them, and they shall not be few; I will also glorify them, and they shall not be small. Their children also shall be as aforetime, and their congregation shall be established before me, and I will punish all that oppress them" (Jer 30:19-20; cf. Eze 47:22).

SOCIAL CONDITIONS

PEACE

The history of the human race has been one long succession of wars and conflicts, which is one of the works of the devil brought about by sin. When man sinned he declared war on God. Instead of being in submission to Him and dependent upon Him, he rebelled because he wanted to become independent. When man is out of fellowship and has enmity with God he cannot get along with his fellowman. War has proven costly in money, foolish in results, and wasteful in lives. At times man has ended his wars, but peace is short-lived when God is left out. In recent years man has attempted to use the World Court, the League of Nations, and the United Nations, and now cries are heard about the necessity of a world police force. In the end time, the world will give power to a strong leader who will promise "peace and safety" (1 Th 5:3). He is a false Messiah or the Antichrist.

Jesus came as a Prince of Peace (Is 9:6). At His birth the angels said, "Glory to God in the highest, and on earth peace, good will toward men" (Lk 2:14). Although the Prince of Peace was rejected by the nation of Israel, He made it possible for man to have peace with God (Ro 5:1-10). Through the ministry of the Holy Spirit, He makes it possible to have the peace of God in the heart (Gal 5:22). There will be wars and rumors of wars to the very end time (Mt 24:6), and the greatest wars that the world will ever see will introduce the kingdom age (Is 2:12-22).

There may be temporary peace in the world, but when Christ comes He will bring permanent peace (Mic 4:1-5). Herman Hoyt says:

> There will be the socialization of the saved elements of society. This is accomplished by the complete organization of society into segments of divisions over which administrators such as kings would preside (Rev. 21:24). This will produce an efficient industrialization of society so that the gifts, skills, and artistry of men can be utilized to create benefits for mankind that will constitute their glory and honor (Rev. 21:24, 26). The dynamic for this constructive enterprise will be the sufficient idealization centering in His Highness, the eternal Son of God. Infinite purpose for men in Christ will provide an ever receding horizon for ambition.[1]

ONE LANGUAGE

Because of the sin of rebellion, God confused the tongues at the tower of Babel (Gen 11:6-9), and the miracle on the day of Pentecost foreshadowed the time in which men will again be able to understand one another. When Jesus reigns on earth He will restore the unity of the language that the human race had before the tower of Babel. Clarence Benson explains:

> The curse of the confusion of tongues will be removed and all of the people will use the same language, which will not only unite the race and remove the possibilities of misunderstandings, but also add greatly to its common comfort and happiness. Zephaniah predicts, "Then will I turn to the people a pure language, that they may all call upon the name of the Lord, to serve Him with one consent" (3:9).[2]

The word "language" in Zephaniah 3:9 is the Hebrew word for "lip" and is the same word used in Genesis 11:1.

This switch to one language will probably be a gradual change, because at the beginning there are men who use many languages going up to Jerusalem to worship (Zec 8:23). What that "official language" will be is not revealed; it could be Hebrew. We do not know what the pre-Babel language was nor that it will be restored, but only that we will understand and communicate in a pure language.

GEOGRAPHICAL CONDITIONS OF THE MILLENNIAL KINGDOM

The warfare, invasion, and judgments of God of the great tribulation will all leave their mark upon the land. The Mount of Olives will split in two when the Lord returns. "And his feet shall stand in that day upon the Mount of Olives, which is before Jerusalem on the east, and the Mount of Olives shall cleave in the midst thereof toward the east and toward the west, and there shall be a very great valley; and half of the mountain shall remove toward the north, and half of it toward the south" (Zec

14:4). There will be great topographical changes to the center of the land of Palestine. A great plain will be raised up. "All the land shall be turned as a plain from Geba to Rimmon south of Jerusalem" (14:10). Geba is about six miles north of the present-day Jerusalem and Rimmon, thirty miles south of Jerusalem. This evidently will be referred to as the mountain of the Lord's house. "And it shall come to pass in the last days, that the mountain of the LORD's house shall be established in the top of the mountains, and shall be exalted above the hills; and all nations shall flow unto it (Is 2:2; cf. Mic 4:1). These geographical changes seem to be in preparation for the building of the millennial temple and the New Jerusalem described in Ezekiel.

DIVISION OF THE LAND

God promised Abraham that He would give him the land (Gen 15:18). In Ezekiel 47:13–48:35 He gives detailed instructions concerning this division. The northern border is at Hamath, which is about 160 miles north of Jerusalem (47:15-17). The southern border is "from Tamar unto the waters of strife in Kadesh, and to the river toward the great sea" (48:28). The western border is the great sea or the Mediterranean (47:20). The eastern border appears to run along a line from Damascus to the Sea of Galilee and the Jordan River to the Dead Sea (47:18). Clarence Larkin, because of God's promise to Abraham, extends these grants to the river Euphrates (Gen 15:18).[3]

The reed and the cubit. In understanding the exact divisions of the land it is necessary to know that the cubit was used in Egypt, Israel, Greece and Babylon, but the exact length differed. There was the normal cubit and the royal cubit, which was longer by about a hand breadth. Unger says that ancient Babylon used three cubits: The smallest was 10.8 inches or three palms, the second was four palms or 14.4 inches, and the third was five handbreadths or eighteen inches. He says,

> As the prophet is very specific in stating the unit of measurement in his vision as a "cubit and a hand breadth" (40:5; 43:13), he, no doubt, meant the smallest cubit of three hand breadths as a basic measure, plus one hand breadth, or what is equivalent to the middle cubit of 14.4". Upon this calculation the reed would be 7.2".[4]

There are several reasons for choosing this size cubit, the most important being that the measurements given for the division of the land fit within the boundaries of the land to be divided (see Fig. 21).

Tribal divisions. In the division of the land among the twelve tribes, Levi has no part, but Joseph's two sons, Ephraim and Manasseh, each has

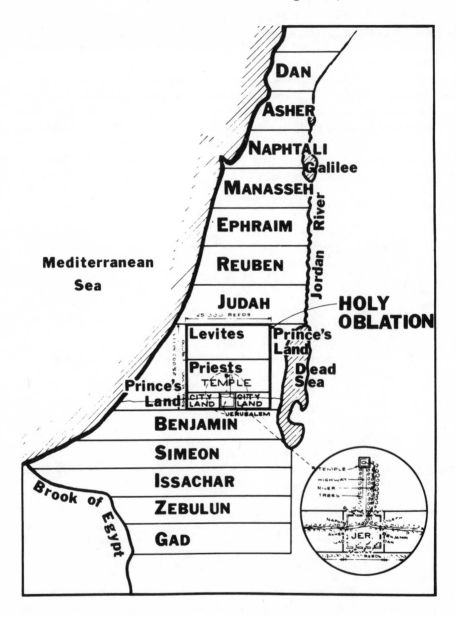

Fig. 21. Division of the Land

a part. Levi will receive his inheritance in the part set aside as the holy oblation. The northern tribe is Dan, followed by Asher, Naphtali, Manasseh, Ephraim, Reuben and Judah (Eze 48:1-7). Under the holy oblation come the tribes of Benjamin, Simeon, Issachar, Zebulun and Gad (48:23-29). It is interesting that the last two tribes to go into captivity, Judah and Benjamin, are given land adjoining God's portion. At the time the kingdom was disrupted under Rehoboam they remained true to the house of David, so perhaps this is their reward. The land itself within the tribal portions is to be divided by lot (48:29).

Holy oblation. In the midst of the land will be the holy oblation, which is to be 25,000 reeds long and 25,000 reeds high. Using a 7.2-foot reed, it would be about thirty-four miles each way. The top section, which will be given to the Levites, is 10,000 reeds wide and 25,000 long (48:13-14). The center section, 10,000 reeds wide, is given to the priests (48:10-12). In the center of the priest's section the temple is built. The southern section, which is 5,000 reeds wide, is set aside as a profane (common) place for the city, its suburbs, and farming areas. The city with its suburbs will be about six miles square (48:15-17). In Bible times, Jerusalem was never over one mile wide. The farming areas on each side of the city will be 5,000 reeds wide and 10,000 reeds long (48:18). This makes the total holy oblation 25,000 reeds square (48:20).

Location of New Jerusalem. If the holy oblation is located upon the great plain mentioned in Zechariah 14:10, New Jerusalem will be south of the present site. Note that the new temple will not be located in New Jerusalem. Isaiah describes this New Jerusalem (65:18-23); it should not be confused with the heavenly Jerusalem described by John in Revelation 21:2. During the millennial kingdom the new city of Jerusalem will have twelve gates named after the twelve tribes of Israel. The heavenly Jerusalem will also have twelve gates named after the twelve tribes of Israel (Rev 21:12).

While the temple will not actually be built within the city limits, Jerusalem will be the capital of Israel and, because Israel will be the foremost nation in the world, it will be the most important city in the world. This will be where the Lord has His throne.

The river of the sanctuary. From the temple will flow a river of living water which will go down to the city of Jerusalem and divide, with one part going to the Mediterranean Sea and one to the Dead Sea. On each bank of the stream will grow trees, the fruit of which will be for meat (food), and whose leaves that never fade can be used for medical purposes. When the water enters the Dead Sea it will make it fruitful so that fish can live there in abundance (Eze 47:1-12). Some feel that there will be a literal highway called "The Way of Holiness" from Jerusalem to the millennial temple.[5] Chapter 35 of Isaiah speaks of the beauty and wonders of the kingdom after the curse of nature has been lifted. The desert blossoming as a rose, streams in the desert, joy and singing, "and an highway shall be there, and a way, and it shall be called The way of holiness; the unclean shall not pass over it; but it shall be for those: the wayfaring men, though fools, shall not err therein. No lion shall be there, nor any ravenous beast shall go up thereon, it shall not be found there; but the redeemed shall walk there" (vv. 8-10).

Prince's portion. The area between the holy oblation and the Great Sea on the west and between the holy oblation and the Jordan on the east will be given to the prince and is called the prince's portion (Eze 45:7-9).

Jerusalem described. The city itself will be a square of 4,500 cubits. There is a space of 250 cubits on each side, making a total of 5,000 cubits per side. Residence in the city will be an honor and will be regarded as a public service. The twelve gates are named after the twelve tribes of Israel, and the population will represent all twelve tribes (48:19). Whether they will reside permanently in the city or not is not stated. Alfred Edersheim in describing the priestly ministry during the time of Christ says,

> The number of priests to be found at all times in Jerusalem must have been very great, and Ophel a densely inhabited quarter. According to Jewish tradition, half of each the twenty-four courses into which the priesthood were divided, were permanently resident in Jerusalem; the rest scattered over the land. It is ordered, that about one-half of the latter had settled in Jericho and were in the habit of supplying the needful support to their brethren while officiating in Jerusalem.[6]

Ezekiel, in speaking of the city lands adjacent to the city, says that they "shall be for food unto them that serve the city" (48:18).

After the Babylonian captivity there was a problem in peopling Jerusalem: "And the rulers of the people dwelt at Jerusalem: the rest of the people also cast lots, to bring one of ten to dwell in Jerusalem the holy city, and nine parts to dwell in other cities. And the people blessed all the men, that willingly offered themselves to dwell at Jerusalem" (Neh 11:1-2). John Skinner suggests, "There may have been causes for this general reluctance which are not known to us, but the principle reason was doubtless the one which has been hinted at, that the new colony lived mainly by agriculture, and the district in the immediate vicinity of the capitol was not sufficiently fertile to support a large agricultural population."[7] While there was a reluctance after the Babylonian captivity, probably there will be an eagerness to live in Jerusalem during the kingdom. Perhaps again lots will be cast to determine who will dwell and serve at Jerusalem from among Israel. This would be apart from any assigned positions that the Lord might give to His resurrected believers.

Summary

1. Most of the curse upon creation will be lifted at the beginning of the kingdom.

2. Life will be lengthened and most sickness removed, but death will still occur in the millennial era.

3. The Prince of Peace will bring peace to the earth, and war will cease.

4. Justice will characterize His kingdom.

5. The people will learn to speak one language.

6. Israel will inherit the land and it will be divided into tribal areas.

7. There will be a holy oblation about thirty-four miles square for the temple, Jerusalem, and for the priests and Levites.

8. Jerusalem will be the capital city.

20

Positions in the Kingdom

WHAT ARE GOD'S PURPOSE and plan for His kingdom? Peters explains:

The Wonderful Plan of God is shown in gathering out an elect body which shall, in the coming Theocracy, be associated with the Christ in rulership in order to promote the redemptive process of the race, and to fill the earth with the praises and glory of the Lord. Instead of being defeated in His Theocratic purpose, God has been steadily making preparation for its sudden and overwhelming appearance . . . these risen and glorified saints . . . form a chosen body, a peculiar distinctive people who alone inherit the Kingdom (for flesh and blood cannot inherit), while the Jewish and spared Gentile nations form the willing subjects of the Kingdom. Being thus a select corporate body to whom the Kingdom is given . . . who alone are crowned as the kings and priests of the restored Theocracy, we find deep reasons for the astonishing expressions recorded of the union, oneness, and fellowship with the Father and Son.[1]

This leads to two important subjects: the heirs of the kingdom and their assignment to positions in the kingdom.

HEIRS OF THE KINGDOM

How do you become an heir? Does being an heir guarantee you a position in the government of the kingdom? Will some be honored more than others? These are important questions because the kingdom is eternal.

BECOMING AN HEIR

Bible students studying the spiritual life often compare the Christian's standing and his state. Because of his union with Christ, the Christian's standing is in "heavenly places" with Him (Eph 2:6). In contrast, his state or spiritual condition in this world may be very "carnal." "For ye are yet carnal: for whereas there is among you envying, and strife, and divisions, are ye not carnal, and walk as men?" (1 Co 3:3).

There is a similar contrast in relation to the Christian and his inheritance. Because of his faith he becomes a Christian and an heir, "for the promise, that he should be the heir of the world, was not to Abraham, or to his seed, through the law, but through the righteousness of faith" (Ro 4:13). Because of the faith of the believer, Paul could say, "Giving thanks unto the Father, which hath made us meet to be partakers of the inheritance of the saints in light: who hath delivered us from the power of darkness, and hath translated us into the kingdom of his dear Son" (Col 1:12-13). The Amplified Bible translates "made us meet" by the words "qualified and made us fit to share." Because of personal faith in Christ, the believer can say that he is an heir and is a part of Christ's kingdom; although that kingdom is yet future, this is positional truth. In Christ he is now a fellow heir: "Which in other ages was not made known unto the sons of men, as it is now revealed unto his holy apostles and prophets by the Spirit; that the Gentiles should be fellowheirs, and of the same body, and partakers of his promise in Christ by the gospel" (Eph 3:5-6).

Commenting upon Luke 18:16, Peters says:

> Every believer, who runs the race successfully, is *heir* to a kingdom, *heir* to a substantial kingship. He is *a prince* in his minority, although perhaps struggling with poverty and without owning a foot of land, or house to shelter himself and family. He may be despised and overlooked by the rich, or by his neighbors, and yet he is destined to a position *far higher and more honorable* than that occupied by the proudest, richest, greatest monarch that ever lived.[2]

RELATIONSHIP OF THE HEIR TO HIS INHERITANCE

W. E. Vine says that the word "inheritance" in Galatians 3:18 stands for "the title to the inheritance."[3] This is an important distinction. We don't become eligible for inheritance because of the works of the law but by faith, but there is a definite relation between faithful service on the part of believers and their reward or inheritance. Paul calls it the "reward" of the inheritance: "Knowing that of the Lord ye shall receive the reward of the inheritance: for ye serve the Lord Christ" (Col 3:24). The Bible does give conditions for ruling with Christ: "And if children, then heirs; heirs of God, and joint-heirs with Christ; if so be that we suffer with him, that we may be also glorified together" (Ro 8:17). Second John 8 warns against losing our reward: "Look to yourselves, that we lose not those things which we have wrought, but that we receive a full reward." Revelation 3:11 warns us against losing our crown: "Behold, I come quickly: hold that fast which thou hast, that no man take thy crown."

FOUR WAYS TO LOSE THE INHERITANCE

A Christian's inheritance can be missed or lost in four different ways:

1. by laziness or poor stewardship
2. by worthless works
3. by evil conduct
4. by despising his birthright

1. *Laziness or poor stewardship.* Paul compares the judgment of a Christian to a stewardship: "But why dost thou judge thy brother? Or why dost thou set at nought thy brother? For we shall all stand before the judgment seat of Christ. For it is written, As I live, saith the Lord, every knee shall bow to me, and every tongue shall confess to God. So then every one of us shall give account of himself to God" (Ro 14:10-12). There is an individual responsibility to give account of all the Lord has given of money, strength, time, and natural and spiritual gifts. The stress is upon faithfulness (1 Co 4:2). It is reassuring to realize that a Christian is *not* responsible for goods which have *not* been committed unto him, for it is easy for a Christian to get discouraged if he compares his achievements with others. Two of the great Old Testament prophets, Isaiah and Jeremiah, had very little outward response from their ministry. They were even hated and mistreated, but they were faithful. The general principle laid down in Scripture is that future greatness in the kingdom will be proportionate to faithfulness in present labor and suffering (Mt 20:21-28; Lk 22:24-30). Even "a cup of cold water" (Mt 10:42) shall be rewarded.

Jesus illustrated in the parable of the pounds what would happen to stewards. He gave each servant a pound. One gained ten more pounds and was rewarded with authority over ten cities. Another gained five pounds and was likewise rewarded with authority over five cities. But one who had done nothing with the pound, but kept it "laid up in a napkin," had his pound given to the one who had been faithful and gained ten pounds. While we are not saved by works, yet we are told, "See then that ye walk circumspectly, not as fools, but as wise, redeeming the time, because the days are evil" (Eph 5:15-16). And again, "That being justified by his grace, we should be made heirs according to the hope of eternal life. This is a faithful saying, and these things I will that thou affirm constantly, that they which have believed in God might be careful to maintain good works. These things are good and profitable unto men" (Titus 3:7-8).

2. *Useless works.* A Christian is also compared to a builder building upon the foundation of Jesus Christ (1 Co 3:11-15). Some Christians' work will go through the fire of Christ's judgment as gold, silver and precious stones. The work of others will be consumed as hay, wood and

stubble, for it is useless busy work, work done for personal glory, or other unworthy motives.

It would be hard to estimate the percentage of work being done today that is truly spiritual work. Many things go under the title of "Christian works" that are a reproach to His name, but these will all be manifest and revealed in their true character at the judgment seat of Christ.

3. *Evil conduct.* Paul compares himself to a runner: "Know ye not that they which run in a race run all, but one receiveth the prize? So run, that ye may obtain" (1 Co 9:24). The apostle explains that runners train and are temperate in all things so that they may win a prize (9:25-26). He does the same: "But I keep under my body, and bring it into subjection: lest that by any means, when I have preached to others, I myself should be a castaway [disapproved]" (9:27). If Christians want to win an incorruptible crown they must also keep the rules of the game and discipline themselves. They must not bring reproach upon the name of the Lord by sinning or they will find that they are disproved and unable to serve Him now and in the age to come.

A Christian can lose his inheritance, not his salvation, by his evil conduct:

> Be ye therefore followers of God, as dear children; and walk in love, as Christ also hath loved us, and hath given himself for us an offering and a sacrifice to God for a sweetsmelling savour. But fornication, and all uncleanness, or covetousness, let it not be once named among you, as becometh saints . . . but rather giving of thanks. For this ye know, that no whoremonger nor unclean person, nor covetous man, who is an idolater, hath any inheritance in the kingdom of Christ and of God (Eph. 5:1-5; see the parallel passage in Gal. 5:19-21).

After listing the long, terrible lists of the works of the flesh, Paul tells the Galatians that "they which do those things shall not inherit the kingdom of God." The word "do" is in the present tense and would point to a habitual manner of life. The usual explanation of this verse is that if a person practices these sins habitually it indicates that they are not really believers, but this is not necessarily true. It is very unfortunate, but there are many Christians who practice these things and are a reproach upon the name of Christ. This verse does not mean that they are not saved, or that they will lose their salvation, but that they will forfeit their inheritance or right to rule in the kingdom. Lot is an example of one who, from outward appearances looked unsaved, but the Scriptures called him "just Lot" (2 Pe 2:7). This same warning against evil conduct is repeated again in 1 Corinthians 6:9-10. When the Lord warns three different times that evil conduct will cause us to lose our inheritance, we should take heed.

There is an example in the Old Testament of a descendant of David who lost his right to reign through sin. King Jehoiakin is told that his son Coniah will never reign: "Thus saith the LORD, Write ye this man childless, a man that shall not prosper in his days: for no man of his seed shall prosper, sitting upon the thone of David, and ruling any more in Judah" (Jer 22:30).

A poor testimony will also cause us to be denied a place of honor. Paul exhorted Timothy to be a good soldier, "endure hardness," and not be "entangled" with the affairs of this life. He warned him that a person is "not crowned, except he strive lawfully" and that "the husbandman that laboureth must be first partaker of the fruits" (2 Ti 2:3-6). "If we suffer, we shall also reign with him: if we deny him, he also will deny us" (2 Ti 2:12; cf. Ro 8:17).

4. *Despising his birthright.* God is training rulers, and Hebrews 12 teaches some important things concerning this training:

1. All true sons receive this training (v. 8).

2. We are not to despise this training (v. 5).

3. We are not to faint or grow weary when rebuked by the Lord (v. 5).

4. We are to reverence the Lord and not be bitter concerning this training (v. 9).

5. This training is to change our character so that we might be partakers of His holiness (v. 10).

6. If we are exercised thereby, our training will bring forth the peaceable fruit of righteousness (v. 11).

An example is given in verse 16 of a wrong attitude that a believer might take concerning this training by God: the despising of the inheritance. "Lest there be any fornicator, or profane person, as Esau, who for one morsel of meat sold his birthright" (12:16). Pentecost says:

> The birthright (Gen. 25:27-34) which Esau despised was a promise to which he was heir under the Abrahamic Covenant. Since it rested on the integrity of God, Esau must be seen to be a man who did not believe God could or would fulfill His word. In like manner the blessing forfeited (Gen. 27) was that blessing due him under the covenant, which must be forfeited because of his unbelief manifested in surrendering the birthright.[4]

Many today mistakenly feel that all they must do is say "Lord forgive me" and their record is all cleaned up. It is true that God has provided confession as a means for restoration to fellowship (1 Jn 1:9), and the penalty of sin has been paid for once and for all at the cross of Christ. Yet, the record of the Christian will go with him to the judgment seat of Christ for rewards and the assignment of position in the kingdom. Esau could not undo what he had done: "For ye know how that afterward, when he would have inherited the blessing, he was rejected: for he found no place of repentance, though he sought it carefully with tears" (12:17).

The parable of the prodigal son is used to illustrate many things. The Lord gave it to point out the hypocrisy of the scribes and Pharisees. Thousands of sermons have been preached, using it to illustrate how God is willing to receive repentant sinners. It also illustrates the loss of an inheritance through a sinful life. In the parable (Lk 15:11-32) the young son in the family was dissatisfied with his manner of life. So the father divided among the two sons their inheritance, and the younger took his and went to a far country and consumed it with riotous living. After his money was gone and he had come to himself, he realized he would be better off in his father's house as a servant. So he decided to go home and ask to be permitted to serve in that position. When he arrived home his father received him, not as a servant but as a son. The older brother, who was out working in the field and heard the noise of the celebration, found out the reason for it and became angry.

It's easy for the faithful working Christian today to also have bitter thoughts concerning the many careless, unconcerned Christians. It has been estimated that 90 percent of the work in most churches is done by 10 percent or less of the members. The elder brother said, "Father, Lo these many years do I serve thee, neither transgressed I at any time thy commandment: and yet thou never gavest me a kid, that I might make merry with my friends" (v. 29). But the father reminded him, "Son, thou art ever with me, and all that I have is thine" (v. 31). While the father provided food, clothing and shelter for the prodigal and considered him a son, he did not restore unto him his inheritance nor make his elder brother divide with him. He reminded the elder brother that for his faithful service, "all that I have" is your inheritance. This parable illustrates that God will reward faithful service.

BEING WORTHY OF THE KINGDOM

After commending the Thessalonians for their faith and love and patience in all persecutions and tribulations, Paul said, "which is a manifest token of the righteous judgment of God, that ye may be counted worthy of the kingdom of God, for which ye also suffer" (2 Th 1:5; cf. v. 11).

Peter encourages Christians in their spiritual growth in 2 Peter 1:3-11, concluding by saying, "Wherefore the rather, brethren, give diligence to make your calling and election sure: for if ye do these things, ye shall never fall: for so an entrance shall be ministered unto you abundantly into the everlasting kingdom of our Lord and Saviour Jesus Christ" (1:10-

11). And abundant entrance is promised to those who have grown spiritually in contrast to the previous warnings that a life of sin will cause the inheritance to be forfeited. In Matthew 20:1-16 Jesus gives the parable of the labourers in the vineyard, concluding with: "For many be called, but few chosen." After giving the parable of the marriage feast in Matthew 22:1-14, He again repeats these words. In Revelation 17:14 these words are used once again, with the addition of one more important word: "These shall make war with the Lamb, and the Lamb shall overcome them: for he is the Lord of lords, and King of kings: and they that are with him are called, and chosen, and faithful." Sinners are called to salvation but there is a higher calling mentioned throughout the New Testament—the call to holy living and faithfulness which issues into the reign with Jesus Christ in His kingdom. Yes, many are called but few are chosen, and those that are chosen to reign are the faithful.

ASSIGNMENTS IN THE KINGDOM

Believers of the church age will receive their assignments at the judgment seat of Christ. Old Testament believers and tribulation martyrs will receive their assignments after Christ's second coming (see chap. 15).

PURPOSE OF THE ASSIGNMENTS

Believers will be assigned by Christ to their respective and proper places in the kingdom. Unger says:

> If a wise earthly monarch is judicious and discriminating in his selections and assignments for offices and positions of trust and power, how much more so will be the returning all glorious "King of kings, and Lord of lords" (Rev. 19:16). In the coming kingdom, the rule of the heavens upon the earth, some will be least and some greatest; some will rule over many cities, others over a few. In the kingdom, Christ, who is now with His Father on His Father's throne, will then take His own throne, the throne of David. Overcomers of the Laodicean church, as a reward, are going to be assigned the dignity and authority of sitting down with Christ on His throne (Rev. 3:21). Those who endured or suffered with Christ, Paul said, would also reign with Him (II Tim. 2:12). In Revelation 19:14, the all-glorious Christ is seen coming with the saints "clothed with fine linen, white and pure," to smite the nations and rule them with a rod of iron.
>
> Overcomers of matured and ripened (rotten) Balaamism and Nicolaitanism in the orgy of Romish corruption in the church of Thyatira are promised the reward of the gift of "authority over the nations," millennial nations, to rule them with a rod of iron, with Christ, as the vessels of a potter are broken to shivers (Rev. 2:26-27; Ps. 2:9). The blessed and holy who have part in the first resurrection are said to be "priests of God, and of Christ," and to "reign with him a thousand years" (Rev. 20:6).[5]

THE NATURE OF THE ASSIGNMENTS

One should not divide the assignments into secular and spiritual ministries because they will be closely related, even as believers are called "kings and priests" (Rev 1:6). "It seems apparent that these assignments will not only embrace *executive* and *administrative* offices, ruling and reigning, but *judicial* duties as well."[6]

The structure of the government is studied in detail in chapter 21, the spiritual life in chapter 22, and activities in eternity in chapter 24.

THE BASIS FOR ASSIGNMENTS

He values faithfulness in His servants and will reward them accordingly:

> To appertain these various executive and administrative and judicial honors, and appoint the various incumbents of offices of trust and power, the judgment seat of Christ will be a necessity. Intrinsic faithfulness and meritorious service will be the criteria; and one thing is sure: politics and unjust favoritism will have no place in these assignments, as Christ Himself will make them.[7]

The service of the believer has a definite relationship to his kingdom service. Raud says,

> Let us rather look upon our earthly life and service as a divinely ordained training which fits us for our occupation in the ages to come. The Lord has prepared for each believer a definite service in the eternal Kingdom. We must learn to think of that service as our "life's work," the ministry which God has planned and for which He seeks to make us ready. Let us perform with all our hearts and all our strength whatever the Lord gives us to do for Him on this earth, knowing that in the glory awaits us our fullest, most powerful, most joyous eternal service. The solemn thought for us to grasp now is that our life on earth has direct bearing upon our eternal future.[8]

For this coming glory the Christians must be trained in obedience, suffering, temptation and trial just as the King was.

The present life is important because as Raud points out,

> The only time God has to prepare His rulers is this brief life on earth. His training is necessary; it is real and thorough; and it is most precious to His trusting child. . . . Our training is made up of continual tests of obedience, some of them weighty, some of them apparently trivial, but how important they really are. We are being trained to do as the Lord commands, no matter what it costs us. Rulers in the eternal kingdom will be examples of prompt, wholehearted obedience. Our obedience to God at that time must be perfect, a pattern for men to study and imitate it. We are being trained now in obedience.[9]

Retarded Spiritual Christians

What will be the position of the lazy, selfish or rebellious Christian in heaven? These improper attitudes come about because of a lack of spiritual growth and can be attributed to a lack of growth as a result of an improper response on the part of the Christian to the grace of God and the teaching ministry of the Holy Spirit. Their position in the kingdom can be illustrated by the position of a retarded child in the home.

The parents can, and often do, love their retarded children as much as they do their other children. Because of this love they protect them and look after them, supplying food, shelter, and necessary clothing. They try to make life as happy for the retarded one as they can. These children are often as happy as possible in relation to their capacity to enjoy life.

In the same way, retarded spiritual children have eternal life because they have been born into the family of God. God loves them and will provide all the necessities, protection, and care necessary. Their responsibilities will be very limited. Their ability to serve Him will be practically nonexistent, and their capacity for happiness and enjoyment will be more limited than those who have experienced the normal or desired spiritual growth.

Summary

1. A person becomes an heir because of his faith in Christ.

2. Being an heir does not guarantee that one will receive the inheritance.

3. There are four ways in which an heir can lose his inheritance: laziness or poor stewardship, worthless works, evil conduct, or by despising his birthright.

4. The assignments will be made by Christ.

5. The assignments will be related to both governmental and spiritual ministries (kings and priests).

6. Faithfulness and meritorious service will be the criteria for assignments.

7. The believer undergoes training in this life to fit him for the ministry to come.

8. The spiritually "retarded" believer's ability to serve the Lord will be almost nonexistent. Few, if any, assignments will be given them.

9. The spiritually "retarded" believers' capacity for happiness will be more limited than those who have matured spiritually through faithful service.

21

The Government of the Kingdom

THE GOVERNMENT of Christ's kingdom will be unique and will accomplish what other governments have not been able to do. Many details have been given concerning the type of government, the structure of His government, the personnel of His government, and the character of His government.

THE TYPE OF GOVERNMENT

The government in the kingdom will be a theocracy or the government of the state by the immediate direction of God.

THE STRUCTURE OF THE GOVERNMENT

The system of government will be unique. We are accustomed to thinking of government as divided into three divisions: executive, legislative and judicial. But in the kingdom government these will be unified under the leadership of Christ. These divisions are necessary now to serve as a system of checks and balances, because of the imperfection of human government.

Our country was established on the principle of the separation of church and state, but in the kingdom the spiritual life will be directly related to the government, which was foreshadowed in the relationship between God and Israel. He was the supreme Lawgiver in all civil and religious affairs (Deu 4:12-14; 12:32). At times He even acted as Judge (17:8-13), and He acted as King of Israel until rejected by them (1 Sa 8:7-8). God partially delegated authority to others to be exercised under a restricted form (Deu 16:18; 33:4-5), but all people were expected in their civil, religious, social and family relationships to acknowledge and be obedient to God's express will (29:10-13).

Daniel prophesied of Christ's reign and His *executive function* of government: "And there was given him dominion, and glory, and a kingdom, that all people, nations, and languages, should serve him: his dominion

219

is an everlasting dominion, which shall not pass away, and his kingdom that which shall not be destroyed" (7:14).

The *legislative function* is seen in Isaiah 2:3, "Out of Zion shall go forth the law, and the word of the LORD from Jerusalem." The *judicial function* of government is seen in the next verse: "And he shall judge among the nations, and shall rebuke many people" (2:4). The *religious function* of His reign is seen in Zechariah 6:13, "Even he shall build the temple of the LORD; and he shall bear the glory, and shall sit and rule upon his throne; and he shall be a priest upon his throne."

KING OF KINGS

Jesus came as the seed of David to fulfill the promise made in the Davidic covenant: "He shall be great, and shall be called the Son of the Highest: and the Lord God shall give unto him the throne of his father David: and he shall reign over the house of Jacob for ever; and of his kingdom there shall be no end" (Lk 1:32-33). The wise men asked, "Where is he that is born King of the Jews?" When asked at His trial, He stated that He was King of the Jews. He was crucified and an inscription was placed on the cross over Him: "THIS IS JESUS THE KING OF THE JEWS" (Mt 2:2; 27:11, 37).

But there will be other kings under Him in His kingdom. Psalm 72:11 says, "Yea, all kings shall fall down before him: all nations shall serve him" and again, "Also I will make him my firstborn, higher than the kings of the earth" (Ps 89:27). He is to be "KING OF KINGS, AND LORD OF LORDS" (Rev 19:16; 1 Ti 6:14-15).

NATIONAL KINGS

Israel will be the leading nation in the world during Christ's kingdom reign. Under the King of kings, Jesus Christ, there will be the King of Israel who is of special interest: "And David my servant shall be king over them; and they all shall have one shepherd: they shall also walk in my judgments, and observe my statutes, and do them" (Eze 37:24). To take this passage in any but a literal sense does injustice to the Scriptures. All through the Bible the resurrected saints are promised a place in the coming kingdom of God. Very little is said in the Scriptures concerning who the other kings will be, but the overcomers mentioned in Revelation 2:26-27 are promised power or authority "over the nations" when ruling them with a rod of iron. While nothing definite is promised in the Scriptures, it seems possible that Joseph and Daniel will also have positions of honor because of what the Lord has promised David. They both served faithfully in troubled times in Gentile governments, and they were faithful to both God and their governmental responsibilities (Dan 12:13). Zerubbabel is promised he will be as a signet (Hag 2:23).

TRIBAL KINGS

"And Jesus said unto them, Verily I say unto you, That ye which have followed me, in the regeneration, when the Son of man shall sit in the throne of his glory, ye also shall set upon twelve thrones, judging the twelve tribes of Israel" (Mt 19:28). The twelve tribes will be regathered in the land, separated into tribes, and given an allotment of land (see Fig. 21). They will be ruled by the twelve apostles as tribal kings or governors, the ministry that Peter was probably referring to when Matthias was chosen to replace Judas when he quoted Psalm 69:25 and said that his bishopric or overseership should be taken by another (Ac 1:20).

CITY KINGS

The parable of the pounds given in Luke 19:11-27 tells of a nobleman who went into a far country to receive unto himself a kingdom and then returned. Before he left he gave a pound to each of his ten servants, and they were to do business with it until he returned. When he returned they were called to account and the faithful were rewarded with the rule over cities. One was given authority over ten cities, another five. Jesus used this parable to teach of Himself. It seems likely that He will appoint city kings or mayors.

OTHER GOVERNMENTAL POSITIONS

Isaiah promises that princes will rule and that judges and counselors will be restored to Israel as at the first (1:26; 32:1). The Old Testament judge was not just a judicial judge but also a leader of the people both in war and in peace. God appointed five ranks of officials in ancient Israel: "So I took the chief of your tribes, wise men, and known, and made them heads over you, captains over thousands, and captains over hundreds, and captains over fifties, and captains over tens, and officers among your tribes" (Deu 1:15). Whether Christ's kingdom will be reestablished in this order or not, it will be the most competent, efficient government the world has ever known.

Satan's forces are organized into principalities, powers, rulers of the darkness of this world and spiritual wickedness in high places (Eph 6:12). Raud suggests an interesting thought: "These enemy spirits must be ejected from their seats of power. God will replace these principalities and powers, these world rulers, with His own administrators. To wield authority in these heavenly regions, He may well appoint members of the church; for he has called the church to reign over the world and the angels."[1]

When the Corinthians were arguing among themselves, Paul reproved them: "Do ye not know that the saints shall judge the world? And if the world shall be judged by you, are ye unworthy to judge the smallest matters? Know ye not that we shall judge angels? How much more things that pertain to this life?" (1 Co 6:2-3). It seems safe to say that there will be many thousands of positions for those who rule with Christ.

SUBJECTS OF THE KINGDOM

Everyone cannot be a ruler. Who will be the subjects in the kingdom? Walvoord says:

> It is clear from Scripture that there will be a believing remnant on the earth when Christ comes back to establish His millennial kingdom. This remnant is never identified with the church and is never spoken of as translated. It is composed of believing Jews and Gentiles living at the close of the tribulation (Ezek. 20:34-38; Matt. 25:31-46). After the second coming, they are still in the flesh and are not free from death. They till the ground, raise crops, bear children, and repopulate the earth (Isa. 65:20-23; 66:20-24; Zech. 8:5; Matt. 25:31-40). . . .
> The church after the Lord's coming is not going to raise crops in the earth, bear children, repopulate the earth, and be subject to death. An interval of time is demanded, then, during which another generation of believers will come into existence. While every believer will be translated when Christ comes for His church, a new body of believers will be formed in the awful days of the tribulation. Those of this group who escape martyrdom will be the believing godly remnant on the earth when the Lord returns with His church from heaven to establish His millennial kingdom.[2]

Jesus very clearly says that only born-again believers can enter the kingdom (Jn 3:3, 6), which will start with subjects who have survived the terrible judgments of the great tribulation and the personal judgment by Jesus Christ. All unbelievers will be put to death.

In the kingdom, children will be born to these believers, but before the first thousand years have ended, they will either have trusted in Christ or rebelled against Him. The Scriptures seem to teach that the government will be given to the resurrected believers, but the subjects of the kingdom will be mortals who pass through the tribulation and the children who are born to them.

THE PERSONNEL OF HIS GOVERNMENT

COMING REIGN OF RESURRECTED AND NONRESURRECTED SAINTS

Some object to the church returning to have a part in the earthly reign during the millennial era. They claim it will be impossible for resurrected and unresurrected people to mingle, but Christ mingled with His disciples in the postresurrection period between His resurrection and His ascension. The Old Testament records that the angels who carried the message to Sodom ate with Abraham and were in the house of Lot. Walvoord says:

> It is clear that even at the present time there is a ministry of angels to human beings even though angels are of an entirely different order of being than men and are invisible in their earthly activities under ordinary circumstances. Though the free mingling of resurrected and nonresurrected beings is contrary to our present experience, there is no valid reason why there should not be a limited amount of association in the millennial era.[3]

ANGELS IN THE KINGDOM

The exact position of angels in the kingdom is not disclosed. Now they are spoken of as the "ministering spirits, sent forth to minister for them who shall be heirs of salvation" (Heb 1:14). "For unto the angels hath he not put in subjection the world to come, whereof we speak" (2:5). First Corinthians 6:3 says that they will be under the authority of the ruling saints.

ISRAEL'S PLACE IN THE KINGDOM

When Christ institutes His kingdom at His second coming, He will be sitting upon the throne of David, ruling over Israel as well as the rest of the world (Is 9:6-7; Zec 14:9; Eze 37:21-25). Israel will be exalted above the other nations (Deu 28:13), occupy the place of religious leadership in the world (Is 2:1-5), become God's witness during the millennium (44:8, 21), and will be prepared for her ministry through the new covenant (Heb 8:10-13).

CHARACTER OF HIS GOVERNMENT

CHRIST'S ATTRIBUTES REFLECTED IN GOVERNMENT

The great characteristics of the Lord's government are justice (Ps 72:2-5), mercy and truth (Is 16:5); equality and faithfulness (11:2-5); and glory. Clarence Benson says:

> Truly it will be an age of glory; glory for the earth, glory for the vegetable kingdom, glory for the animal kingdom, glory for the redeemed of the human race, and above all glory for the King of kings and Lord of lords. "His name shall endure for ever: his name shall be continued as long as the sun: and men shall be blessed in him: all nations shall call him blessed" (Ps. 72:17).[4]

His government will be a shepherd-type government. Isaiah 11:4 says, "He shall smite the earth with the rod of his mouth, and with the breath of his lips shall he slay the wicked." Some have thought that because the expression "rod of iron" is used that if anyone should sin in His kingdom He will immediately be punished by being slain.

Siess says, "To shepherdize with an iron sceptre, is to exercise dominion which is inflexible, irrefragable, and that cannot be withstood. Strength, absoluteness and perpetuity of rule, is unmistakably indicated; and that rule is specifically said to be over *'all nations.'* "[5] In the New Testament where He is said to "rule them with a rod of iron" (Rev 2:27; 12:5; 19:15) the word "rule" is literally "shepherd." Six times it is translated "feed." Christ as the chief Shepherd will meet their every need, whether it is for care, feeding, protection, training or discipline.

The method of government is closely connected to the spiritual life of the people. Isaiah shows that it will have three phases: teaching, judging and rebuking:

> And it shall come to pass in the last days, that the mountain of the LORD's house shall be established in the top of the mountains, and shall be exalted above the hills; and all nations shall flow unto it. And many people shall go and say, Come ye, and let us go up to the mountain of the LORD, to the house of the God of Jacob; and he will teach us of his ways, and we will walk in his paths: for out of Zion shall go forth the law, and the word of the LORD from Jerusalem. And he shall judge among the nations, and shall rebuke many people: and they shall beat their swords into plowshares, and their spears into pruninghooks: nation shall not lift up sword against nation, neither shall they learn war any more (2:2-4).

National punishment. All people will not be obedient and some will require rebuking or disciplining. Zechariah gives an example of the Lord withholding the rain and sending a plague. These will be dramatic judgments because in the kingdom the fruitfulness of the earth will be restored and the curse of disease will largely be lifted:

> And it shall come to pass, that every one that is left of all the nations which came against Jerusalem shall even go up from year to year to worship the King, the LORD of hosts, and to keep the feast of tabernacles. And it shall be, that whoso will not come up of all the families of the earth unto Jerusalem to worship the King, the LORD of hosts, even upon them shall be no rain. And if the family of Egypt go not up, and come not, that have no rain; there shall be the plague, wherewith the LORD will smite the heathen that come not up to keep the feast of tabernacles. This shall be the punishment of Egypt, and the punishment of all nations that come not up to keep the feast of tabernacles (Zec 14:16-19; see Is 60:12).

Individual punishment. Attention has often been drawn to a one-hundred-year-old person being called a child in Isaiah 65:20, but very little is said of the sinner in the latter part of that verse: "There shall be no more thence an infant of days, nor an old man that hath not filled his days: for the child shall die an hundred years old; but the sinner being an hundred years old, shall be accursed." The rebellious are "destroyed from among the people," perhaps at the end of each hundred years during the millennium. If this is the case, the rebels mentioned in Revelation 20:7-8 are those born during the last one hundred years of Christ's reign on earth.

The Jews today practice a ritual called Bar Mitzvah on the first Sabbath after a boy's thirteenth birthday. He is then allowed to take part in public worship. More important, he is considered morally responsible for his actions and is then supposed to keep the commandments, for the term Bar Mitzvah means "son of commandment." In the millennium, grace may be extended until the age of one hundred before judgment is exercised. Whether or not this idea is correct concerning the method of capital punishment during the millennial period, this is sure: it will be a perfect government with every sentence right and just, with no innocent person ever being punished for a crime which he did not commit, nor no sentence but what matches the crime committed.

SUMMARY

1. The type of government of the kingdom is a theocracy: the government of the state by the immediate direction of God.

2. The principle of separation of "church and state" or the spiritual and the secular will come to an end in the kingdom.

3. Jesus Christ will be King of kings. David will rule Israel (other national kings are not named); the twelve apostles will rule the twelve tribes of Israel; and rulers of cities and other positions will be appointed.

4. The subjects of the kingdom will be the believing remnant of the tribulation and the children who are then born to them.

5. Israel as a nation will be exalted above the Gentiles to a place of religious leadership.

6. Christ's government will be characterized by justice, mercy, truth, equality and faithfulness—a shepherd-type government.

7. Christ will exercise discipline and judgment in His kingdom.

22

Spiritual Life in the Kingdom

AT MOUNT SINAI God promised the nation of Israel that they would be a kingdom of priests, a holy nation (Ex 19:6). This promise was conditioned upon their obedience to Him, but Israel failed to keep her covenant and God promised a new covenant (Jer 31:31). In this new covenant He would write His laws upon the table of their heart and give them a new heart and put His spirit in them so that they could keep His covenant. After Israel's regathering and conversion, God will institute this covenant with His people and they will become a kingdom of priests unto Him.

THE TEMPLE IN THE MILLENNIUM

Spiritual life in the kingdom will revolve around the new temple that will be built. The temple and the religious service connected with it are described in Ezekiel 40—48. Some have questioned how these prophecies should be interpreted. James Gray gives a good summary:

> (1) Some think they describe the temple at Jerusalem prior to the Babylonian captivity, and are designed to preserve a memorial of it. But the objection is that such a memorial is unnecessary because of the records in Kings and Chronicles; while the description is untrue because in many particulars it does not agree with that in the books named.
>
> (2) Some think these chapters describe the temple in Jerusalem after the return from the seventy years in Babylon, but this can not be, because there are more marks of contrast than likeness between the temple here described and that.
>
> (3) Some think they describe the ideal temple which the Jews should have built after the seventy years' return, and which they never realized. But this lowers the character of the divine Word. Why should this prophecy in Ezekiel have been given if it was never to be fulfilled?
>
> (4) Some think this temple in Ezekiel symbolizes the spiritual blessings of the church in the present age. But this appears unlikely, because even those who hold the theory can not explain the symbolism of which they speak. Moreover, even as symbolism it leaves out several important features of Christianity, such as the atonement and intercession of the high priest.

(5) The last view is that in the preceding comments, that we have here a prediction of the temple that shall be built in the millennial age. This appears a fitting and intelligent sequel to the preceding prophecies.[1]

Too many details and measurements are given if the temple and service are just symbolical. Since the prophecy has never been fulfilled historically, the only satisfying interpretation is that Ezekiel's temple is a literal future temple to be constructed in Palestine during the millennium. The words of the prophet need to be taken in their natural grammatical and literal sense and not symbolically unless so indicated by the text.

THE TEMPLE'S LOCATION

The temple will be built in the heart of Palestine in the midst of the twelve tribes in the center of the holy oblation on a high mountain (see Fig. 21).

THE TEMPLE BUILDERS

This temple will not be the temple of the tribulation period, but it will be built under the supervision of Christ Himself. "Behold the man whose name is The BRANCH; and he shall grow up out of his place, and he shall build the temple of the LORD: even he shall build the temple of the LORD; and he shall bear the glory, and shall sit and rule upon his throne; and he shall be a priest upon his throne: and the counsel of peace shall be between them both" (Zec 6:12-13). He will serve in a dual capacity as King of kings and High Priest and evidently will be assisted in the building by many from all over the world (6:15). It may take 1,040 days to complete it (2,300 days after the desolation of the tribulation temple; see Dan 8:13-14).

THE TEMPLE'S DESCRIPTION

The dimensions of the temple are given in detail, but it is suggested that the reader refer to several other translations. *Living Psalms and Proverbs with Major Prophets, The American Standard Version* of 1901, *The Amplified Bible,* and *The Berkley Version* are all helpful. No attempt has been made to cite all the differences in the King James Version and other translations, but this brief list of buildings and main features will give a basic understanding of the temple.

The wall. Ezekiel first describes a wall which separates against all that would defile (40:5). This wall is five hundred cubits or about one-eighth of a mile on each side (40:5; 42:20) and is six cubits high and six cubits thick (see Fig. 22).

The eastern gate. This is one of three gates in the outer wall, there

EZEKIEL 40-46

NORTH

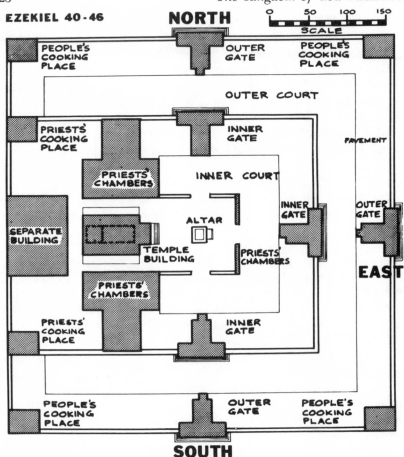

Fig. 22. Ezekiel's Temple

being none in the west. All are of the same design. Seven steps lead to the gate, and the door of each gate is ten cubits wide (40:11). A hall or porch is connected to each gate, and on each side of each porch hallway are three little chambers, one reed square in size, and separated by a space of five cubits (Eze 40:7-10). The Hebrew word here is also used in 1 Kings 14:28, where it is translated "guard chamber," which is probably what the six chambers are for.

Five chambers were on each side of the gate in the outer court in the wall, making a total of thirty chambers. All are joined together, with one leading into another (40:17-18). The exact internal division is not given (see Fig. 23).

The outer court. The outer court is the area of general assemblage where people gathered. In the outer court in front of the chambers and around the edges is a pavement (40:17-18).

Kitchens. In each corner of the outer court there is a kitchen of forty cubits long and thirty cubits wide where the ministers of the house shall boil the sacrifices of the people, evidently the peace offering (46:21-24). The location of the priest's cooking places (46:19-20) are not given, so they have been placed opposite the people's cooking places.

The inner court. The inner court is one hundred cubits square (40:47). Three gates with eight steps leading to them are in the inner court directly opposite the gates in the outer court (40:37). Thus this portion of the temple is elevated from the outer court. By the north gate are tables and instruments to prepare the sacrificial animals (40:39-43). On each side of the gate toward the inner court are the chambers for the singers, priests, and keepers of the charge (40:44-46).

The altar. In the midst of the inner court is the altar, whose size is between that of the altars in the tabernacle and in the temple of Solomon. The base is sixteen cubits square, the ledge fourteen cubits square and

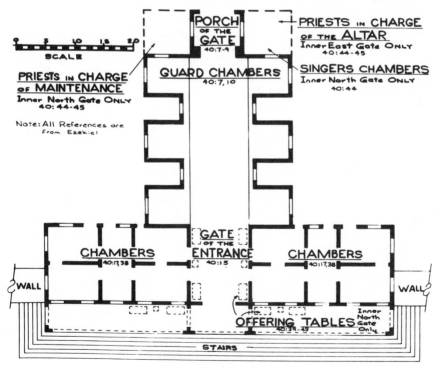

Fig. 23. Detail of the Gates

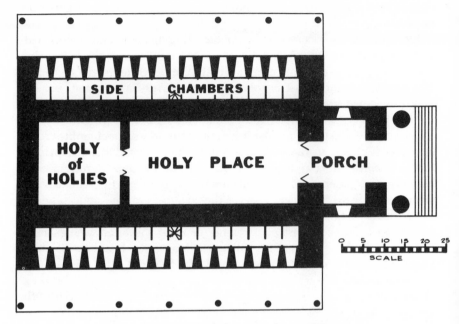

Fig. 24. Detail of the Temple Building

two cubits high, with the altar itself being twelve cubits square and four cubits high (40:47; 43:13-17).

The porch of the temple. The porch is twenty cubits by eleven. Two large pillars are on it, and it must be reached by steps, although the number is not given (40:40, 49; see Fig. 24).

The holy place. The porch leads into the holy place which is forty by twenty cubits. The holy place and the holy of holies are the same size as those in Solomon's temple and twice as big as the tabernacle. It has only one piece of furniture called an altar of wood which probably compares to the altar of incense in the tabernacle. There is no mention of the candlestick, table of shewbread, or veil.

The Holy of Holies. Connected to the holy place is the most holy place which is twenty cubits square (41:4). No ark of the covenant or any furniture is seen in the holy of holies, but Ezekiel prophesies in his vision that the Shekinah glory will fill this most holy place. The inside of the temple was paneled with wood and ornamented with palm trees and cherubim, a contrast to Solomon's temple because of the conspicuous absence of silver and gold (41:15-26).

Side chambers. There are three stories of side chambers with thirty chambers to a story. It is not disclosed what their purpose is, but they are probably for the use of the priests.

The separate place or court of the priests. This is twenty cubits wide and surrounds the temple building on every side except the east.

Doors. "And the temple and sanctuary had two doors" (Eze 41:23). The prophet does not tell exactly where the doors are located, but evidently they are between the court and holy place.

The hinder building. The hinder building is built adjoining the separate place to the west of the temple building. It is seventy cubits broad and ninety cubits long with a wall five cubits thick around it. The purpose of this building is not known. A. C. Gaebelein suggests that it is probably used for the disposal of refuse from the sacrifices and other unclean things.[2]

The priest's chambers. Opposite the temple building on the north and south are the priest's chambers. They are three stories high with galleries. Following the King James text, there appears to also be a row of chambers in the wall east of the altar (42:1-14).

Living waters. An unusual feature is the living waters which come out of the south side of the altar and flow to the right of the house, out of the eastern side of the court and then down to Jerusalem (47:1-12). The stream divides, part of it flowing into the Dead Sea and part of it into the Mediterranean (see Fig. 21).

THE SHEKINAH GLORY IN THE MILLENNIAL TEMPLE

The children of Israel were led out of Egypt by a fiery cloud. The Shekinah glory was seen when the tabernacle was dedicated: "Then a cloud covered the tent of the congregation, and the glory of the LORD filled the tabernacle. And Moses was not able to enter into the tent of the congregation, because the cloud abode thereon, and the glory of the LORD filled the tabernacle" (Ex 40:34-35).

The same thing happened when Solomon finished the temple: "The cloud filled the house of the LORD, so that the priests could not stand to minister because of the cloud: for the glory of the LORD had filled the house of the LORD" (1 Ki 8:10-11). Evidently the Shekinah glory remained in the holy of holies until just before the destruction of Jerusalem. God showed Ezekiel in a vision the departure of the glory of the Lord from the temple and from Jerusalem (Eze 10:18-19; 11:22-23).

When the Jews returned from the Babylonian captivity and rebuilt the temple under Zerubbabel, the Shekinah glory never returned to Zerubbabel's temple, nor was it seen in Herod's. Haggai prophesied, "For thus saith the LORD of hosts; Yet once, it is a little while, and I will shake the heavens, and the earth, and the sea, and the dry land; and I will shake all nations, and the desire of all nations shall come: and I will fill this house with glory, saith the LORD of hosts" (2:6-7). The Lord visited that temple, because Herod's temple was really only the remodeled temple of Zerubbabel, but His glory was veiled in human flesh.

When the Millennial temple is built, the Shekinah glory of the Lord will return. Ezekiel saw the glory of the Lord come in through the eastern gate: "And the glory of the LORD came into the house by the way of the gate whose prospect is toward the east. So the spirit took me up, and brought me into the inner court; and, behold, the glory of the LORD filled the house" (43:4-5). This is a visible glory and God will now dwell in the midst of the children of Israel forever (43:7). It will be as it was when the children of Israel made their exodus from Egypt: "And the LORD will create upon every dwelling place of mount Zion, and upon her assemblies, a cloud and smoke by day, and the shining of a flaming fire by night: for upon all the glory shall be a defence. And there shall be a tabernacle for a shadow in the daytime from the heat, and for a place of refuge, and for a covert from storm and from rain" (Is 4:5-6).

ANIMAL SACRIFICES RESUMED

In the worship of the temple, animal sacrifices are resumed. The sacrifices and offerings will not be exactly the same as under the Mosaic covenant, but there will be sin offerings, trespass offerings, peace offerings, and burnt offerings. A lamb will be offered as a burnt offering every morning, but no mention is made of the evening sacrifice. Some object to the literal interpretation of these passages, especially as they feel there is a conflict between Hebrews 7:27; 9:12, 26.

In Old Testament times the animal sacrifices had no efficacy in themselves but only pointed to Jesus, the Lamb of God (Jn 1:29). In the millennium there still will be no efficacy in the sacrifice itself. While the Old Testament sacrifice was typical and pointed toward Christ, the millennial sacrifice is commemorative and points back to the death of Christ. There are four other reasons to believe the sacrifices will be resumed: (1) In the millennium, death will be much more infrequent. These sacrifices will help keep in mind the terrible cost to the Saviour in redeeming us from the curse of sin.. (2) The church has a memorial today, the Lord's Supper. When we partake of this we do show the Lord's death until He comes (1 Co 11:26). (3) The early Christians continued to participate in the temple services (Lk 24:53). Paul went to the temple as late as A.D. 50 (Ac 21:26). (4) Jeremiah also mentions animal sacrifices in the millennium (33:15-18).

TEMPLE MINISTRIES

Because in the vision the glory of the Lord goes through the eastern gate, the Lord orders it to be closed and not to be used as a gate, but the prince can "sit in it to eat bread before the Lord." The prince is not identified. Some have thought that he is the Lord, but chapter 46 shows him worshiping and bringing burnt offerings, so this could not be Christ because He has no need for offerings. Also, it speaks of him having sons. The prince probably is a descendant of David.

WORSHIP OF THE PRINCE AND THE PEOPLE

In chapter 46 Ezekiel gives detailed instructions concerning worship. No unsaved person is to enter the temple (44:9), there are special observances of the eastern gate, and the inner court is only open on the Sabbath and the new moon. When the people come in to worship through the northern gate they must leave by the southern gate, or if they enter by the southern gate they must exit by the northern gate.

Under the old system all Jews who were able were to come to Jerusalem for the three great feasts: Passover, Pentecost, and the Feast of Tabernacles (Deu 16:16). In the millennium only the Passover and Feast of Tabernacles will be observed. The feast of Pentecost seems to foreshadow the calling out of Jew and Gentile into a new body of believers, the church, which was born on the day of Pentecost. The Day of Atonement is also missing from the calendar. This we can understand because it was fulfilled in the ministry of Jesus Christ when He died upon the cross and ascended into heaven.

When the temple is rebuilt, it is to be a house of prayer for all nations: "Even them will I bring to my holy mountain, and make them joyful in my house of prayer: their burnt-offerings and their sacrifices shall be accepted upon mine altar; for mine house shall be called an house of prayer for all people. The Lord GOD which gathereth the outcasts of Israel saith, Yet will I gather others to him, besides those that are gathered unto him" (Is 56:7-8). Jesus Himself quoted from this passage when He cleansed the temple: "It is written, My house is the house of prayer: but ye have made it a den of thieves" (Lk 19:46).

The kingdom starts with only those who are born again, but there will be children born who will have to make their own personal decision concerning Christ. In that day, even as now, there will be some who don't care to worship the Lord and they will be punished (Zec 14:16-19). Some suggest that the annual trip to Jerusalem to worship and to sacrifice, spoken of in these verses, is to be performed on a representative basis

rather than an individual basis. This seems probable and would solve
many problems such as transportation and housing.

The Jews will have a ministry unto the Gentiles. While there will be
many Gentiles saved out of the tribulation, their knowledge of God will
doubtless be very limited (Zec 8:20-23; Is 11:9).

THE HOLY SPIRIT IN THE MILLENNIUM

An important aspect of spiritual life in the kingdom will be the ministry
of the Holy Spirit. He will indwell believers (Eze 36:25-28). There isn't
any reason to believe that this promise is exclusively for the Jews, for the
Lord will also give the Holy Spirit unto Gentiles as He does in this age.

THE CHURCH'S SPIRITUAL MINISTRY

Believers are promised that they are kings and priests (1 Pe 2:9; Rev
1:6), but there is no indication that the church will minister in the millennial temple. Pache suggests a threefold grouping patterned after the
tabernacle:

> a. The Church in the most Holy Place, namely, in the heavenly places,
> sharing with Christ's royalty and priesthood;
> b. Israel in the Holy Place, serving God below in the sanctuary as the
> ancient Levites;
> c. The nations in the forecourt, coming to bring the Lord their wor-
> ship as did formerly the twelve tribes.[3]

The grouping probably should be changed rather to "resurrection
saints," "living Israel," and "the living nations." (The church will still

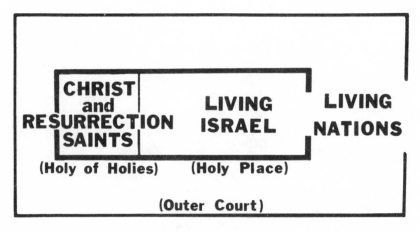

Fig. 25. Tabernacle Outline

have a unique relationship to Christ within the general category of resurrected saints.) The outline of the tabernacle can illustrate this (see Fig. 25).

HIGH PRIEST

Jesus Christ is not only King of kings and Lord of lords, He is also a High Priest after the order of Melchizedek (Heb 5:10). He is presently ministering and making intercession for us (7:25). The exact nature of His priestly ministry during the millennium is not disclosed (Zec 6:13).

SUMMARY

1. A temple will be rebuilt in the millennium which will be the center of spiritual activity in the kingdom.

2. A detailed description of their temple is given by Ezekiel.

3. No unsaved person will be allowed to enter it, but believers from all nations will come up to worship.

4. A stream of living water will flow from the temple down to Jerusalem, where it will divide and flow into the Dead Sea and the Great Sea.

5. The Shekinah glory of God will reside in the temple.

6. Commemorative animal sacrifices will be offered in the temple worship.

7. The faithful descendants of Zadok will minister as priests in the temple.

8. The church and other resurrected believers probably will not minister in this earthly temple, but in the New Jerusalem.

23

Eternal Destinies

MAN'S EXISTENCE does not cease at death, for he is a being of eternity. But mankind will be divided into two main categories: the saved and the lost, each of which has its destiny. At the end of the millennial era the final division of the living will be made. We will consider (1) the final revolt, (2) eternal punishment of the lost, and (3) the eternal blessedness of the saved.

THE FINAL REVOLT

Why does God release Satan? After one thousand years of blessed rule under Christ, God will release Satan for at least four reasons: (1) God will prove that good conditions do not make a good man. Many, when given the choice, will rebel against God. (2) God will use Satan, who is incurably wicked and rebellious, to gather the unbelievers from over the world together. (3) God will purge the earth of these evil men and angels. (4) the righteousness of God's judgment will be demonstrated on the wicked who have been giving "lip service" unto Christ during the long millennial era.

GOOD CONDITIONS DO NOT MAKE GOOD MEN

Many people today think that if we could defeat disease, hunger, poverty, ignorance, and corruption in government we would have our own heaven on earth. After one thousand years of unparalleled blessing the people of the earth will be put to a final test. For one thousand years there will have been no war. No young man will have received notice that he must fight in the defense of his country. Crime will sharply decrease, and sickness and disease will be largely eliminated. Man's life will have been extended to hundreds of years of useful service. Climatic conditions will have been so changed that the very desert will bloom like a rose. For one thousand years the world will have been governed without graft and corruption, for the government will have been under the

236

rule of Jesus Christ and His saints. While it will have been very different from the present age, yet there still will have been sin and death in the millennial era, but for one thousand years Satan and the forces of evil will have been restrained. Satan himself will have been bound in the bottomless pit and man freed of his temptations.

SATAN USED TO GATHER THE UNGODLY

"And when the thousand years are expired, Satan shall be loosed out of his prison, and shall go out to deceive the nations which are in the four quarters of the earth" (Rev 20:7-8). Satan in his desire to be as God will desperately make one last attempt to gather followers. His exact appeal unto the nations is not given, but perhaps it will be as he said unto Eve, "Ye shall be as gods" (Gen 3:5). It won't be a passive decision on the part of his followers, however, for he is gathering them to battle against the saints of the Lord (Rev 20:8-9). Satan will be very successful in his appeal, for his armies will be "as the sands of the sea" in number (20:8). "And they went up on the breadth of the earth, and compassed the camp of the saints about, and the beloved city: and fire came down from God out of heaven, and devoured them" (20:9). The length of the "little season" during which Satan is loosed is not given, but evidently it is not very long. It will end with the judgment of God upon those who have rebelled and followed Satan. When Satan is released, God uses him like a magnet to draw unbelievers unto himself from all over the world.

POPULATION EXPLOSION

When Christ establishes His kingdom, only believers will be permitted to enter it (Jn 3:3-5). The judgments of the great tribulation will destroy a large percentage of the population. Only one-third of Israel will go through the great tribulation, and it seems very likely that there will be even less than this of the Gentile population.

The long life, low death rate, plentiful food supply, and favorable conditions will cause the population to expand rapidly. At the present time about three billion people are in the world, and at the present growth rate this figure will double by A.D. 2,000. Some have estimated that from one-tenth to one-fifth of all the people who have ever lived are living today. At the end of the millennial era, the world will probably have its record population. It seems probable that there will be more people living at that time than the total who have lived from Adam to the kingdom.

FINAL PURGING OF THE EARTH

The ungodly are defeated "and fire came down from God out of heaven, and devoured them" (Rev 20:9). Sodom is an Old Testament type of God's judgment by fire (Lk 17:28-30).

Without trying to decide the exact nature of the fire that fell on Sodom, it is important to notice that the fire came from God. It was selective; it did not harm Lot and his two daughters. The scriptural account, while very simple and short, does convey the idea that it was an unusual and terrible judgment.

This is the final purging of sin and sinners from the face of the earth. The last traces of sin, disease, germs and virus will probably be removed at this time, perhaps by the very fire that judges unbelievers. Most important of all, where there is no sin, there is no longer any need for a curse, and consequently no death. Death is described as the last enemy: "For he must reign, till he hath put all enemies under his feet. The last enemy that shall be destroyed is death" (1 Co 15:25-26). The new heavens and new earth can then take on their final form.

The scene in John's vision divides, with first a view of the lost and then the saved: "And the devil that deceived them was cast into the lake of fire and brimstone, where the beast and the false prophet are, and shall be tormented day and night for ever and ever" (Rev 20:10).

The dead of all ages are raised and brought before a great white throne for judgment. This throne's location is not given, but it is not upon the earth (20:11). John uses personification to describe heaven and earth fleeing away like a person: "And I saw a great white throne, and him that sat on it, from whose face the earth and the heaven fled away; and there was found no place for them" (20:11).

TERMINOLOGY

The doctrine of hell is ridiculed, spurned and hated by many liberal theologians and teachers in false cults, and there are also false conceptions among evangelical believers. Several words are used in the Bible for the place the soul goes after death:

Sheol. The Hebrew word *Sheol* is used sixty-five times in the Hebrew Old Testament, but it is not translated consistently. Three times it is translated *pit;* thirty-one times, *grave;* and thirty-one times, *hell.* When the Old Testament was translated into Greek, the translators used the word *hades;* for all practical purposes *sheol* and *hades* are equivalents. *Sheol* is never used to denote a place of final punishment; its basic meaning is "the place of departed spirits." It has the same relation to the soul as the grave has to the body, and both good and bad are spoken of as going there. Seiss says that it is the "invisible place where the soul that leaves their bodies live, whether it be a place of bliss or torment. In this sense it is taken in Scripture, the Apocrypha, the Fathers, yea, and in the heathenish authors, too."[1]

Hades. The Christian's concept of heaven is entirely lacking in Old Testament thinking. "The ancient saints gained satisfaction in the thought of being gathered to their fathers, and in resting there with the holy dead: but never as enjoying there the bright presence of God and the society of angels. All the higher and the better recompenses to which they looked, they invariably connected with the resurrection."[2]

Jesus revealed several additional facts about hades in Luke 16:19-31: (1) It is divided into two compartments, one side a place of torment and the other a place of blessing. In this passage He calls it "Abraham's bosom," which seems to be a synonym for paradise, and is probably what Paul saw (2 Co 12:1-4). (2) A great gulf is between these two compartments so there can be no traffic between them. (3) The destinies of men are fixed in this life and cannot be changed when they get to hades. (4) This is a conscious experience, not soul sleep, and the memory will continue to function. (5) The unsaved in the place of torment do not want their friends to come there.

Paradise. Jesus promised the thief on the cross that "to day shalt thou be with me in paradise" (Lk 23:43). Christ and the thief went to the paradise side of hades, but He went as a Conqueror of death, proclaiming His victory to the spirits that were imprisoned there (1 Pe 3:18-19). On the day of Pentecost, Peter quoted from Psalm 16 and said of Jesus, "Because thou wilt not leave my soul in hell [hades], neither wilt thou suffer thine Holy One to see corruption" (Ac 2:27). While Christ went to hades, He did not come out alone but He brought captivity captive (Eph 4:8-9). Jesus said that He had the keys of hades and death (Rev 1:18). Paradise is no longer in hades but above, in the heavens (2 Co 12:1-4), and the destination of believers today is no longer hades but the presence of the Lord. Speaking of the church, He promised that the "gates of hell [hades] shall not prevail against it" (Mt 16:18). Or this can be paraphrased, "The gates of hades shall never close on any true member of His church."

Abaddon, abyss, tartarsus. Another place in the underworld is spoken of in the Old Testament. Called *abaddon*, it is usually translated "destruction" (Job 26:6; 28:22). Literally Proverbs says, "Hades and *abaddon* are never full" (27:20). *Abaddon* seems to be a deeper and darker and more wretched place than hades, evidently identified with the *abyss* in Revelation 9:1-3. This *abyss* is mentioned nine times in the New Testament and seems to be an abode of the demons. Some identify this with *Tartarsus:* "For if God spared not the angels that sinned, but cast them down to hell [*tartarsus*] and delivered them into chains of darkness, to be reserved unto judgment" (2 Pe 2:4). Seiss says, "*Abaddon* and the *abyss* would therefore seem to be the abode of demons, a sort of deeper pit beneath hades, where the wickeder and baser spirits of dead men, and other foul spirits of the lower order, are for the most part held as melancholy prisoners till the day of final judgment"[3] (see Lk 8:26-31; Rev 11:7; 17:8; 20:1-3).

Gehenna. A new word, Gehenna, is used as a name for the place of eternal punishment eleven times in the New Testament, every time but once by Christ Himself. *Gehenna* is the Greek rendering of the Hebrew word *Hinnom.* The beautiful valley of Hinnom was located just southeast of Jerusalem, and here Israelites killed and sacrificed their own children to the Ammonite idol Molech in direct disobedience to God's command (Deu 18:10). Two kings of Judah performed this terrible act: Ahaz, who began to rule in 742 B.C. (2 Ki 16:3) and Manasseh, whose rule began in 698 B.C. (2 Ch 33:6). Just before the Babylonian captivity in the day of Jeremiah, the Israelites were systematically sacrificing their children in this valley, which they called *Tofeth*, "a place of burning." Jeremiah warned that instead of a place of idol worship it would be a place of slaughter where they would be forced to bury their dead in large numbers (7:32-34), which was literally fulfilled when Jerusalem was destroyed in 586 B.C.

In New Testament times the Valley of Hinnom, instead of being the place of idol worship, had become the dumping grounds and sewage plant of Jerusalem where fires smoldered continually and there were all kinds of decay and corruption from the garbage. So in Jesus' day the idea that Gehenna was a picture of eternal punishment was firmly identified in the minds of the people, and He used it as a name for eternal punishment. It is translated in our English Bibles by the word *hell* (see Mt 5:22, 29-30; 10:28; 18:9; 23:15, 33). In describing this place, Jesus spoke of the place where "their worm dieth not, and the fire is not quenched" (Mk 9:44), evidently quoting from Isaiah 66:24. This appears to be the same place of punishment described later in Revelation 14:9-11; 19:20; 20:10, 14-15.

The lake of fire. The lake of fire which burneth with brimstone is prepared for the devil and his angels: "And the devil that deceived them was cast into the lake of fire and brimstone, where the beast and the false prophet are, and shall be tormented day and night for ever and ever" (Rev 20:10). All the wicked dead, along with death and hades, are cast into it. There won't be any more use for hades, the temporary place of confinement, and death itself will then become the second death or eternal separation from God. This is the final defeat of the forces of evil. At this time the curse and the promise given in Genesis 3:15 will have been fulfilled, for Satan will have been defeated. Man will have been redeemed; he will be back in his place of dominion, ruling over the world led by the last Adam, the God-Man, Christ Jesus.

ETERNAL BLESSEDNESS OF THE SAVED

PROPHECIES OF THE NEW JERUSALEM

The book of Hebrews contains the earliest recorded idea concerning the city of God: "For he [Abraham] looked for a city which hath foundations, whose builder and maker is God" (11:10).

The New Jerusalem will be the capital city of the new earth: "But ye are come unto mount Sion, and unto the city of the living God, the heavenly Jerusalem, and to an innumerable company of angels, to the general assembly and church of the firstborn, which are written in heaven, and to God the Judge of all, and to the spirits of just men made perfect" (12:22-23).

Paul, writing to the Galatians, said, "But Jerusalem which is above is free, which is the mother of us all" (4:26). Jesus, in His letter to the overcomers at the church at Philadelphia, said, "Him that overcometh will I make a pillar in the temple of my God, and he shall go no more out: and I will write upon him the name of my God, and the name of the city of my God, which is new Jerusalem, which cometh down out of heaven from my God: and I will write upon him my new name" (Rev 3:12). Note that this city is to come *down* from heaven. Many feel that Jesus was speaking of the New Jerusalem when He said, "In my Father's house are many mansions: if it were not so, I would have told you. I go to prepare a place for you" (Jn 14:2). It may have been the New Jerusalem that Paul saw when he was caught up into the third heaven and was given revelations that he was not permitted to tell about (2 Co 12:1-7).

A LITERAL CITY

Some have tried to spiritualize the heavenly city, but God goes to great length to show the city's materials, dimensions, appearance, inhabitants and contents. As William R. Newell has so aptly said, "If gold does not mean gold, nor pearls—pearls, nor precious stones—stones, nor exact measurements—real dimensions, then the Bible gives nothing accurate nor reliable."[4]

THE SHAPE OF NEW JERUSALEM

In describing the city, John said, "And the city lieth foursquare, and the length is as large as the breadth: and he measured the city with the reed, twelve thousand furlongs. The length and the breadth and the height of it are equal" (Rev 21:16). There are three different ideas regarding the shape of the holy city. Clarence Larkin believes it will be in the shape of a pyramid.[5] It is true that all three dimensions for a pyramid can be equal but it is just one of the possibilities, for Scripture does not support the idea of a pyramid in preference to a cube.

J. Vernon McGee has an unusual idea that the city is a cube within a crystal sphere and that the bride will live outside the planet earth within the planet called New Jerusalem.[6] Although the sun, moon and earth have spherical shapes nothing is given in Scripture to support this idea.

Most commentators look at New Jerusalem as being in the shape of a cube. When God told Moses to tell the children of Israel to build a sanctuary so He could dwell among them, the pattern that He gave for the holy of holies was shaped like a cube—ten cubits wide, ten cubits long, and ten cubits high. This same shape was repeated in Solomon's temple but the measurements were double the size of the tabernacle. Zerubbabel's temple, that was remodeled by Herod, and the millennial temple, described in Ezekiel, have a cube-shaped holy of holies. Because of this it has been suggested that the holy city is the holy of holies of the future, for God will dwell in it. It seems significant that Moses was admonished to carefully construct a tabernacle after the heavenly pattern (Heb 8:1-5).

THE SIZE OF THE NEW JERUSALEM

When John saw New Jerusalem he said the city was 12,000 furlongs, or about 1,342 miles, on each side. This would make a tremendous city covering about half the United States or all of Europe. Some, thinking that this would be too large, have interpreted Revelation 21:16 as being the sum of the dimensions, but there is no valid basis for doing this. New Jerusalem would cover about 1,750,000 square miles in contrast to New York City which covers 315 square miles. New York City's present population is 7,800,000, or 24,700 people per square mile. If New Jerusalem were populated with the same density it would hold over 43 billion people, or fourteen times the present population of the earth. This would be from two to six times the estimated total population of the world since Adam. But even this doesn't take the height of the city into consideration, for it is 1,342 miles high. While too much stress should not be put upon its actual dimensions, the city obviously will be immense.

THE LOCATION OF THE NEW JERUSALEM

John saw "the holy city, new Jerusalem, coming down from God out of heaven" (Rev 21:2). Three times it is said to be coming down, but it never says that it actually settles upon the earth. The earth will be changed but there is no reason to believe that there will be any great difference in its size. The earth is approximately 8,000 miles in diameter, the moon is approximately 2,100 miles in diameter, and New Jerusalem will be a cube of 1,342 miles. If New Jerusalem settled on the site of earthly Jerusalem it would cover an area from Greece to the Persian Gulf and most of Egypt. Since Revelation 21:24 says the nations of the earth will walk in the light of the city, apparently it will come near the earth but not actually settle upon it. (See Fig. 26. The earth, moon and New Jerusalem are all drawn to scale.)

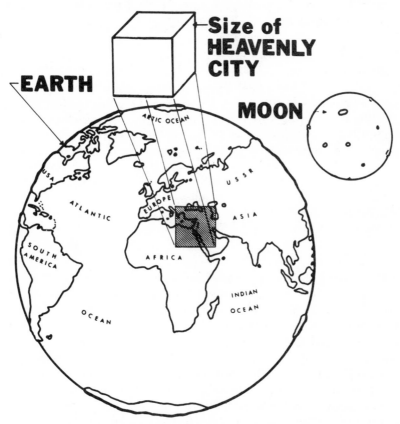

Fig. 26. New Jerusalem, the Heavenly City

In the book of Genesis, Jacob had an interesting dream as he fled from his brother Esau after stealing the blessing: "And he dreamed, and behold a ladder set up on the earth, and the top of it reached to heaven: and behold the angels of God ascending and descending on it. And, behold, the LORD stood above it, and said, I am the LORD God of Abraham thy father, and the God of Isaac: the land whereon thou liest, to thee will I give it, and to thy seed" (28:12-13). At this time God confirmed the Abrahamic covenant with Jacob and promised him the land, which is perhaps a foreshadowing of the relationship of the holy city to the earth.

The word translated *angel* comes from the Hebrew *malak*, which is used about one hundred times in the Old Testament, half the time translated *angel*, and the other half as *messenger*. In Malachi 3:1, in the prophecy about John the Baptist, *malak* is translated *messenger*. The messengers in Jacob's vision do not necessarily have to be angelic beings but could be referring to the servants of God, the resurrected saints. God is at the top of the ladder. If this is the picture, then there is the same basic outline seen in the tabernacle.

E. W. Rogers says, "The 'tabernacle of God' is the 'holy city' which, coming down from heaven, is brought into association with 'men,' that is [we suggest], the inhabitants of the new earth."[7]

Using the tabernacle as a pattern, New Jerusalem would represent the holy of holies and be occupied by God and the resurrection saints. Living Israel would represent the holy place as Israel ministers as a nation of priests to the world. The living nations of the world would represent the outer court of the tabernacle, which of course needs to be visualized in a vertical position with the holy of holies at top, above Israel (see Fig. 25). The holy city has this twofold idea of being God's sanctuary as well as His capital city.

THE EXTERIOR OF NEW JERUSALEM

It is impossible to read Revelation 21 and the description of the New Jerusalem without being impressed with John's attempt to describe the city's beauty. Although he uses figures of speech to describe the various parts of the city, it must be kept in mind that it is a literal city, for when figures of speech are used there is always a direct relationship between the figure and the thing described. When the light of the city is described as a precious stone, even like a jasper, clear as crystal (Rev 21:11), John is using something that we can understand, a jasper, and then he qualifies it with an additional beauty. Jasper is beautiful and often contains many colors, but it is not clear as crystal. His idea can be paraphrased "If you'll look at a jasper stone and think about all its beautiful color and then think of how it would look if it were clear as crystal you will have some idea about the light that comes from the New Jerusalem."

A wall measuring 144 cubits surrounds the city. Some who believe this measurement to be the wall's height, point out that it is not nearly as high as the city, so they think the wall will be a boundary line rather than being for defensive purposes, as in ancient cities. However, this dimension may be the thickness or breadth of the wall, so the wall may reach to the height of the city.

Three gates on each side of the city are named for the twelve tribes of the children of Israel, and the city's foundations are named for the twelve apostles. Some have pictured the foundations as being one on top of another, but Clarence Larkin pictures each side as being divided into three foundations located side by side.[8] The foundations are garnished with all manner of precious stones (Rev 21:19-20) of many different colors, calling to mind the precious stones placed on the high priest's breastplate. Many attempts have been made to attach a meaning to the various stones, but none is very satisfactory. One thing is evident: in the description he attempts to express a beauty unknown to us today. Each city gate is a great pearl, and an angel is at each gate (Rev 21:12, 21).

THE INTERIOR OF NEW JERUSALEM

Seiss suggests that many streets of gold will extend into the holy city: "streets over streets, and stories over stories, up, up, up, to the height of 1500 miles and each street 1500 miles long."[9] This may be an exaggeration, but surely roads will lead from each gate because that is the very purpose of a gate. The gates themselves will never be shut.

One significant thing that will be missing is a temple: "And I saw no temple therein: for the Lord God Almighty and the Lamb are the temple of it" (Rev 21:22). As suggested before, the holy city itself can be compared to a sanctuary.

The city itself will have no need for street lights or other forms of lighting, for the glory of God will illuminate it. When Moses constructed the tabernacle, no provision for light was made in the holy of holies. It was covered on all sides but it was lighted by the presence of God: "Then a cloud covered the tent of the congregation, and the glory of the LORD filled the tabernacle" (Ex 40:34). New Jerusalem will be constantly lit by the presence of God, and there will be no night there (Rev 21:25). But the glory of the Lord will not be contained within New Jerusalem; it will shine and light the nations of the world: "And the nations of them which are saved shall walk in the light of it: and the kings of the earth do bring their glory and honour into it" (Rev 21:24; cf. 21:11).

In the midst of the city will be located the throne of God (Rev 22:1, 3); for He will make New Jerusalem His capital city, His headquarters for the universe.

The river of the water of life. In the beginning, at Eden, there was a river: "And a river went out of Eden to water the garden" (Gen 2:10). When Jesus talked to the woman at the well He told her of living water that He would give (Jn 4:10-14; cf. 7:37-39). There is a similarity between the description of the river in the New Jerusalem and the one coming from the millennial temple described in Ezekiel 47:1-12. The psalmist said, "There is a river, the streams whereof shall make glad the city of God, the holy place of the tabernacle of the most High" (46:4). The stream in Ezekiel comes from the side of the altar, flows down to Jerusalem, and then parts and goes to the Mediterranean Sea and Dead Sea (Zec 14:8). The river in the New Jerusalem comes from the throne of God and the Lamb (Rev 22:1).

The tree of life. The tree of life was first seen in the Garden of Eden: "the tree of life also in the midst of the garden" (Gen 2:9). After Adam and Eve sinned they were driven from the garden so that they might not partake of the tree of life and live forever in their sinful state. Ezekiel described trees that grew on each bank at the river that flowed from the temple: "And by the river upon the bank thereof, on this side and on that side, shall grow all trees for meat [food], whose leaf shall not fade, neither shall the fruit thereof be consumed: it shall bring forth new fruit according to his months, because their waters they issued out of the sanctuary: and the fruit thereof shall be for meat, and the leaf thereof for medicine" (47:12). The trees, although described as being good for food, are not called the tree of life. This description is not the same as the description in New Jerusalem, but the earthly one is a type of the heavenly. Or expressed differently, Ezekiel's description is a reflection of what will be found in New Jerusalem.

In both descriptions the trees line each side of the river. John says, "In the midst of the street of it, and on either side of the river, was there the tree of life, which bare twelve manner of fruits, and yielded her fruit every month: and the leaves of the tree were for the healing of the nations" (Rev 22:2). It's hard to understand exactly what it means to eat of the fruit of the tree of life, but the Scripture does teach that if Adam and Eve had eaten of the tree of life, physical death would have been an impossibility (Gen 3:22). The tree in New Jerusalem seems to have the same purpose. The word translated "healing" can mean "health." Walvoord says,

The word for "healing" is *"therapeian,"* from which the English word *therapeutic* is derived, almost directly transliterated from the Greek. Rather than specifically meaning "healing," it should be understood as "health-giving," as the word in its root meaning has the idea of serving or ministering. In other words, the leaves of the tree promote the enjoyment of life in the New Jerusalem, and are not for correcting ills which do not exist. This, of course, if confirmed by the fact that there is no more curse as indicated in verse three.[10]

No more curse. When New Jerusalem appears one thing will make a real contrast between it and the present world: there will be no more curse. Sin, sickness, disease and death, with all the problems of war, poverty and strife that come from the curse of sin, will be gone. When sin is eliminated there will be no more curse, and mankind will be what the theologians call "confirmed in holiness," or no longer subject to sin. R. I. Humberd describes this as "crystalized character."[11] "He that is unjust, let him be unjust still: and he which is filthy, let him be filthy still: and he that is righteous, let him be righteous still: and he that is holy, let him be holy still" (Rev 22:11).

TIME OF THE APPEARANCE OF THE NEW JERUSALEM

Some people have identified New Jerusalem with the church during this present age, while others believe it is the earthly city of Jerusalem as seen in the millennial era. Still others think it will descend and hover over the earth at the beginning of the millennium.[12]

The chronological order of the Bible places the appearance of New Jerusalem after the millennial era, and there seems to be no valid reason to consider that Revelation 21:10–22:5 is a flashback into millennial times. As Wilbur M. Smith says, "This refers to our eternal state."[13]

Without being dogmatic, we would place it as a climax at the end of the millennium when the program of redemption has been fulfilled and the eternal character of the kingdom assumed, but it could be near the beginning of the thousand years.

INHABITANTS OF NEW JERUSALEM

New Jerusalem becomes the habitation of God: "But ye are come unto mount Sion, and unto the city of the living God, the heavenly Jerusalem, and to an innumerable company of angels, to the general assembly and church of the firstborn, which are written in heaven, and to God the Judge of all, and to the spirits of just men made perfect, and to Jesus the mediator of the new covenant" (Heb 12:22-24). This verse says that the following will inhabit New Jerusalem:

1. God

2. holy angels
3. the church
4. just men made perfect (all other resurrected believers)

No unsaved persons will ever defile it (Rev 21:27). Apparently the believers who lived through the millennium will continue to live on the earth and walk in the light of it: "And the nations of them which are saved shall walk in the light of it: and the kings of the earth do bring their glory and honour into it" (21:24). It is hard to tell whether these kings are the believers of this age who are to rule and reign with Christ, or earthly kings ruling under Christ and His church.

JEREMIAH 31:31-34
HEBREWS 8:7-13

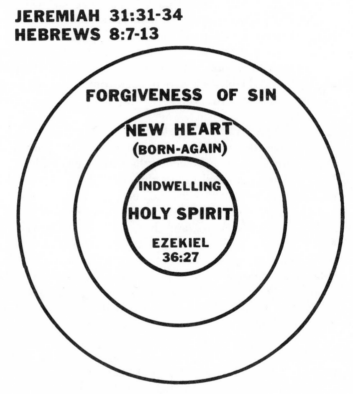

Fig. 27. The New Covenant

THE NATIONS IN THE ETERNAL STATE

Will nations continue to exist? Walvoord says:

> It is an error, however, to assume that national identity will be lost in eternity. Just as there will be individual identity, so also there will be

racial identity, and individuals will inevitably carry throughout eternity an identification related to some extent to their place in the history of the world. Hence, Israelites will be Israelites throughout eternity and Gentiles will be Gentiles as well.

Although there has been some resistance to this idea, national identity seems a natural corollary to individual identity. If Abraham is to remain Abraham throughout eternity and David is to remain David, it is inevitable that they would be considered in their historical context in time.[14]

The people will be living under the benefits of the new covenant (see Fig. 27).

THE BRIDE OF THE LAMB AND NEW JERUSALEM

New Jerusalem is compared to a bride in Revelation 21:2. The angel tells John, "Come hither, I will shew thee the bride, the Lamb's wife. And he carried me away in the spirit to a great and high mountain, and shewed me that great city, the holy Jerusalem, descending out of heaven from God" (21:9-10). This does not mean that *"the* bride" and New Jerusalem are necessarily synonyms. For example, if you were riding in an airplane approaching New York City you could say, "Look, I want you to see the Empire State Building." It is in New York, but it is not New York City. In the same way the angel could have been referring to the bride as an inhabitant of New Jerusalem. In Galatians 4:26 New Jerusalem is called "our mother." Walvoord, in commenting on Revelation 21:2 where New Jerusalem is compared to a bride, says:

> The use of the marriage figure, however, in both the Old and New Testaments is sufficiently frequent so that we cannot arbitrarily insist that figures are always used in precisely the same connotation. The subsequent description of the new Jerusalem in this chapter makes plain that saints of all ages are involved and that what we have here is not the church per se but a city or dwelling place having the freshness and beauty of a bride adorned for marriage to her husband.[15]

There is a possibility that the word "bride" is used of the city of New Jerusalem and is not referring to its inhabitants. In the Old Testament, Jerusalem is called the bride (Is 62:5). Peters, referring to an Oriental custom, says:

> In the usage of the east when a king entered his capitol to rule therefrom, or a prince ascended the throne, it was represented under *the figure of a marriage*, i.e. he was wedded, *intimately and permanently united* to the city, or throne, or people. The use of the figure in Scripture shows that we are not to limit it unless specified to the Church. While employed to denote *Christ's union with the Church*, it has been used to mean *other unions*. It designates *the permanent union* of a people *with the land*, as in Isa. 62 where in the Millennial description the land is called *"Beulah,"*

that is *"married"* (marg. read.) and it is said: *"thy land shall be married, for as a young man marrieth a virgin, so shall thy sons marry thee . . ."* Then the figure rises still higher, including *God's marriage* (i.e. dwelling again with man on the earth) *with the land*, for it is added: *"as the bridegroom rejoiceth over the bride, so shall thy God rejoice over thee."* The *earthly Jerusalem* is personified as a woman, and God, when dwelling there by a visible representation, is declared *to be married* to her, i.e. *to the city itself.* But just as soon as the city was filled with wickedness, she is represented as an *adulterous woman,* and God withdraws from her. In Ezek. 16, is such a description of marriage, which in view of the alleged birth, parentage, etc., *can only* be applied directly to the city, which become by virtue of this relationship the representative of the nation. . . . Then again, God is spoken of *as married to the nation,* because abiding with them, as Ruler in a special manner. How, considering that . . . Jesus has gone before to prepare a place for us to be incorporated into the Father's house, that this place or inheritance is "ready to be revealed in the last time" (so context demands, including saints); that when the last time does come it is represented as descending from God out of heaven upon the new earth, that the figure of marriage is applied to a literal city (as the old Jerusalem), there is no impropriety but rather eminent fitness *that the union of the King of kings with His metropolitan city should be designated under the same figure, including the most intimate and permanent relationship.* . . . Now the setting up of this Throne in it, *is the act of marriage*; it is that which makes *the union.* For, just as God was *formerly married* to the earthly Jerusalem when His Theocratic Throne was there, so, carrying out the same beautiful prophetical figure, He is again married, when the New Jerusalem comes down from heaven upon the earth, *by the very act of erecting His Theocratic Throne* there and ever abiding in it in His glorified humanity as David's Son, "The Christ."[16]

An Old Testament example is quoted by Seiss as he compares the opening of the tabernacle with the entrance into the New Jerusalem:

> Just what the ceremony of this marriage is we are nowhere told. Some have thought that it is the first opening of the city of God, the New Jerusalem, to the footsteps of the redeemed. Jesus says that he is now preparing a place for us. The ancient saints looked for a city whose maker and builder is God. That city John saw and describes in a subsequent chapter. That city was shown him as the Bride, the Lamb's Wife, so called on account of those who inhabit and dwell in it. The placing of the redeemed with their Redeemer in that sublime and eternal home necessarily involves some befitting formality. Nor is it far-fetched to connect that first formal entrance into that illustrious heaven-built city with the ceremonial of what is described as the marriage of the Lamb. When the sacred tabernacle was first opened and used it was with great solemnities, which God himself prescribed, and in the observance of which there was also a marked coming together of God and his people. By visible manifestations of Deity a point of union and communion was then and there established between man and Jehovah, so direct and close that the

holy prophet could say of Israel, Thy Maker is thy Husband. And the fact that God so ordered and honoured the occasion is ample warrant for taking it as the type of a corresponding formality in the heavens, answering to the coming together of the Lamb and his affianced people for the first time in that glorious city, which even the great voice from the throne calls "THE TABERNACLE OF GOD."[17]

It is hard to be dogmatic about the identity of the bride and the significance of the marriage, but the church will reside with the Lord in the New Jerusalem.

RELATION OF THE NEW JERUSALEM TO HEAVEN

The word *heaven* has the general idea of that which is above and it usually refers to one of three things: (1) the atmospheric heavens, (2) the heavens of the universe, or (3) the abode of God. Wilbur M. Smith in his classic *The Biblical Doctrine of Heaven* points out that six different words or phrases are used to describe heaven as the abode of God: tabernacle, sanctuary, habitation, house, temple, and throne of God.[18] He goes on to show that the abode of God has the characteristics of holiness, glory and fellowship. A careful study will show that the Old Testament saints did not have our popular concept of "going to heaven after they die." Gustave Oehler says:

> (1). *Of the traces of belief in a heavenly life beyond the grave* which have been supposed to be found in the Pentateuch, the translation of Enoch, Gen. 5:24, can alone come into consideration. But that is not a testimony to a higher existence of the soul *after death*; for the meaning of the passage is that Enoch never died—that is, his body and soul were never separated. (2). In it, as in the history of Elijah's translation (II Kings 2), there lies rather the declaration, that even before the coming of death's vanquisher some specially favored men were excepted from the curse of death and of the kingdom of death which hangs over man. These narratives, then, contain an indirect corroboration of the position that according to the Old Testament, death is not unconditionally connected with human nature.[19]

Daniel 12:2 shows that they did not think of a departure at death to heaven or hell but that after resurrection there would come blessing or torment. At death the soul went to *sheol*, "the place of departed spirits."

Robert Girdlestone also emphasizes that the future reward of the saint is connected with the heavenly city:

> The usage of the word "heaven" in the N.T. generally answers to that which is to be traced through the Hebrew Bible, but more stress is laid upon the spiritual heaven, upon the Father who is there, and upon the Son who came from heaven, and who has returned thither to remain hidden from the eye of man until the time of the restitution. . . . The

popular phraseology about "going to heaven" represents the truth, but certainly not in the form in which it is generally presented in Scripture. We rarely read that the godly will go *to heaven*, either at death or after the resurrection. We are rather told of a kingdom being set up *on earth*, of a heavenly city descending from above, and taking up its abode in the new or renewed earth.[20]

It was Paul who revealed, "We are confident, I say, and willing rather to be absent from the body, and to be present with the Lord" (2 Co 5:8). He revealed that at physical death the soul and spirit are separated from the body and they go to be with Christ (who is in heaven). But this is really an intermediate state because when Christ returns from heaven to rapture His church, the dead will return with Him. Their bodies are changed, resurrected, and reunited with the soul and spirit. While it is true in this sense in the present age that we go to heaven, our eternal reward is connected with this earth. It would be more accurate to say that God will bring "heaven" to us rather than taking us to live in heaven. Most of the knowledge that we have of the eternal state (often called heaven) is taken from the description of New Jerusalem and the eternal state of the kingdom.

SUMMARY

1. Good conditions do not make good men.

2. Many who are born during the millennial era will rebel against Christ.

3. God will destroy with fire the great army of unbelievers that Satan will gather.

4. This fire will purge the earth of all sinners.

5. The unsaved of all ages will be judged and cast into the lake of fire as their eternal punishment.

6. The relation of New Jerusalem can be shown to be above the earthly Jerusalem (it's not clear whether it will remain stationary there or whether the earth will revolve under it, or how high it will be above the earth).

7. New Jerusalem is the capital city and sanctuary of the new heavens and the new earth from which God will rule His creation.

8. The nations of the world will live under it.

9. New Jerusalem is not heaven as we think of it now, but it will become the abode of God.

24

Activities of Eternity

THE QUESTION is often asked, "What will we do when we get to heaven?" or perhaps more appropriately, "What will we do throughout eternity?" Revelation 22 gives a brief glimpse of life in heaven. The picture is not one of idleness, but one of activity in the midst of unparalleled blessing.

In New Jerusalem the redeemed will have access to the "water of life" and "the tree of life" (Rev 22:1-2). It is interesting to compare this to man's position in Eden. Seiss says:

> Being innocent, man ate of the tree of knowledge of good and evil, and learned to know *evil*. For all these many ages he has been tasting and experiencing the bitternesses of evil. Through the redemption that is in Christ Jesus, they that believe in him come to know *good*: and knowing good, there will be no more turning of their hearts away from him, and hence no more sinning and no more curse. And man being finally and permanently redeemed, everything that has been disordered, disabled, or cursed for man's sake, shall also be permanently delivered (Rom. 8:9-23).[1]

Peters points out that the redeemed will not be idle:

> The priesthood, as well as the kingship, shows that God in the Coming Kingdom has *something for His saints to perform*. Idleness and selfishness enfeeble and degrade; activity and imparting to others are elevating and joy-producing. It will still, then, be true, that "*it is more blessed to give than to receive.*" To be made instrumental of doing good to others is Christ-like, God-like. And this activity in honor of God, in behalf of others, in joyfulness to ourselves, is unceasing. Being glorified, there is no need of recuperation to remove fatigue of weakness, and therefore, as expressive both of a constant activity and a never-decaying vigor, they are represented, e.g. as serving God "*day and night*" (Rev. 7:15-17).[2]

The eternal activities of the saved can be expressed in four ideas found in Revelation 22:3-5: (1) service, (2) fellowship, (3) worship, and (4) dominion.

SERVICE

"His servants shall serve him" (Rev 22:3). Exactly what form this service will take is not revealed. However, the general teaching of Scripture is that this present life is a "workshop for eternity." Who would want to spend eternity in idleness? One of the great thrills during the present age is the thrill of being a colaborer with Christ. John, describing the martyrs who came out of the great tribulation, says, "They . . . [shall] serve him day and night in his temple" (7:15).

How close our future service will resemble our present service is difficult to say. There will be some important differences: the work will be free from the fatigue and care, it will not be burdensome but a delight and an expression of our ability acquired through obedience to the Spirit of God in this age.

"The race of man, as a race, continues on the new earth, and there realizes its complete and final recovery from all the effects and ill consequences of the fall. Ransomed nations in the flesh are therefore among the occupants of the new earth, and blessed and happy dwellers in it, as Adam and Eve dwelt in paradise."[3]

Some have suggested that perhaps part of the service of the inhabitants of New Jerusalem will be to dispense the benefits of the water of life and the tree of life to the nations on the earth. "The leaves of the tree were for the healing [or health] of the nations" (Rev 22:2).

Others have turned their eyes on the universe itself, believing that surely God has a plan for all the billions of stars and planets. His future program for His universe is not revealed, and man can only speculate. But because of our intimate relationship with Christ, we will share in His activities.

FELLOWSHIP

"And they shall see his face" (22:4). We have a preview in this life of what fellowship can be like in the next. One of the great purposes of our ministry is declared by John: "That which we have seen and heard declare we unto you, that ye also may have fellowship with us: and truly our fellowship is with the Father, and with his Son Jesus Christ" (1 Jn 1:3).

Peter said of Jesus, "Whom having not seen, ye love; in whom, though now ye see him not, yet believing, ye rejoice with joy unspeakable and full of glory" (1 Pe 1:8). Think how that joy will increase when we "see his face." God will not be off "somewhere" in heaven, but His tabernacle will be with man forever.

WORSHIP

One of the themes that run through the book of Revelation is worship. In chapters 4 and 5 are the four living creatures and the twenty-four elders worshiping: "And when those beasts [living creatures] give glory and honour and thanks to him that sat on the throne, who liveth for ever and ever, the four and twenty elders fall down before him that sat on the throne, and worship him that liveth for ever and ever, and cast their crowns before the throne, saying, Thou art worthy, O Lord, to receive glory and honour and power: for thou hast created all things, and for thy pleasure they are and were created" (4:9-11). The martyrs who come out of the great tribulation add their voices to the angels and the elders and the living creatures: "And cried with a loud voice, saying, Salvation to our God which sitteth upon the throne, and unto the Lamb. And all the angels stood round about the throne, and about the elders and the four beasts, and fell before the throne on their faces, and worshipped God" (7:10-11). Before Christ returns to the earth (11:15-19) and before the great Battle of Armageddon there will be other great scenes of worship (19:1-6).

Music will have an important place in worship. As Smith points out, "Much of this worship will be conducted within the framework of music. The Book of Revelation contains more songs than any other book in the Bible, with the exception, of course, of the Psalter—fourteen of them, all sung by groups appearing in heaven, some by the angels, some by the elders, but a number of them by the redeemed."[4]

Directly connected with this worship will be our position as priests: "His name shall be in their foreheads" (22:4). The high priest in Israel had the words "HOLINESS TO THE LORD" engraved on a golden crown that he wore on his forehead (Ex 39:30). During the tribulation period, the beast will cause people to wear his name or number, 666. The harlot who sits upon the beast has upon her forehead, "BABYLON THE GREAT, THE MOTHER OF HARLOTS AND ABOMINATIONS OF THE EARTH" (Rev 17:5). But Jesus has promised the overcomers in the church at Philadelphia, "Him that overcometh I will make a pillar in the temple of my God, and he shall go no more out: and I will write upon him the name of my God, and the name of the city of my God, which is new Jerusalem, which cometh down out of heaven from my God: and I will write upon him my new name" (3:12).

DOMINION

"They shall reign for ever and ever" (22:5). God created man and intended for him to rule the earth, but due to the fall, man lost his privilege.

This responsibility was transferred to Christ, or the last Adam, who will accomplish that in which Adam failed. As previously discussed, the church and resurrected believers will rule with Him. His dominion will include all nations (Isa 2:2), the whole earth (Dan 2:34-35; Zec 14:9), and all people, nations and languages (Dan 7:14; Ps 2:8, 11).

The millennial era will start with Israel in the land as the chief nation on earth, but there will also be the sheep nations as described by Christ in the Olivet discourse. Only those who have been born again will be allowed to enter into the millennial kingdom. But there will be many children born during this age, and from among them Satan will gather his army in his last revolt. The believers of that age will never die, and when the curse of sin is finally lifted from the earth apparently they will enter into an existence similar to what Adam and Eve would have known had they not sinned. The people that populate the new earth will then rule as God had originally planned for Adam. They will have dominion over all the lower creation, and all animals, fish and birds will be subject unto them. M. R. DeHaan says,

> Evidently there will be nations of people on the earth throughout eternity. This may be a rude shock to men who have conceived of eternity as a time when all men will be the same and dwell together in heaven as spirits or, at least, angels, but such is not true, . . . believers will be literal human beings in perfect resurrection bodies, but there will be other people also. There must be, for it is said of us, the saints of God, that we shall reign with Him forever and ever.
>
> Note the words "reign with Him." If we are to reign, there must be subjects over which we are to reign. You cannot reign over nothing. A king implies a kingdom. All the details are not clear, but the teaching of Scripture seems clearly to indicate that there will always be nations upon the earth, even the new earth, and we shall reign over them.[5]

CONTINUED PROCREATION?

The question arises, will man continue to procreate and will the population continue to grow? Seiss contends it is necessary for the race to continue in a self-multiplying order, or otherwise Satan's mischief would not be overruled.[6] But this idea poses some real problems. If man is created with a will and permitted to have freedom of choice, he has proven time and time again through many dispensations and different kinds of conditions that he will fall into sin. Sin must be punished, and yet Scripture says there is no more curse. If man is created without a will he would not be of the same "kind of man" but a subnormal type of being.

Scripture clearly teaches that the resurrected saints will not procreate. Jesus said that in the resurrection they would be as angels (each of which is a direct creation of God). Luke 20:35-36 says, "But they which shall be accounted worthy to obtain that world, and the resurrection from the dead, neither marry, nor are given in marriage: neither can they die any more: for they are equal unto the angels; and are the children of God, being the children of the resurrection." It seems improbable that procreation will continue.

THE DURATION OF CHRIST'S KINGDOM

How long will the kingdom last? Will it end after the millennial era? No, Scripture says that it will endure forever (Ps 72:15-17); be an everlasting dominion (Dan 7:14); there shall be no end (Is 9:7); and never be destroyed, and stand forever (Dan 2:44). As Walvoord says, "The concept that the reign of Christ must cease at the millennium, based on I Corinthians 15:24-25, is a misunderstanding. It is the character of His reign that changes. Christ continues for all eternity as King of kings and Lord of lords."[7]

Chafer explains:

> The Son is to rule during the thousand years by the authority of the Father and that, therefore, the Father is excepted from the authoritative rule of the Son. This verse reads: "For he (the Father) hath put all things under his (the Son's) feet. But when he saith all things are put under him (the Son), it is manifest that he (the Father) is excepted, which did put all things under him" (i.e., the Son). The declarations of verses 24 and 28 become the point of misunderstanding. The delivery to God of a now unmarred kingdom does not imply the release of authority on the part of the Son. The truth asserted is that at last the kingdom is fully restored—the kingdom of God to God. The distinction to be noted lies between the presentation to the Father of a restored authority and the supposed abrogation of a throne on the part of the Son. The latter is neither required in the text nor even intimated. The picture presented in Revelation 22:3 is of the New Jerusalem in the eternal state, and it is declared that "the throne of God and of the Lamb shall be in it."[8]

McClain, in commenting on this same passage, said, "This does not mean the end of our Lord's regal activity, but rather from here onward in the unity of the Godhead He reigns with the Father and the eternal Son. There are no longer two thrones: one His Messianic Throne and the other His Father's throne, as our Lord indicated in Rev 3:21. In the final kingdom there is but one throne, and it is 'a throne of God and the Lamb' (Rev. 22:3)."[9]

We could close with no finer words than those of Clarence H. Benson:

> Now we have reached the apex and finale of the eternal state in a culmination which brings the Bible's most far-reaching prophecy to a

close, "And they shall reign forever and ever." Not, "They live and reign a thousand years," but rather, "They reign until the ages of ages." And here the final words of Scripture leave the sons of God. They are clothed as princes of eternity, the supreme officers through whom the throne acts with regal activities and enormous responsibilities. Here we have fulfilled our Lord's words, fathomless and supreme, "The glory which thou gavest me I have given them" (John 17:22). Here is realized in all its marvelous magnificence that glorious, golden promise, "He that overcometh shall inherit all things; and I will be his God, and he shall be my son" (Rev. 21:7). Sons of God! Heirs of glory! Princes of supreme sovereignty! Participants of endless bliss! . . . The earth ceases to be the theater of the universe and commences its eternal career as the center of creation and the capital of the kingdom of God.[10]

To this we can only echo the words of John at the close of the book of Revelation, "Even so, come, Lord Jesus."

Summary

1. The resurrected saints in the New Jerusalem will be active in service, fellowship, worship and dominion.

2. Because of our relationship to Christ, we will share in His activities.

3. The nations of the earth will be ruling over nature in an existence similar to what Adam and Eve would have experienced if they hadn't sinned.

4. Procreation probably will not continue in the eternal state.

5. Christ will rule forever, and believers will rule with Him.

Appendix A: Kingdom Terminology

THE GREEK WORD *basileia* that is translated "kingdom" occurs 161 times in the Authorized Version, in the majority of cases referring to the kingdom of God. The expression "the kingdom of God" occurs four times in Matthew, fourteen times in Mark, thirty-two times in Luke, twice in John, six times in Acts, eight times in Paul's epistles, and once in Revelation. The phrase "kingdom of heavens" occurs thirty-three times in Matthew and only in that book. The word "kingdom" is used in various combinations: my kingdom, his kingdom, thy kingdom, the kingdom of His beloved Son, His heavenly kingdom, the eternal kingdom, the kingdom of their father, the kingdom of Christ and of God, the kingdom of our Lord and of His Christ, the kingdom of the son of man, the gospel of the kingdom, the word of the kingdom, and the sons of the kingdom.

What are the essential ingredients of a kingdom concept? McClain says:

> A general survey of the Biblical material indicates that the concept of a "kingdom" envisages a total situation containing at least three essential elements: first, a ruler with adequate authority and power; second, a realm of subjects to be ruled; and third, the actual exercise of the function of rulership.[1]

Commentators offer many different ideas and concepts concerning the use of the word "kingdom." We are especially interested in the kingdom of God and its related uses. Pache has a good outline. He says:

> From one end of the Bible to the other, the kingdom of God is presented to us under seven different aspects. It is very important to distinguish these carefully. They are:
>
>   I. The Earthly Paradise
>   II. The Theocracy in Israel
> III. The Kingdom of God Announced by the Prophets
> IV. The Kingdom Offered and Rejected at the First Coming of Christ
>   V. The Kingdom Hidden in the Heart
> VI. The Glorious Kingdom Established on Earth During a Thousand Years
> VII. The Eternal Kingdom and Heaven.[2]

259

By expanding this outline and adding a few related concepts we can examine most of the popular interpretations. The doctrine of the Jehovah Witnesses is considered in Appendix B by itself.

THE EARTHLY PARADISE

As God created the heavens and earth, He is the Lord and can be called the King of all. Man was placed in the Garden of Eden and given dominion over all the animals, but he was under God's authority. When man rebelled he put himself under the subjection of Satan who is now called the "prince of this world," and the kingdoms of this world are now subject to him (Lk 4:5-6). Pache argues that Bible history records God's effort to restore this long-lost kingdom as He seeks to bring man to voluntary submission to His will.

UNIVERSAL KINGDOM

A related idea is expressed by Scofield: "The kingdom of God is universal, including all moral intelligences willingly subject to the will of God, whether angels, the church, or saints of past or future dispensations (Luke 13:28-29; Heb. 12:22-23)."[3]

James Orr, in contrast, does not exclude those in rebellion but places all objects, persons, events and nations without exception under the natural or universal kingdom or dominion of God.[4]

No one would question the fact that God is sovereign and that no one can do anything except as He permits. The main criticism is one of terminology. This is a misuse and unbiblical use of the term "kingdom" in an attempt to show the relationship of God to His creation. The references usually given to support this usage are Psalm 10:16; 24:1-2, 9-10; 103:19. These psalms are Messianic and probably look forward to their fulfillment in the future kingdom just as do many other portions of the Psalms.

While God is, in a sense, ruling through or over the present governments of this world (Ro 13:1), this still could not be called the kingdom of God. This world is a rebellious planet, but He is still the Creator and keeps the rebellion within limits. Yet, this is not the promised kingdom.

THE THEOCRACY IN ISRAEL

When the nations of the world turned from God, He called out Abraham to raise up unto Himself a new nation:

> Ye have seen what I did unto the Egyptians, and how I bare you on eagles' wings, and brought you unto myself. Now therefore, if ye will obey my voice indeed, and keep my covenant, then ye shall be a peculiar

> treasure unto me above all people: for all the earth is mine. And ye shall be unto me a kingdom of priests, and an holy nation. These are the words which thou shalt speak unto the children of Israel (Ex 19:4-6).

This is the first occurrence of the word "kingdom" in the Bible, where the idea is directly associated with God's rule. Peters defines theocracy thus: "A theocracy is a government of the State by the immediate direction of God; Jehovah condescended to reign over Israel in the same direct manner in which an earthly king reigns over his people."[5]

Peters makes an important distinction: "The theocracy is something then *very different* from the Divine Sovereignty, and must not be confounded with the same."[6] Some would make a distinction between the typical theocracy and the kingdom, but it probably should be considered as typical and/or an initial stage of the kingdom.

THE MEDIATORIAL KINGDOM

McClain in his classic work on the kingdom defines the mediatorial kingdom thus:

> The Mediatorial Kingdom may be defined tentatively as: (a) the rule of God through a divinely chosen representative who not only speaks and acts for God but also represents the people before God; (b) a rule which has special reference to the earth; and (c) having as its mediatorial ruler one who is always a member of the human race.[7]

It was within God's plan for Israel to have a king, for He promised a ruling seed in Genesis 3:15 and had given instructions concerning a king (Deu 17:14-20). But the Israelites wanted a king like the surrounding nations and were not content to wait for God's time.

McClain, who believes the mediatorial kingdom is a phase of the larger universal kingdom,[8] uses the term "mediatorial" to refer to the *method* of God's rule.[9] He describes God's working through the ages up to and including the millennium as the "mediatorial kingdom," saying it will finally come to an end when the "last enemy . . . death" (1 Co 15:26) is destroyed and the final kingdom appears.[10] With all due respect, I believe that the use of this term tends to confuse the biblical usage of the term "kingdom" and places an improper emphasis on the millennial era of the kingdom.

THE KINGDOM ANNOUNCED BY THE PROPHETS

Even as the people were in a spiritual decline under the theocracy, God through the prophets began to prophesy that His kingdom would be established eternally (Ps 89:21, 29, 36-38). In Psalm 2 He promised a coming King who would rule all nations. Looking beyond the captivity, the prophets foretold many details about the kingdom (Is 2, 11, 65), and during the captivity, God promised through Daniel that the kingdom would stand throughout all eternity (2:44; 7:14, 18). In the postexilic period Zechariah told about the establishment of this eternal kingdom (chap. 14).

THE KINGDOM OF GOD OFFERED AND REJECTED AT THE FIRST COMING OF CHRIST

When the angel told Mary of the coming birth of Jesus, he said, "He shall be great, and shall be called the Son of the Highest: and the Lord God shall give unto him the throne of his father David: and he shall reign over the house of Jacob for ever; and of his kingdom there shall be no end" (Lk 1:32-33). John the Baptist called upon the people to repent for the kingdom of heaven was at hand (Mt 3:2), and Jesus and His disciples preached the same message, authenticating their ministry with miracles. Note that neither John nor Jesus nor His disciples ever explained what kingdom they were talking about. They didn't have to, for the Old Testament very fully explained what was meant and the people understood. Peters says:

> The language and whole tenor of the Word is so explicit that both Jews and Gentiles thus understand it. Whatsoever views may be entertained respecting the interpretation of the prophecies themselves, there is no writer, within our knowledge, who has ventured to suggest that *two* kingdoms are denoted.[11]

Israel rejected their Messiah and crucified Him, as foretold by Jesus in the parable of the vineyard (Lk 20:9-16). After Pentecost the kingdom was reoffered to Israel through Peter:

> Repent ye therefore, and turn again, that your sins may be blotted out, that so there may come seasons of refreshing from the presence of the Lord; and that he might send the Christ who hath been appointed for you, even Jesus: whom the heaven must receive until the time of restoration of all things, whereof God spake by the mouth of his holy prophets that have been from of old (Ac 3:19-21, ASV).

The final rejection by that generation in the land probably took place at the stoning of Stephen in Acts 7 and in the dispersion by Acts 28.

THE KINGDOM HIDDEN IN THE HEART

Because of Israel's rejection of Christ, some feel that the kingdom of God is only a spiritual kingdom where He rules in the hearts of men. After quoting Matthew 6:20, "Thy kingdom come. Thy will be done in earth, as it is in heaven," E. Stanley Jones defines the kingdom of God as "the doing of the will of God on earth as it is done in heaven."[12]

Another says it is the "way of life in which the rule of God as revealed in Jesus Christ is accepted."[13] In his book, *Jesus and the Kingdom*, George Eldon Ladd says:

> The central thesis of this book is that the kingdom of God is the redemptive reign of God dynamically active to establish His rule among men, and that this Kingdom, which will appear as an apocalyptic act at the end of the age, has already come into human history in the person and mission of Jesus to overcome evil, to deliver men from its power, and to bring them into the blessing of God's reign. The kingdom of God involves two great moments: fulfillment within history, and consummation at the end of history.[14]

There is a spiritual aspect to the kingdom, but it is not correct to refer to it as a "spiritual kingdom" in contrast to a literal, earthly kingdom nor to speak of the kingdom as a present reality. Acts 1:6-7 and Revelation 11:15 show the establishment is yet future. Christians are to be yielded unto God (Ro 12:1), but to use the term "kingdom" is a misuse of terms.

THE CHURCH AND THE KINGDOM

A related idea, which identifies the church as the kingdom, has done much to confuse many. Augustine, who is considered the father of the church-kingdom idea, in his book *The City of God* identifies the church as the kingdom, consequently denying that there will be a literal millennial reign of Christ upon earth. He contends that the present age of conflict is the millennium. But in the first few centuries after Pentecost, the church was not identified as the kingdom. Archibald Robertson, quoting Cyprian, an early church Father, says, "He cannot hope to reach the kingdom, who deserts her [the church] who *is destined* to reign."[15] Although *church* and *kingdom* are not synonymous terms, yet the church is related to the kingdom in that the church will reign in the kingdom.

KINGDOM IN MYSTERY FORM

Because of the rejection of the kingdom by Israel it is quite popular for many commentators to speak of the present "mystery form" of the kingdom, an idea based upon a supposed difference between the "kingdom of heaven" and the "kingdom of God." Scofield defines the kingdom of heaven as the "earthly sphere of the universal kingdom of God. . . . The kingdom of heaven merges into the kingdom of God when Christ having put all enemies under his feet, 'shall have delivered up the kingdom to God, even the father' (I Cor. 15:24-28)."[16] The kingdom of heaven is usually described as *Christendom* and is said to include both saved and unsaved. It is acknowledged that it is similar to the kingdom of God in many ways.

McClain says that the idea of a present kingdom of heaven established on earth in the church is "fiction." He continues:

> Now it is true that these parables present certain *conditions* related to the kingdom which are contemporaneous with the present age but nowhere in Matthew 13 is the establishment of the kingdom placed within this age. On the contrary, in two of these parables the setting up of the kingdom is definitely placed at the end of the "age" (vss. 39 and 49, ASV, with 41-43). And it is noted that in each of these references, our Lord is speaking as the infallible interpreter of His own parable.[17]

Merrill F. Unger defines the kingdom of heaven as follows:

> The Phrase "Kingdom of Heaven," literally, "of the heavens," is peculiar to Matthew and denotes the Messianic rule on the earth of Christ as the Son of David. The designation is appropriate because it is the rule of the heavens over the earth (Matt. 6:10). The phrase is derived from the O.T. (Dan. 2:34—36:44; 7:23-27), and it is said that the "God of heaven" will set up this kingdom covenanted to David's posterity (II Sam. 7:7-10) after the destruction of Gentile world powers by the returning Christ, "the Stone cut out without hands."[18]

Jesus used the two expressions in an interchangeable fashion in Matthew 19:23-24, "Then said Jesus unto his disciples, Verily I say unto you, That a rich man shall hardly enter into the kingdom of heaven. And again I say unto you, It is easier for a camel to go through the eye of a needle, than for a rich man to enter into the kingdom of God." It is difficult to see how any distinctions can be made between the expressions used here. The kingdom of Christ and the kingdom of God are also the same: "For this ye know, that no whoremonger, nor unclean person, nor covetous man, who is an idolater, hath any inheritance in the kingdom of Christ and of God" (Eph 5:5). "And the seventh angel sounded; and there were great voices in heaven, saying, The kingdoms of the world are become the kingdoms of our Lord, and of his Christ; and he shall reign for ever and ever" (Rev 11:15).

Does Matthew intend a distinction between the term "kingdom of heaven" and "kingdom of God"? Gerhard Kittel gives three reasons why he believes that they are interchangeable, summarized as follows:

1. The parables in the synoptic gospels using "kingdom of God" are interchangeable.

2. The idea suggests lordship or the coming down from heaven into this world, the main idea being to reign and not the realm. But the reign

cannot be a realm by human effort, natural development of earthly relationships, but only by divine intervention.

3. Heaven can be substituted for God according to later Jewish usage.[19]

Jewish theologian S. Schachter says, "The term *kingdom of heaven* must
be taken in the sense in which heaven is equivalent to God, not locally, as
if the kingdom were located in the celestial sphere."[20] Some examples of
this usage are in Mark 11:30 and Matthew 16:17.

The background must be understood concerning the giving of the kingdom of heaven parables. Religious Israel had just reached a crisis, for
they had rejected Jesus as the Messiah (Mt 12). Consequently the character of His ministry changed at this point and He purposely taught in
parables in order to hide His message from those who were rejecting Him
and to illustrate the message for those who were receiving Him. The
question that would naturally come to the mind of His disciples is: "What
about the kingdom now that the religious rulers are rejecting You, the
King?"

In this series of parables He begins to reveal something that has been
hid, a mystery or truth that can only be known by revelation from God.
This mystery is that there is going to be a delay between the time when
the kingdom is offered and the time that it is actually established. This is
more fully developed in the parable of the pounds (Lk 19:11-27) and in
the parables given in the final week before His death.

Jesus compared His kingdom to a seed in one parable: "The kingdom
of heaven is likened unto a man which sowed good seed in his field" (Mt
13:24). The verb "is likened" is in the aorist passive tense and can be
better translated "the kingdom of heaven has been made like unto." Notice
in the parable of the tares that the tares are sowed in the field, not in the
kingdom, and Jesus said that the field is the world (Mt 13:38). This
parable shows the relationship during this age between the two seeds—
those who receive the message of the kingdom, and the children of the
wicked one. Kittel, who suggests that these parables teach the important
thought that the kingdom is brought in by an act of God, says that the
parable of the seed (Mk 4:26-29), the mustard seed (Mt 13:31-32), and
the leaven (Mt 13:33-35; Lk 13:20) all carry the same lesson.[21] They also
teach that there will be a delay in the establishment of the kingdom, for
there is a period of time from the planting of the seed until it brings forth
the ear of corn. The tiny mustard seed grows to be the greatest among
the herbs and then becomes a tree, and the leaven will finally leaven all
of the meal, but both call for a period of time to complete their work.
Notice that the parable of the leaven is repeated as a description of the
kingdom of God in Luke 13:20. The argument that leaven must represent

evil was previously considered in the discussion of the kingdom of heaven parables.

Some argue that there is a present form of the kingdom from this verse: "Who hath delivered us from the power of darkness, and hath translated us into the kingdom of his dear Son" (Col 1:13). But this verse is speaking of positional truth, just as 2 Peter 1:11 refers to the future reality: "For so an entrance shall be ministered unto you abundantly into the everlasting kingdom of our Lord and Saviour Jesus Christ." Colossians 1:13 can be compared to Ephesians 2:6, "And hath raised us up together, and made us sit together in heavenly places in Christ Jesus." Positionally we are with Christ in the heavenlies but actually we are still living on this earth.

At the time Christ gave the kingdom of heaven parables, the church was still unknown. He did not mention it until a year later, and then He did not explain it. Almost two years later the church was founded at Pentecost. Yet He asked His disciples, "Have ye understood all these things? They said unto him, Yea, Lord" (Mt 13:51). It would have been impossible for them to have understood that He meant the church here, when they didn't know anything about the church. Many applications of these parables can be made to the church in this age, but the primary purpose was to reveal that there was going to be a delay between the offer of the kingdom by the King and His establishment of the kingdom.

The Glorious Kingdom Established on Earth During a Thousand Years

When Christ returns in His glory He shall establish His kingdom and reign on the earth for one thousand years. At the end of this time certain things will happen: Satan will be released; he will gather a great army of unbelievers; God will destroy them; the unsaved dead of all ages will be raised and judged; the curse will be lifted from the earth, and New Jerusalem will descend from heaven— but the kingdom will not end, for it is eternal.

The millennial kingdom is not a synonym for the kingdom of God. A better term would be "the millennial era of the kingdom."

The Eternal Kingdom in Heaven

One form of the idea of the eternal kingdom in heaven simply identifies the kingdom with the reign of God in heaven. For other people, "entering the kingdom" means going to heaven at death. A third group holds the view of a future reign of God in eternity at the close of human history. An overemphasis on the dispensation of the kingdom is partially respon-

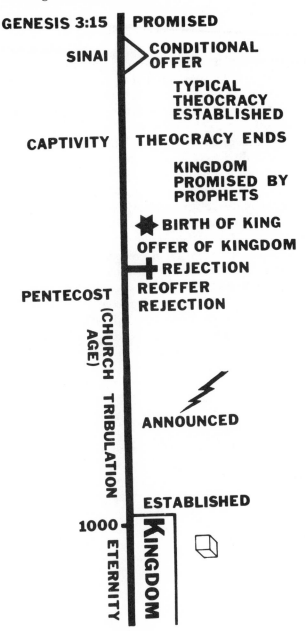

Fig. 28. The Kingdom in History and Prophecy

sible for this, because commentators have tended to separate the millennial era and to forget the eternal aspect of the kingdom.

While there is a certain amount of truth in each of the seven usages suggested by Pache, yet the proper use of the terms as used in Scripture would suggest that there is one kingdom of God. The initial form of this was the theocracy in Israel, and the other prophecies and statements in Scripture are talking about the eternal kingdom that Christ will set up at His second coming.

See Figure 28. Briefly summarized, the kingdom was first promised in Genesis 3:15. A conditional offer was made at Sinai, and a typical theocracy was established. With the captivity the theocracy ended but the prophets promised a future eternal kingdom. The King was born and He offered the kingdom to Israel, but they rejected Him. At Pentecost and in later ministries the King and kingdom were again offered to Israel, but they were rejected again. In the present age God is calling out a people to reign with Christ in His kingdom. After He returns for His church, His 144,000 witnesses will announce His second coming to establish His kingdom. One thousand years later, the curse of death will be lifted and the kingdom will take on its eternal character.

Some may not agree with this but the author only asks that you study the Scripture in this simple, straightforward approach to see if this does not solve many more problems than do other interpretations.

Appendix B: Jehovah's Witnesses and the Kingdom

THE KINGDOM PLAYS an important part in the doctrine of Jehovah's Witnesses. We summarize their teaching as found in their publication, *Let God Be True*.

They contend that God made a kingdom covenant in the Garden of Eden (Gen 3:15) and later expanded this original kingdom covenant with Abraham, Isaac and Jacob and their seed. However, they contend that the theocracy established in Israel was not the promised kingdom but that God made an everlasting kingdom covenant with David.[1] Jesus Christ is acknowledged as the rightful Heir of David,[2] and from this point they begin to develop their peculiar doctrine.

THE NATURE OF THE KINGDOM

What is the kingdom like? The kingdom is heavenly, not earthly, and is the invisible part of the new world.[3] Who can enter the kingdom? Its inhabitants are limited to 144,000.[4] It is still possible for a few to join this heavenly congregation, but they must "be faithful to death."[5] These 144,000, who will serve as a royal priesthood for one thousand years,[6] are also referred to as the body of Christ, the bride of the Lamb, and the congregation of God.[7] All others who receive life through God's hand will live on the earth, but under the rule of Jesus Christ and His congregation in the heavens.[8] When did this kingdom begin? It began in 1914[9] at which time Satan was ousted from heaven and his activities limited to the earth.[10]

What is the purpose of the kingdom? It has three purposes: (1) to crush out all wickedness, (2) to restore righteousness, and (3) to repopulate the earth.[11]

What is the new earth? It is a new human society under new social arrangements. Nature will be changed, and there will be a paradise earth,"[12] which will be like Eden.

SUBJECTS OF THE KINGDOM

Who will be the subjects of the kingdom? First, there will be many angels,[13] and the earth will be full of many faithful children of King Jesus.[14] There will be many resurrected "forefathers" of Jesus, extending all the way back to Abel.[15] There is no salvation for Adam. Some of these forefathers will be "princes," and many are called "other sheep" from all nations, tribes and tongues.[16] Included among the people on the earth will be the "unrighteous dead"[17] who will be resurrected and then instructed in God's laws during the thousand-year reign. At the end of the thousand years Satan and his demons will be released to tempt nations, and some of the people will still be "misled" after one thousand years of instruction.[18] Satan and these "misled" individuals will then be cast into the "lake of fire and sulphur," which is the second death.[19]

This doctrine of a second chance is clearly unscriptural, for the Bible nowhere teaches a second chance; in contrast, it says, "And as it is appointed unto men once to die, but after this the judgment" (Heb 9:27).

Jehovah's Witnesses do not like the idea of eternal punishment, but say that those who spurn God's loving provisions will "be perpetually asleep." Some who are living upon the earth may never die, but they will live right on through the coming great Battle of Armageddon.[20] This favored class will receive a divine mandate to procreate and fill the earth with a righteous race[21] and they will raise these children under the direction of the King. Of this new race, any who want to serve Jehovah may live through Christ the King, but any who do not want to serve Him will be executed.[22]

THE KING

While Jesus Christ is acknowledged as the rightful Heir of David, He is not recognized as God. They believe His baptism was His anointing as king over the heavenly government, at which time, through God's Holy Spirit, He was begotten as a spiritual son.[23] After His resurrection He became an invisible spirit creature,[24] and the world will never see Him again.[25] Yet, He is supposed to have returned to the earth in 1914 in an invisible, secret return.[26] Although He is not considered as God, they say He was existing in God's form[27] and was the first thing God created. He was David's son according to prophecy, for He was born of the virgin Mary.[28] He is a perfect human, absolutely sinless, guileless, and undefiled.[29] They call Him mankind's redeemer, saying that Jehovah God accepted Him as a sacrifice as mankind's redeemer.[30] When Jehovah God raised Him from the dead, it was not as an human son but as an immortal spirit son.[31] God made Him the "head under Jehovah of God's capital organization over the entire universe."[32] Yet, with all their talk about

Jesus being a redeemer, if asked the way to heavenly glory they give a three-part answer: (1) faith in Jehovah God and Jesus Christ; (2) dedication to do God's will; (3) faithfully carry out that dedication. Those who do this will be rewarded with everlasting life.[33] The whole system is a religion of works.

The very danger in the doctrine of the Jehovah's Witnesses is the mixture of truth and error, especially as it concerns the person of Christ and salvation. The Scripture says, "For Christ also hath once suffered for sins, the just for the unjust, that he might bring us to God, being put to death in the flesh, but quickened by the Spirit" (1 Pe 3:18). Salvation is by faith in this work of Christ and not by our works: "For by grace are ye saved through faith; and that not of yourselves: it is the gift of God: not of works, lest any man should boast" (Eph 2:8-9).

Notes

CHAPTER 1

1. Erich Sauer, *From Eternity to Eternity*, p. 89.
2. C. F. Hogg and W. E. Vine, *The Epistle to the Thessalonians*, p. 70.
3. Alva J. McClain, *The Greatness of the Kingdom*, p. 17.

CHAPTER 2

1. Charles L. Feinberg, *Premillennialism or Amillennialism?* p. 33.

CHAPTER 3

1. Erich Sauer, *The Dawn of World Redemption*, p. 106.
2. John F. Walvoord, *The Millennial Kingdom*, p. 146.
3. George N. H. Peters, *The Theocratic Kingdom of Our Lord Jesus, the Christ*, 1:302.
4. Sauer, p. 98.
5. Arthur W. Kac, *The Rebirth of the State of Israel*, pp. 16-22.
6. J. P. Lange, *Commentary on Exodus*, p. 66.
7. Peters, 1:216.
8. Kenneth S. Wuest, *Galatians in the Greek New Testament*, p. 110.

CHAPTER 4

1. Walter C. Wright, *The Sacrificial System of the Old Testament*, p. 26.
2. Erich Sauer, *Eternity to Eternity*, p. 35.
3. C. I. Scofield, *Scofield Reference Bible*, p. 250, n. 1.
4. Sidlow Baxter, *Explore the Book*, 1:224.

CHAPTER 5

1. George N. H. Peters, *The Theocratic Kingdom of Our Lord Jesus, the Christ*, 3:582.
2. W. S. Hottel, *Through the Bible Book by Book*, 4:20.
3. Arthur E. Smith, *The Temple and Its Teaching*, p. 21.

CHAPTER 6

1. Lewis S. Chafer, *Systematic Theology*, 4:350.

CHAPTER 7

1. A. C. Gaebelein, *The Prophet Daniel*, p. 187.

CHAPTER 8

1. Charles L. Feinberg, *Premillennialism or Amillennialism?* pp. 57-58.
2. George N. H. Peters, *The Theocratic Kingdom of Our Lord Jesus, the Christ*, 1:245.
3. W. B. Hill, *The Life of Christ*, pp. 39-40.
4. Ibid., p. 40.
5. Alfred Edersheim, *The Life and Times of Jesus the Messiah*, 1:160.
6. Ibid., p. 167.
7. O. C. S. Wallace, *The Life of Jesus*, pp. 33-34.
8. Ibid., 2:710-37.

CHAPTER 9

1. Samuel Andrews, *The Life of Our Lord upon the Earth,* p. 125.
2. Ray E. Baughman, *The Life of Christ Visualized,* p. 22.
3. Cunningham Geikie, *Life and Words of Christ,* 2:203-4.
4. Alfred Edersheim, *The Life and Times of Jesus the Messiah,* 1:273-74.

CHAPTER 10

1. Ray E. Baughman, *The Life of Christ Visualized,* pp. 200-1.
2. Charles Ryrie, *The Bible and Tomorrow's News,* p. 125.
3. Ryrie, *The Basis of the Premillennial Faith,* p. 93.
4. Alva J. McClain, *The Greatness of the Kingdom,* pp. 406-7.
5. Ryrie, *The Basis of the Premillennial Faith,* p. 94.
6. McClain, p. 441.
7. Samuel Adams, *The Life of Our Lord upon the Earth,* p. 126.
8. Lewis S. Chafer, *The Kingdom in History and Prophecy,* pp. 56-57.

CHAPTER 11

1. Herman A. Hoyt, *The End Times,* p. 187.
2. Robert Anderson, *The Silence of God,* p. 175.
3. Ibid., p. 162.
4. Ibid., p. 177.
5. J. R. Lumby, *The Acts of the Apostles,* pp. 36-37.
6. A. C. Gaebelein, *The Annotated Bible,* p. 203.
7. Hoyt, p. 188.

CHAPTER 12

1. See Ray E. Baughman, *The Abundant Life.*
2. Erich Sauer, *Eternity to Eternity,* p. 93.
3. George N. H. Peters, *The Theocratic Kingdom of Our Lord Jesus, the Christ,* 1:402.
4. Herbert Lockyer, *All the Doctrines of the Bible,* p. 153.
5. W. E. Vine, *Vine's Expository Dictionary,* p. 32.
6. Peters, p. 396.
7. Richard Wolff, *Israel, Act III,* p. 25.
8. John Walvoord, *The Millennial Kingdom,* pp. 49-50.
9. Peters, p. 402.

CHAPTER 13

1. C. I. Scofield, *Scofield Reference Bible,* p. 1192.
2. R. E. Neighbour, *If They Shall Fall Away,* p. 135.

CHAPTER 14

1. George N. H. Peters, *The Theocratic Kingdom of Our Lord Jesus, the Christ,* 3:361.
2. Ibid., p. 573.
3. Alva J. McClain, *The Greatness of the Kingdom,* p. 442.

CHAPTER 15

1. Charles Ryrie, *The Bible and Tomorrow's News,* p. 131.
2. John Walvoord, *The Return of the Lord,* pp. 87-88.
3. W. E. Blackstone, *Jesus Is Coming,* pp. 101-2.
4. George N. H. Peters, *The Theocratic Kingdom of Our Lord Jesus, the Christ,* 2:596.
5. Elsa Raud, *Introduction to Prophecy,* p. 158.
6. Ibid., p. 157.
7. Walvoord, *Prophetic Truth Unfolding Today,* p. 158.

CHAPTER 16

1. James Gray, *Great Epochs of Sacred History,* p. 93.
2. René Pache, *The Return of Jesus Christ,* p. 217.
3. Merrill F. Unger, *Unger's Bible Dictionary,* p. 116.
4. Erich Sauer, *The Triumph of the Crucified,* p. 125.
5. Ibid., p. 125.
6. Alexander Hislop, *The Two Babylons, or the Papal Worship,* p. 5.
7. Martin O. Massinger, *Babylon in Biblical Prophecy,* p. 223.
8. Lewis S. Chafer, *Systematic Theology,* 7:62.
9. Merrill F. Unger, *Unger's Bible Handbook,* pp. 872-73.
10. J. A. Seiss, *The Apocalypse,* p. 430.

CHAPTER 17

1. L. M. Haldeman, *The Coming of Christ,* pp. 245-46.
2. J. Dwight Pentecost, *Things to Come,* pp. 354-55.
3. Charles L. Feinberg, *The Prophet Ezekiel,* pp. 218-19.
4. John Walvoord, *The Revelation of Jesus Christ,* p. 279.

CHAPTER 18

1. R. C. Trench, *Synonyms of the New Testament,* pp. 206-7.
2. J. A. Seiss, *The Apocalypse,* p. 484.
3. Robert D. Culver, *Daniel and the Latter Days,* p. 190.
4. Seiss, p. 485.
5. Wilbur M. Smith, *The Atomic Age and the Word of God,* p. 132.
6. Culver, pp. 29-30.
7. Ibid., pp. 24-25.

CHAPTER 19

1. Herman Hoyt, *The End Times,* p. 229.
2. Clarence Benson, *The Earth, the Theater of the Universe,* p. 130.
3. Clarence Larkin, *Dispensational Truth,* p. 95.
4. Merrill F. Unger, *Great Neglected Bible Prophecies,* p. 67.
5. J. Hoffman Cohn, "Disputed Passage" in *Light for the World's Darkness,* p. 25; and Larkin, p. 93.
6. Alfred Edersheim, *The Temple, Its Ministry and Services,* p. 83.
7. John Skinner, *The Book of Ezekiel* in *The Expositor's Bible,* p. 495.

CHAPTER 20

1. George N. H. Peters, *The Theocratic Kingdom of Our Lord Jesus, the Christ,* 2:587-88.
2. Ibid., p. 593-94.
3. W. E. Vine, *Expository Dictionary,* 2:259.
4. J. Dwight Pentecost, *Things to Come,* p. 81.
5. Merrill F. Unger, *Great Neglected Bible Prophecies,* p. 117.
6. Ibid.
7. Ibid., p. 118.
8. Elsa Raud, *Introduction to Prophecy,* p. 161.
9. Ibid., pp. 227-28.

CHAPTER 21

1. Elsa Raud, *Introduction to Prophecy,* pp. 224-25.
2. John Walvoord, *The Return of the Lord,* pp. 86-87.
3. Walvoord, *The Millennial Kingdom,* p. 330.
4. Clarence Benson, *The Earth, the Theater of the Universe,* p. 133.
5. J. A. Seiss, *The Apocalypse,* pp. 298-99.

CHAPTER 22

1. James Gray, *Christian Worker's Commentary on the Whole Bible,* pp. 265-66.
2. A. C. Gaebelein, *The Prophet Ezekiel,* p. 292.
3. René Pache, *The Return of Jesus Christ,* p. 415.

CHAPTER 23

1. J. A. Seiss, *The Apocalypse*, p. 447.
2. Ibid., p. 448.
3. Ibid., p. 449.
   3:42-43.
4. William R. Newell, *The Book of Revelation*, p. 348.
5. Clarence Larkin, *Dispensational Truth*, p. 146.
6. J. Vernon McGee, *Reveling Through Revelation*, 2:104-5.
7. E. W. Rogers, *Concerning the Future*, p. 114.
8. Larkin, p. 148.
9. Seiss, p. 498.
10. John Walvoord, *The Revelation of Jesus Christ*, p. 330.
11. R. I. Humberd, *The Book of Revelation*, p. 271.
12. J. Dwight Pentecost, *Things to Come*, p. 577; cf. James Gray, *Progress in Things to Come*, p. 47.
13. Wilbur M. Smith, *The Biblical Doctrine of Heaven*, p. 258.
14. Walvoord, *The Nations in Prophecy*, pp. 169-70.
15. Walvoord, *The Revelation . . .*, p. 313.
16. George N. H. Peters, *The Theocratic Kingdom of Our Lord Jesus, the Christ*, 3:42-43.
17. J. A. Seiss, *The Apocalypse*, pp. 430-31.
18. Smith, pp. 55-61.
19. Gustave Oehler, *Theology of the Old Testament*, p. 173.
20. Robert Girdlestone, *Synonyms of the Old Testament*, pp. 266-67.

CHAPTER 24

1. J. A. Seiss, *The Apocalypse*, p. 508.
2. George N. H. Peters, *The Theocratic Kingdom of Our Lord Jesus, the Christ*, 2:614-15.
3. Seiss, p. 492.
4. Wilbur M. Smith, *The Biblical Doctrine of Heaven*, p. 191.
5. M. R. DeHaan, *Revelation*, pp. 303-4.
6. Seiss, p. 483.
7. John Walvoord, *The Revelation of Jesus Christ*, p. 332.
8. Lewis S. Chafer, *Systematic Theology*, 5:373-74.
9. Alva J. McClain, *The Greatness of the Kingdom*, p. 513.
10. Clarence H. Benson, *The Earth, the Theater of the Universe*, p. 140.

APPENDIX A

1. Alva J. McClain, *The Greatness of the Kingdom*, p. 17.
2. René Pache, *The Return of Jesus Christ*, p. 46.
3. C. I. Scofield, *Scofield Reference Bible*, p. 1003.
4. James Orr, "Kingdom of God" in *Dictionary of the Bible*, 2:844.
5. George N. H. Peters, *The Theocratic Kingdom of Our Lord Jesus, the Christ*, 1:216.
6. Ibid., p. 217.
7. McClain, p. 41.
8. Ibid., p. 36.
9. Ibid., p. 21.
10. Ibid., p. 512.
11. Peters, p. 245.
12. E. Stanley Jones, *Is the Kingdom of God Realism?* p. 52.
13. *My Confirmation*, p. 198.
14. George Eldon Ladd, *Jesus and the Kingdom*, p. 214.
15. Archibald Robertson, *Regnum Dei*, p. 175.
16. Scofield, p. 1003.
17. McClain, pp. 440-41.
18. Merrill F. Unger, *Unger's Bible Dictionary*, p. 719.
19. Gerhard Kittel, ed., *Theological Dictionary of the New Testament*, 1:582.
20. S. Schachter, *Some Aspects of Jewish Theology*, p. 89.
21. Kittel, 1:535.

APPENDIX B

1. *Let God Be True,* pp. 134-35.
2. Ibid., p. 136.
3. Ibid., p. 138.
4. Ibid., pp. 130, 136.
5. Ibid., p. 129.
6. Ibid., p. 137.
7. Ibid., p. 130.
8. Ibid.
9. Ibid., p. 141.
10. Ibid.
11. Ibid., p. 142.
12. Ibid., p. 264.
13. Ibid., p. 138.
14. Ibid., p. 139.
15. Ibid., p. 263.
16. Ibid., p. 260.
17. Ibid., pp. 139, 270.
18. Ibid., p. 270.
19. Ibid.
20. Ibid., p. 265.
21. Ibid., p. 268.
22. Ibid., p. 269.
23. Ibid., p. 136.
24. Ibid., p. 138.
25. Ibid.
26. Ibid., p. 141.
27. Ibid., p. 32.
28. Ibid., p. 35.
29. Ibid., p. 39.
30. Ibid.
31. Ibid., p. 40.
32. Ibid.
33. Ibid., p. 298.

Bibliography

Anderson, Sir Robert. *The Silence of God.* New York: Hodder & Stoughton, n.d.

Andrews, Samuel J. *The Life of Our Lord upon the Earth.* Grand Rapids: Zondervan, 1954.

Baughman, Ray E. *Bible History Visualized.* Chicago: Moody, 1963.

———. *Seeking Bible Treasures.* Oak Park, Ill.: Emmaus Bible School, 1965.

———. *The Abundant Life.* Chicago: Moody, 1959.

———. *The Life of Christ Visualized.* Chicago: Moody, 1968.

Baxter, J. Sidlow. *Explore the Book.* London: Marshall, Morgan, & Scott, 1951. 6 vols.

Benson, Clarence H. *The Earth, The Theater of the Universe.* Chicago: Bible Institute Colportage Assn., 1929.

Blackstone, W. E. *Jesus Is Coming.* New York: Revell, 1908.

Bradbury, John W., ed. *Light for the World's Darkness.* New York: Loizeaux, 1944.

Braun, Ralph C. *The Evangelistic Home Bible Class*, McCook, Nebr.: Braun, 1966.

Bullinger, E. W. *The Foundation of Dispensational Truth.* London: Eyre & Spottiswoode, 1930.

Chafer, Lewis Sperry. *The Kingdom in History and Prophecy.* Chicago: Bible Institute Colportage Assn., 1936.

———. *Systematic Theology.* Dallas: Dallas Seminary, 1948. 8 vols.

Cohn, J. Hoffman. "Disputed Passage" in *Light for the World's Darkness*, ed. John W. Bradbury. New York: Loizeaux, 1944.

Culver, Robert D. *Daniel and the Latter Days.* Chicago: Moody, 1954.

Dean, I. R. *The Coming Kingdom: The Goal of Prophecy.* Cleveland: Union Gospel, 1928.

DeHaan, M. R. *Revelation.* Grand Rapids: Zondervan, 1946.

Edersheim, Alfred. *The Life and Times of Jesus the Messiah.* 2 vols. New York: Longmans, Green, n.d.

———. *The Temple, Its Ministry and Services.* Grand Rapids: Eerdmans, 1950.

Feinberg, Charles L. *Premillennialism or Amillennialism?* Wheaton, Ill.: Van Kampen, 1954.

———. *The Prophecy of Ezekiel.* Chicago: Moody, 1969.

———. *Prophetic Truth Unfolding Today.* Westwood, N. J.: Revell, n.d.

Gaebelein, A. C. *The Annotated Bible.* New York: Our Hope, 1913.

———. *The Prophet Daniel.* New York: Our Hope, 1911.

———. *The Prophet Ezekiel.* New York: Our Hope, 1918.

Geilkie, Cunningham. *Life and Words of Christ.* 2 vols. New York: Appleton, 1880.

Girdlestone, Robert B. *Synonyms of the Old Testament.* Grand Rapids: Eerdmans, 1948.

Gray, James. *Great Epochs of Sacred History.* New York: Revell, 1910.

——. *Christian Worker's Commentary on the Whole Bible.* Westwood, N. J.: Revell, 1953.

——. *Progress in Things to Come.* New York: Revell, 1910.

Haldeman, I. M. *The Coming of Christ: Both Premillennial and Imminent.* Los Angeles: Bible House of Los Angeles, 1905.

Hill, Willima Bancroft. *The Life of Christ.* New York: Revell, 1917.

Hislop, Alexander. *The Two Babylons or the Papal Worship.* New York: Loizeaux, n.d.

Hogg, C. F. and Vine, W. F. *The Epistle to the Thessalonians.* Fincastle, Va.: Bible Study Classics, 1959.

Hottel, W. S. *Typical Truth in the Tabernacle.* Cleveland: Union Gospel, 1943.

——. *Through the Bible Book by Book.* Cleveland: Union Gospel, 1948.

Hoyt, Herman A. *The End Times.* Chicago: Moody, 1969.

Humberd, R. I. *The Book of Revelation.* Florida: Humberd, 1944.

Jones, E. Stanley. *Is the Kingdom of God Realism?* New York: Abingdon-Cokesbury, 1940.

Kac, Arthur W. *The Rebirth of the State of Israel—Is It of God or of Men?* Chicago: Moody, 1958.

Kittel, Gerhard, ed. *Theological Dictionary of the New Testament.* Grand Rapids: Eerdmans, 1964.

Ladd, George Eldon. *Jesus and the Kingdom.* New York: Harper & Row, 1964.

Lang, J. P. *Commentary on Exodus,* trans. Charles N. Mead. New York: Scribner, 1876.

Larkin, Clarence. *Dispensational Truth.* New York: Larkin, 1920.

Let God Be True. Brooklyn, N. Y.: Watchtower Bible and Tract Society, 1946.

Lockyer, Herbert. *All the Doctrines of the Bible.* Grand Rapids: Zondervan, 1964.

Lumby, J. R. *The Acts of the Apostles.* Cambridge: U. Press, 1897.

McClain, Alva J. *The Greatness of the Kingdom.* Chicago: Moody, 1968.

McGee, J. Vernon. *Reveling Through Revelation.* Los Angeles: Church of the Open Door, n.d.

Massinger, Martin Otto. "Babylon in Biblical Prophecy." Doctor's dissertation, Dallas Theological Seminary, 1967.

My Confirmation. Philadelphia: Christian Education Press, 1959.

Neighbour, R. E. *If They Shall Fall Away.* Cleveland: Union Gospel, n.d.

Newell, William R. *The Book of The Revelation.* Chicago: Moody, 1935.

Oehler, Gustave Friedrich. *Theology of the Old Testament.* Grand Rapids: Zondervan, n.d.

Orr, James. "Kingdom of God" in *Dictionary of the Bible,* ed. James Hastings. 5 vols. New York: Scribner, 1905.

Pache, René. *The Return of Jesus Christ.* Trans. William Sanford LaSor. Chicago: Moody, 1955.

Pentecost, J. Dwight. *Things To Come.* Findlay, O.: Dunham, 1958.

Peters, George N. H. *The Theocratic Kingdom of Our Lord Jesus, the Christ.* 3 vols. Grand Rapids: Kregel, 1957.
Phillips, Rev. O. E. *Birth Pangs of a New Age.* Los Angeles: Biblical Research Soc., 1941.
Raud, Elsa. *Introduction to Prophecy.* Findlay, O.: Dunham, 1960.
Rice, John R. *The Coming Kingdom of Christ.* Dallas: Rice, n.d.
Robertson, Archibald. *Regnum Dei.* New York: Macmillan, 1901.
Rogers, E. W. *Concerning the Future.* Chicago: Moody, 1962.
Ryrie, Charles Caldwell. *The Basis of the Premillennial Faith.* New York: Loizeaux, 1953.
――――. *The Bible and Tomorrow's News.* Wheaton, Ill.: Scripture Press, 1969.
Sale-Harrison, L. *The Remarkable Jew: His Wonderful Future.* New York: Sale-Harrison, 1934.
Sauer, Erich. *The Dawn of World Redemption.* Grand Rapids: Eerdmans, 1955.
――――. *From Eternity to Eternity.* Grand Rapids: Eerdmans, 1954.
――――. *The Triumph of the Crucified.* Grand Rapids: Eerdmans, 1953.
Schechter, S. *Some Aspects of Jewish Theology.* New York: Macmillan, 1923.
Scofield, C. I. *Scofield Reference Bible.* New York: Oxford U., 1945.
――――. *The Word of Truth Rightly Divided.* Lincoln, Nebr.: Back to the Bible Broadcast, n.d.
Seiss, J. A. *The Apocalypse.* Grand Rapids: Zondervan, 1962.
Skinner, John. *The Book of Ezekiel* in *The Expositor's Bible,* ed. W. Robertson Nicoll. New York: Hodder & Stoughton, n.d.
Smith, Arthur E. *The Temple and Its Teaching.* Chicago: Moody, 1956.
Smith, Wilbur M. *The Biblical Doctrine of Heaven.* Chicago: Moody, 1968.
――――. *This Atomic Age and the Word of God.* Boston: Wilde, 1948.
Talbot, Louis T. *God's Plan of the Ages.* Los Angeles: Talbot, 1936.
――――. *The Revelation of Jesus Christ.* Grand Rapids: Eerdmans, 1946.
Trench, Richard Chenevix. *Synonyms of the New Testament.* London: Clarke, 1961.
Unger, Merrill F. *Great Neglected Bible Prophecies.* Chicago: Scripture Press, 1955.
――――. *Unger's Bible Dictionary.* Chicago: Moody, 1957.
――――. *Unger's Bible Handbook.* Chicago: Moody, 1966.
Vine, W. E. *Expository Dictionary.* London: Oliphants, 1948.
Vos, Geerhardus. *The Teaching of Jesus Concerning The Kingdom of God and The Church.* New York: American Tract Soc., 1903.
Wallace, O. C. S. *The Life of Jesus.* Philadelphia: American Baptist Pubn. Soc., 1893.
Walvoord, John F. *The Millennial Kingdom.* Findlay, O.: Dunham, 1959.
――――. *The Nations in Prophecy.* Grand Rapids: Zondervan, 1967.
――――. *The Return of the Lord.* Findlay, O.: Dunham, 1955.
――――. *The Revelation of Jesus Christ.* Chicago: Moody, 1966.
Wolff, Richard. *Israel Act III.* Wheaton, Ill.: Tyndale, 1967.
Wright, Walter C. *The Sacrificial System of the Old Testament.* Cleveland: Union Gospel, 1942.
Wuest, Kenneth S. *Galatians in the Greek New Testament.* Grand Rapids: Eerdmans, 1951.

Acknowledgments

The author gratefully acknowledges the kindness of authors and publishers in giving permission to reproduce copyrighted material in this volume as follows:

Baker Book House of Grand Rapids, Michigan: *This Atomic Age and the Word of God* by Wilbur M. Smith.

Dallas Theological Seminary, of Dallas, Texas: *The Kingdom in History and Prophecy* and *Systematic Theology* by Lewis Sperry Chafer.

Fleming H. Revell Company of Old Tappan, New Jersey: *The Life of Christ* by Willima Bancroft Hill; *Christian Workers Commentary on the Whole Bible* by James M. Gray; *Prophetic Truth Unfolding Today*, edited by Charles L. Feinberg.

Harper and Row, Publishers, Incorporated, of New York: *Jesus and the Kingdom* by George Eldon Ladd.

Arthur W. Kac of Baltimore, Maryland: *The Rebirth of the State of Israel* by Arthur W. Kac.

Loizeaux Brothers, Inc., Neptune, New Jersey: *The Basis of the Premillennial Faith* by Charles Caldwell Ryrie.

Moody Press of Chicago, Illinois: *Bible History Visualized, The Abundant Life* and *The Life of Christ Visualized* by Ray E. Baughman; *The Earth, the Theater of the Universe* by Clarence H. Benson; *Daniel and the Latter Days* by Robert D. Culver; *The Prophecy of Ezekiel* by Charles Lee Feinberg; *The End Times* by Herman A. Hoyt; *The Greatness of the Kingdom* by Alva J. McClain; *The Book of Revelation* by William R. Newell; *The Return of Jesus Christ* by René Pache; *Concerning the Future* by E. W. Rogers; *The Temple and Its Teaching* by Arthur E. Smith; *The Biblical Doctrine of Heaven* by Wilbur M. Smith; *Unger's Bible Handbook* and *Unger's Bible Dictionary* by Merrill F. Unger; and *The Revelation of Jesus Christ* by John F. Walvoord.

Scripture Press Foundation of Wheaton, Illinois: *Great Neglected Bible Prophecies* by Merrill F. Unger.

Scripture Press Publications, Inc., of Wheaton, Illinois: *The Bible and Tomorrow's News* by Charles Caldwell Ryrie.

Tyndale House Publishers of Wheaton, Illinois: *Israel Act III* by Richard Wolff.

Union Gospel Press of Cleveland, Ohio: *Typical Truth in the Tabernacle and Through the Bible Book by Book* by W. S. Hottel; and *The Sacrificial System of the Old Testament* by Walter C. Wright.

William B. Eerdmans Publishing Company of Grand Rapids, Michigan: *From Eternity to Eternity, The Dawn of World Redemption* and *The Triumph of the Crucified* by Erich Sauer; and *Galatians in the Greek New Testament* by Kenneth S. Wuest.

Zondervan Publishing House of Grand Rapids, Michigan: *Premillennialism or Amillennialism?* by Charles L. Feinberg; *Revelation* by M. R. DeHaan; *Things to Come* by J. Dwight Pentecost; *Introduction to Prophecy* by Elsa Raud; and *The Millennial Kingdom, The Nations in Prophecy* and *The Return of the Lord* by John F. Walvoord.

Special recognition should be given to the classic work of George N. H. Peters, *The Theocratic Kingdom of Our Lord Jesus, the Christ.* Wilbur M. Smith calls it "the most exhaustive, thoroughly annotated and logically arranged study of Biblical prophecy that appeared in our country during the nineteenth century." The three volumes total almost 2,000 pages of small-print text. An estimated 4,000 authors are cited. Because this work, first published in 1883, is out of print, it has been quoted extensively to share Peters' work with this generation.

Selective Subject Index

Selective Scripture Index